Women and Development in Africa

How Gender Works

Michael Kevane

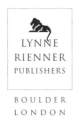

LYNNE
RIENNER
PUBLISHERS

BOULDER
LONDON

Published in the United States of America in 2004 by
Lynne Rienner Publishers, Inc.
1800 30th Street, Boulder, Colorado 80301
www.rienner.com

and in the United Kingdom by
Lynne Rienner Publishers, Inc.
3 Henrietta Street, Covent Garden, London WC2E 8LU

Library of Congress Cataloging-in-Publication Data
Kevane, Michael.
  Women and development in Africa: how gender works / Michael Kevane.
  Includes bibliographical references and index.
  ISBN 1-58826-213-8 (alk. paper)
  ISBN 1-58826-238-3 (pbk. : alk. paper)
  1. Women in development—Africa. 2. Sex role—Africa. I. Title.
HQ1240.5.A35K48 2003
305.3'096—dc22   2003058570

British Cataloguing in Publication Data
A Cataloguing in Publication record for this book
is available from the British Library.

Printed and bound in the United States of America

      The paper used in this publication meets the requirements
 ∞ of the American National Standard for Permanence of
      Paper for Printed Library Materials Z39.48-1992.

  5 4 3 2 1

Contents

Tables and Figures

Tables

Figures

Acknowledgments

What need we have any friends, if we should ne'er have need of 'em?
—*William Shakespeare,* Timon of Athens *(I.ii.95–96)*

Say something once, why say it again? I feel a bit like that when it comes to thanking people. But I may have forgotten, and perhaps thanks (as opposed to blame?) merit repeating. So here goes. First come the students. Over the years at Santa Clara University, a small minority of students have kept my energy levels high because of their interest in Africa and development studies, and because of their active participation in my class on gender and economics in developing countries. Janine Mans, Chris O'Connell, and Charlotte Vallaeys traveled with me to Burkina Faso, and actually read some of the chapters of this book while recovering from unmentionable illnesses in a rat-infested hotel in Bobo-Dioulasso, or was it by the pool at L'Auberge? Other former students to whom I would like to extend my warmest appreciation are Susan Clement, Robin Dayton, Michelle Denatale, Christine Dindia, Molly Fleming, Evan Hughes, Saho Iwamura, Brandon Kitagawa, Jonathan Lautze, Kristin Love, Lauren McCutcheon, Kristin Niedermeyer, Randy Reyes, Michelle Ronco, and Rebecca Warren.

I have had quite a few research assistants over the years working on this and related projects, some MBA students, and some undergraduates. They have all cheerfully trudged on with the most tedious of assignments and been pleasantly excited about some of the more obscure research for the project. Thanks, then, to Hilary Achterkirchen, Kinnari Desai, Magi Diego, Breanne Freeland, Manuella Mignot, Mike Sampias, Heidi Timmons, and Charlotte Vallaeys.

On to colleagues. David Levine, Bruce Wydick, Jonathan Conning, Pierre Englebert, Gabriel Fuentes, and Leslie Gray have been patient and inspiring collaborators on a number of projects. Jeffrey Nugent, Chris Udry, Marcel Fafchamps, Cheryl Doss, Anand Swamy, Biju Rao, Janet Momsen, Sigrun Helmfrid, and Dan Posner have been colleagues in the highest sense, producing work and conversation that give me a reference level to aspire to. Pranab Bardhan, Michael Watts, and George Akerlof provided enduring "formation" as my Berkeley Ph.D. committee, and their intellectual accomplishments are perhaps modestly reflected in this work. Greatly appreciated are the suggestions of participants (especially Matt Warning and Dennis Yang) at various conferences and seminars at the University of California (Davis, Berkeley, and Riverside), University of Southern California, and Yale University, as well as the Working Group on African Political Economy organized by Dan Posner and Ted Miguel and participants at the annual meetings of the African Studies Association, the Western Economics Association, and the Berkeley-Stanford African Studies Centers.

Santa Clara University has been a stimulating home. My colleagues in the Economics Department, especially Helen Popper, Bill Sundstrom, Anu Luther, Deb Garvey, Alex Field, Kris Mitchener, Daniel Klein, and Dongsoo Shin, have always given me much to think about. The university has also been very generous with funding over the years, and in particular I would like to thank Vice-Provost Don Dodson and Leavey School of Business Dean Barry Posner for providing the right "money climate" to encourage research. I have received a number of Santa Clara University Presidential Research grants and Leavey School of Business Summer Research grants, as well as a research fellowship generously endowed by the Dean Witter Foundation. I am grateful for that support for my research.

Part of the chapter on land tenure was prepared for the World Bank, and I thank Tara Vishwanath for giving me the chance to do that work. Part of the chapter on gender policy is based on research I did evaluating a microfinance project in Burkina Faso, and I thank Freedom from Hunger and the Union des Caisses Populaires du Burkina Faso for their support in that evaluation.

There are too many villagers in Burkina Faso and Sudan to thank, and it is unlikely that they will be reading this book. Let me extend instead a message of hope to their children, who may someday have the opportunity to go to college and analyze their own societies. Village chiefs and administrators have kindly let me proceed with my work, and my research assistants and hosts in Sudan and Burkina Faso are fondly remembered, each and every one (Koura Donkoui, Koura Ivette, Gnoumou Anne, Ouedraogo Ousmane, Tapsoba Moumouni, Hassan Idris Suleiman, Mohamed Ahmed al-Bedawi, Ibrahim Abidalla, and Osman Hassan).

Finally, my family deserves to be praised. My children, Elliot and Sukie, are young now, but someday, when they are grown, I will tell them that they didn't bother me at all, sitting on my lap while I typed. My wife, Leslie Gray, has been my coresearcher for many years. I cannot thank her enough. Maybe one day we will go back and find Lily, the baby donkey we had to sell in the drought year in western Sudan. My father taught me numbers, and my mother taught me letters, and hopefully they will find both in this book.

Women and Development in Africa

1

Introduction

> This business of womanhood is a heavy burden. . . . How could it not be? Aren't we the ones who bear children? When it is like that you can't just decide today I want to do this, tomorrow I want to do that, the next day I want to be educated! When there are sacrifices to be made, you are the one who has to make them. And these things are not easy; you have to start learning them early, from a very early age. The earlier the better so that it is easy later on. Easy! As if it is ever easy. And these days it is worse, with the poverty of blackness on one side and the weight of womanhood on the other. Aiwa!
>
> —*Tsitsi Dangarembga,* Nervous Conditions

This book offers an introduction to the analysis of gender in the economies of sub-Saharan Africa. Gender refers to the constellation of rules and identities that prescribe and proscribe behavior for persons, in their social roles as men and women. These rules and identities may be deliberate or unintended, explicit or implicit, conscious or unconscious. All societies of the world are gendered. The focus here will be on Africa south of the Sahara Desert, which means that the Mediterranean and Middle Eastern–oriented countries of Egypt, Libya, Algeria, Tunisia, and Morocco are excluded. Henceforth, sub-Saharan Africa shall be shortened to just plain Africa, in accordance with common usage in the social sciences.

Gender requires analysis because a common outcome of the gendering of social activity is an unequal and inefficient distribution, between men and women, of the capabilities for realizing well-being. Many—if not most—people would agree that women and girls are disadvantaged in life relative to men and boys, even though national statistics sometimes do a poor job of capturing the relevant inequalities (Quisumbing, Haddad, and Pena 2001). The pervasiveness of female disadvantage is one of the most interesting and least understood features of economic life.

Certainly there are people, sometimes very influential and intelligent people, who believe that comparing the well-being of boys and girls, or men and women, is like comparing papayas and lemons. One is sweet and the other sour, and the difference does not imply unequal welfare. Men and

1

boys have their lives to lead and girls and women theirs. Nevertheless, girls and women in Africa face unequal chances for education, less inheritance and ownership of assets, discrimination in employment and occupations, violence at home and in public spaces, and limited political representation. These add up to unambiguously diminished welfare and capacity to fulfill life aspirations.

Gender matters for women, but it also matters for men. Much of the population of sub-Saharan Africa has experienced long-term stagnation or declines in income and general standards of living. Many people still journey from sorrowful, hungry, and frustrating life to early, painful, and diseased death. Perhaps reversing this situation depends on changing structures of gender. The skeptic might immediately want to put down this book. Gender and economic growth? The two have little to do with each other. But consider a few lines of argument. One goes as follows: African economies are poor because of high levels of corruption; men are more corruptible than women; men dominate African governments; therefore the solution is to encourage and campaign for more representation of women in African governments. For those who think this argument a trifle glib, consider this passage from a recent book authored by the World Bank: "Greater women's rights and more equal participation in public life by women and men are associated with cleaner business and government and better governance. Where the influence of women in public life is greater, the level of corruption is lower . . . women can be an effective force for rule of law and good governance" (2001, 12–13).

Take another syllogism: relative to men, women prefer that social spending be higher and more oriented toward the well-being of children; more social spending on local infrastructure, schooling, and antipoverty programs is good for economic growth; thus, empowering women in the political process leads to larger allocations toward growth-enhancing government expenditures. Too obvious? Except for the growth-enhancing part of the story, this is a theory of "big government" in the United States. Lott and Kenny (1999, 1163), for example, find that the period of extension of the franchise to women in the United States "coincided with immediate increases in state government expenditures and revenue and more liberal voting patterns for federal representatives, and these effects continued growing over time as more women took advantage of the franchise." Edlund and Pande (2001) find evidence that recently divorced women, desirous of higher levels of social spending, have increasingly voted for the Democratic Party in the United States. In the context of developing countries, Chattopadhyay and Duflo (2001) find that when the government of West Bengal required that village leadership positions be reserved for women, village councils indeed invested in different kinds of public goods.

A related observation, made frequently in African studies, notes that the market-friendly policies supported by the World Bank and International Monetary Fund have reduced growth because they failed to give consideration to gender inequalities (Gladwin and McMillan 1989; Safilios-Rothschild 1985; Staudt 1987). These policies were supposed to lighten the burden of government regulation of economic activities and encourage farmers and entrepreneurs to work longer and harder, invest more, and shift toward more socially desirable activities (rather than bureaucratically desirable activities). But optimistic expectations of high responsiveness and innovation proved unwarranted. Perhaps African women were simply too downtrodden to take much advantage of new opportunities. Where they did begin to exploit the new opportunities, the surplus generated was wasted in costly political, legal, and cultural struggles with men over rights to control the new surplus.

Another link made between gender and growth emphasizes the importance of fertility. In this view, a major problem in developing countries is that parents want children for old-age security: because child mortality rates are so high, parents try to have many children. The parents do not take into account that their extra children may generate burdens on society as a whole. (Crowded classrooms and health clinics come to mind.) Empowering women seems to be associated with lower fertility rates. If lower fertility rates generate more rapid economic growth, then the syllogism is complete.

The "Economic Method"

Exploring gender issues is an opportunity to master many analytical and empirical tools used in the social sciences. The tools applied in this book are used in all of the social sciences but are most closely associated with economics. Rather presumptuously, some economists call this particular set of analytical tools the "economic method." This method involves model building and verification. The first step is a narrow, careful, and often mathematical exposition of theories, in the form of models of behavior. These theories typically start with assumptions about individual rather than group behavior. This "methodological individualism" is then coupled with logic to make inferences about the interactions among people. Assumptions, logic, and inference constitute a model.

Logic is used to distinguish between causes and effects. Logical statements are often cast as syllogisms. An example of syllogistic reasoning that is common in economics goes as follows: People have a propensity to "truck and barter." People also have different tastes and abilities. Therefore, any equal distribution of resources across society will quickly result in an unequal distribution. Stated another way, people are different, and because people like to trade, any initial equal distribution of resources will lead to situations where people can gain from trade. But trading means the original, equal distribution becomes unequal. The logic is impeccable. It is the often unstated implication of this syllogism that is troublesome: the implication that redistribution of resources is futile, since inequality will inevitably return. But does the logic say that redistribution is futile? Does it say that the same inequality will reappear? No. It says that some kind of inequality will likely reappear, but it is silent on the nature of that inequality. It is important to understand that not every implication that an author insinuates does indeed follow from the argument. Students in the social sciences must be alert to model overbite.

A good model tries to explain and predict the essence of some observed behavior. The economic method then applies statistical techniques to data in order to verify or refute models. The appendix to this book contains a more thorough introduction to models and a discussion of the supply and demand model and the Nash equilibrium approach to modeling strategic situations. There is also discussion in the appendix about regression analysis, the specific statistical technique used in this book. The reader will find a nontechnical and intuitive explanation of regressions and hints about how to interpret regression results. There are many fine introductory textbooks on the subject, and the more mathematically inclined are urged to seek them out (Bacon 1988; Pindyck and Rubinfeld 1998).

It is worth reiterating that the tools used in this book do not belong to economics. John Nash, Nobel laureate and subject of the film *A Beautiful Mind,* whose work has become very important in the analysis of gender in the household, was a mathematician, not an economist. The approaches that he and others have developed are used in many disciplines (Wilk 1996). Hopefully, seeing the tools in action here, in an unfamiliar and compelling setting, may help students apply them to more familiar settings. No special training is required to understand the main ideas of these tools. That is why they are so powerful.

Organization of the Book

The approach adopted in this book emphasizes the interactions between the choices that individuals make and the social environment that structures those choices. Men and women make differing choices, choices that constitute part of the gendering of economic activity. But the motivation for those choices is in part the differing opportunities that men and women experience. The structure of an economy—rights over property and persons, organization of market transfers of property and persons, and rules regarding nonmarket transfers of rights—is itself gendered.

If Africans were rich, the analysis of the economic dimensions of gender would be less urgent. Unfortunately, most African countries are getting poorer. The next chapter offers a broad overview of the problem of declining economic performance in Africa. That sets the context for Chapter 3, on the gendered choices and structures in the economies of sub-Saharan Africa.

Chapters 4–6 concentrate on three examples of economic structures: land tenure, labor control, and marriage markets. The system of land tenure (Chapter 4) is the most basic structure of an agrarian economy. Tenure rules determine the allocation of rights to use and transfer land. Most African societies give women far fewer land-use rights than are given to men. Labor control is discussed in Chapter 5, which provides evidence on the gendering of labor markets, principally in the form of norms that enforce occupational segregation by gender. Many African societies classify certain activities as "male" and others as "female," and rare is the man or woman who will cross those occupational boundaries. Women may also have limited rights to choose how much time to spend in permissible occupations; they may be subordinate to the instructions of their husbands or fathers. Chapter 6 investigates marriage markets, which in many African societies are major economic structures determining the lives of women.

Subsequent chapters look at important choices that men and women make in the context of the structures that they find themselves in as they enter adulthood. Many choices are made in the context of households, discussed in Chapter 7. At the same time, the structures of households are constituted by the choices that the people within them make. One important household choice concerns investments in children (Chapters 8 and 9). If those investment choices are themselves gendered, then right away there is a feedback mechanism between structure and choice. Parents make different investments in girls than they do in boys, which affects the skills, outlooks, and rights that girls take with them into adulthood. Because of this, young women will make choices that are different from those of young men. The social patterns that emerge from these choices become viewed as part of the economic structure of a given society, which in turn shapes the choices of the next generation of parents.

There is a pithy saying that economics is all about how people make choices, while sociology is all about how people don't actually have any choices to make. There is no need to reduce the social sciences to such gross stereotypes, but the saying does capture the essence of how to think about the relationship between structure and agency (Giddens 1984).

Social scientists used to think of economic structures as being "sticky" and persisting through time, experiencing rapid change only as the result of deliberate political action. A more recent line of thinking, however, emphasizes the "tipping point" property of many economic structures (Gladwell

2000). If just enough people change their behavior, then through their spontaneous choices a new economic structure comes to quickly replace the old. Examples of this kind of spontaneous structural change are discussed at various points in the book. Chapters 10 and 11, however, look at the politics and practice of deliberate structural change. Chapter 10 examines how nongovernmental organizations are transforming credit markets through microfinance programs targeted toward women. The most intentional and political change of all, the fundamental, constitutional change that is being brought about by adherence to the Convention for the Elimination of Discrimination Against Women, is discussed in Chapter 11.

2

Explaining Underdevelopment in Africa

We've had a very unfortunate history of military dictatorship in Nigeria, going back to 1966. We sort of got ourselves trapped there, and it just got worse and worse. The last dictator [General Sani Abacha], from whom we were saved just by providence—it wasn't because of anything we did, he just died—was really the most brutal in this line of soldiers. So the country is reeling from the five or six years where he was in power. We now have a democratic government, but it's not something you switch on and off. The damage done in one year can sometimes take ten or twenty years to repair.

—*Chinua Achebe,* Failure Magazine, *June 5, 2001*

Whatever concerns the habits of little chicks, you can be quite sure that the hawk started learning it long ago.

—*Hausa proverb*

On the night of April 6, 1994, a missile destroyed a plane carrying Juvenal Habyarimana, president of Rwanda, and Cyprien Ntaryamira, president of Burundi, as it approached Kigali airport. Both presidents died. The airport was immediately sealed by Rwandan army forces, who prevented United Nations peacekeepers from inspecting the crash site. The peacekeepers were present in Kigali to monitor the Arusha peace agreement signed by Habyarimana with the rebel Rwanda Patriotic Front (RPF). The peace agreement had been negotiated over the course of two years, and Ntaryamira and other East African presidents had acted as witnesses. The Habyarimana regime was to share power with opposition groups within the country and with the RPF, which controlled the northern third of the country. The agreement was intended to forestall the large-scale unrest and killing that had characterized Rwandan society since independence. There is no need to go into the causes of that conflict, other than to note that it was typically interpreted as conflict between two ethnic groups, the Tutsi and Hutu.

Following the death of Habyarimana, a hard-line Hutu faction within the Rwandan government consolidated its power (Prunier 1998). This group propagated a hate-ideology known as Hutu Power and thrust their message into Rwandan political discourse. Rhetoric and imagery of Hutu

Power was used by the Habyarimana regime to justify the government's undemocratic practices. Hutu Power held that Rwanda was in the grip of a constant struggle between a majority, but poor, Hutu population, and a sinister, wealthy, minority Tutsi population. The RPF rebels were *inyenzi,* Tutsi "cockroaches." The hard-liners for months had prepared their Hutu cadres for a genocide—and Habyarimana for his death—with broadcasts from their radio station, Radio Milles Collines.

Military units loyal to the hard-liners searched for and killed opposition politicians. One of their first victims was Agathe Uwinlingiyimana, the prime minister, killed along with her lightly armed guard of Belgian peacekeepers. (The commander of her assailants, Francois Nzuwonemeye, was arrested in France in 2000 and is currently awaiting trial at the International Criminal Tribunal for Rwanda in Arusha, Tanzania.) Other units drove to neighboring districts and organized local groups to kill Tutsis. From April to July these groups used machetes, grenades, bullets, drowning, and incineration to carry out an organized genocide against Tutsi Rwandans and moderate sympathizers of the peace agreement. The rest of the world stood by, even as dramatic television images of the genocide were broadcast (Melvern 2000). Certainly more than 500,000 people died, with the number possibly closer to 800,000. The U.S. Census bureau gives a population figure of 7.5 million Rwandans in the year before the genocide, and 6.4 million after (U.S. Census Bureau 2000). One in ten may have been killed (Gourevitch 1999).

The events may have passed unnoticed by the world, as had been the case for previous mass killings in Rwanda and neighboring Burundi, but not for the dramatic change in power in Rwanda. The RPF, led by a Rwandan exile community from Uganda that had previously helped Yoweri Museveni in his own rise to power in Uganda, broke the cease-fire and advanced rapidly on Kigali. They quickly captured the city, and the Hutu Power regime collapsed. The leaders of the genocide then organized a mass flight of Hutu peasants into neighboring Zaire. Enormous refugee camps were set up and provisioned by international relief agencies. From these refugee camps the *genocidaires,* as they were known, continued to perpetrate raids and killings. The new Rwandan government finally had enough, and sent in an army to destroy the threat. The invaders encountered little resistance, so they continued all the way to Kinshasa, capital of Zaire. The Zairean dictator Mobutu Sese Seko fled, and the mineral-rich, former Belgian colony was thrown into chaos. At the time of this writing, militaries from several neighboring countries occupy parts of what is now known as the Democratic Republic of Congo. There are no good estimates of the number of dead from the ongoing civil conflict in Congo, but the figure of 2 million is often repeated, and sounds reasonable.

The sad story of Rwanda and Congo is not unique to African nations. In fact, the number and intensity of civil conflicts that have occurred in the continent since independence of most countries in the 1960s is heartbreaking. Table 2.1 presents one counting of serious conflicts in sub-Saharan Africa. The more important conflicts have been among the worst the world has seen since World War II. The war in Sudan has now lasted 47 years, with only a brief decade-long hiatus after the Addis Ababa peace accord in the 1970s. Millions have died from the war and resulting destruction of medical and food infrastructure (Burr and Collins 1995; Collins 1983). Somalia has been a "failed state" since the fall of the dictator Siad Barre in 1991. Horrific pictures of children with arms hacked off by rebel soldiers, living warnings of future terror, have been staples of the decades-long civil conflicts of Liberia and Sierre Leone. Until the death of Jonas Savimbi in 2002, his rebel movement UNITA looked set to prolong indefinitely the civil war in Angola, where cities of tens of thousands of people have been besieged into starvation.

While the litany of wars sounds awful, it should be borne in mind that Africa has not actually seen any greater incidence of war than other major regions of the world (Collier and Hoeffler 2000). Nor is there much evidence that African civil conflicts are inordinately ethnic (Collier and Hoeffler 1998; Elbadawi and Sambanis 2000). It is true that African countries are more ethnically fragmented than most other countries. But this fragmentation seems paradoxically to be conducive to peace rather than war, most of the time. The reason for this is somewhat mysterious, but perhaps multiethnic societies develop institutions for defusing tensions. They have to, else they would not survive.

African conflicts are, however, increasing in number and intensity relative to the rest of the world. Dramatic confirmation of this comes from recent violence in Côte d'Ivoire, where an army mutiny in September 2002

Table 2.1 War and Conflict in Sub-Saharan Africa, 1960–2001

Country	Years of conflict	Country	Years of conflict
Angola	1975–1995, 1998–2001	Namibia	1979–1988
Burundi	1997–2001	Nigeria	1967–1970
Chad	1965–1990	Rwanda	1991–1994, 1998–2001
Congo-Brazzaville	1997–1999	Senegal	1997–2000
Congo (Zaire, DRC)	1964–1965, 1978, 1997–2001	Sierra Leone	1994–2000
Eritrea	1998–2000	Somalia	1987–1996
Ethiopia	1974–1991, 1998–2000	South Africa	1989–1993
Guinea-Bissau	1965–1973, 1998–1999	Sudan	1963–1972, 1983–2001
Liberia	1990–1995	Uganda	1979–1991, 1996–2001
Mozambique	1966–1974, 1981–1992	Zimbabwe	1976–1979

Source: Data described in Gleditsch et al. (2002), with some abbreviation (short interruptions in conflicts of one or two years have been glossed over; only conflict intensity levels of "intermediate" and "war" are included). The full conflict list is available at: http://www.prio.no/jpr/datasets.asp.

turned into a general militia free-for-all. The body of the former president, General Robert Guëi, was found lying on the street. One faction accused him of plotting a coup. Another faction took over control of much of the north of the country. Hundreds of others were killed as political and personal scores were settled through violence.

The cause of this relative persistence and rise in conflict probably lies in a vicious circle of economic decline leading to war leading to further economic decline. Poverty fuels conflict, especially when riches are within grasp. Many African countries have lucrative mining and oil enclaves. Whoever controls those enclaves can obtain considerable wealth. It is clear, just by looking at the list of countries in Table 2.1, that this is a defining feature of many conflicts. Liberia and Sierra Leone have diamonds easily mined on the surface. Sudan has oil, with reserves turning out to be far larger than imagined. Angola has a terrifying combination of oil and diamonds. When peasant populations are impoverished, it seems possible to mobilize large numbers of disillusioned young men with the promise of better lives through looting and conquest (Miguel, Satyanath, and Sergenti 2003). The increasingly impoverished countryside provides recruiting grounds for rebel movements that aim to capture riches, all the while further impoverishing the countryside and setting in motion additional rounds of violence.

Gloomy Statistics

The vicious circle of economic decline and civil conflict is reflected in the gloomy statistics on economic growth for the continent. Table 2.2 presents the average rates of growth in per capita gross domestic product (GDP) of African countries. Figure 2.1 shows the evolution of GDP levels of Africa and two other major world regions with substantial poverty, South and East Asia, for the period 1975–2000. The table and figure make clear that growth performance in Africa has been bad. More than half (23 of 45) of African countries experienced negative growth during the period 1975–1990. Only six experienced growth over 2 percent per year, and, of these, two were small island nations (Seychelles and Mauritius) and another was the small kingdom of Lesotho, entirely surrounded by South Africa. Uganda's growth is basically a recovery from years of civil disturbance—no small feat, but still incomes are dismally low. Equatorial Guinea's growth has been due entirely to the very recent discovery and exploitation of oil in the small country. Even Botswana's steady and rapid growth over the decades has been largely fueled by the diamond mining sector and is now endangered by the AIDS pandemic.

African economies in general never recovered from the period of global stagflation that followed the OPEC oil price shocks of the 1970s. Oil

Table 2.2 GDP Growth and Income Levels

	Average growth in per capita GDP 1960–1975	Average growth in per capita GDP 1975–2000	GNI per capita, PPP exchange rate (current U.S.$)	GNI per capita, market exchange rate (current U.S.$)
Sub-Saharan Africa	2.18	0.06	1,600	470
Angola	0.00	−1.95	1,180	290
Benin	0.94	0.46	980	370
Botswana	13.15	4.94	7,170	3,300
Burkina Faso	0.73	1.39	970	210
Burundi	3.14	−0.69	580	110
Cameroon	0.10	−0.58	1,590	580
Central African Republic	0.06	−1.65	1,160	280
Chad	−1.52	0.04	870	200
Congo, Dem. Rep.	0.73	−4.78		
Congo, Rep.	2.26	0.00	570	570
Côte d'Ivoire	4.07	−2.09	1,500	600
Djibouti	−4.61		880	
Equatorial Guinea	0.00	9.86	5,600	800
Eritrea		−0.05	960	170
Ethiopia	0.00	−0.10	660	100
Gabon	6.60	−1.53	5,360	3,190
Gambia	0.81	−0.25	1,620	340
Ghana	0.40	0.06	1,910	340
Guinea		1.31	1,930	450
Guinea-Bissau	0.00	0.37	710	180
Kenya	4.24	0.37	1,010	350
Lesotho	3.42	2.58	2,590	580
Liberia		−3.28		
Madagascar	0.25	−1.73	820	250
Malawi	3.31	0.18	600	170
Mali	0.40	−0.54	780	240
Mauritania	1.01	−0.06	1,630	370
Mauritius	4.41	3.97	9,940	3,750
Mozambique	0.00	1.52	800	210
Namibia		−0.09	6,410	2,030
Niger	−1.81	−2.10	740	180
Nigeria	2.43	−0.75	800	260
Rwanda	0.68	−1.32	930	230
Senegal	−1.06	−0.20	1,480	490
Seychelles		2.86		7,050
Sierra Leone	2.15	−2.59	480	130
Somalia		0.31		
South Africa	3.51	−0.73	9,160	3,020
Sudan	−1.09	0.57	1,520	310
Swaziland	5.11	1.93	4,600	1,390
Tanzania		0.45	520	270
Togo	3.90	−1.18	1,410	290
Uganda	0.00	2.49	1,210	300
Zambia	0.06	−2.36	750	300
Zimbabwe	0.00	0.21	2,550	460

Source: World Bank Development Indicators (2002).
Note: The growth rates are calculated as regression coefficients against a time variable.

Figure 2.1 GDP per Capita for Various World Regions

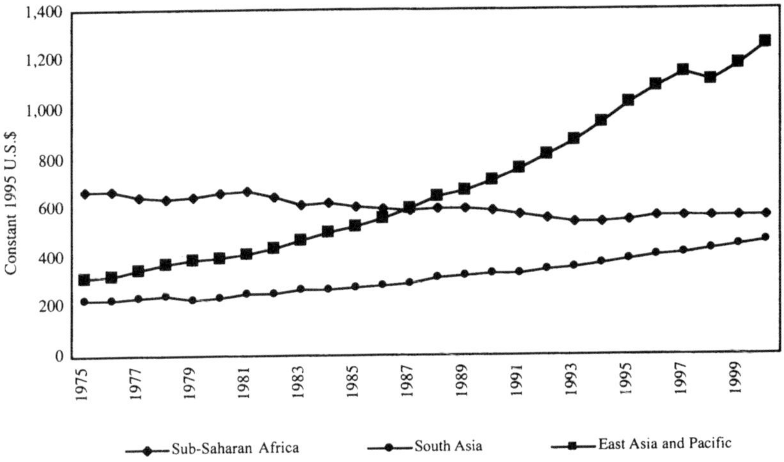

Source: World Bank Development Indicators (2002). Low- and middle-income countries only.

exporters succumbed to the "Dutch Disease," where the large influx of oil revenues quickly led to macroeconomic problems. Nigerian regimes especially could not resist recycling the oil revenues into poorly planned construction projects. The construction boom drove up the price of labor, encouraging rural to urban migration, and exacerbating a rapid decline in the agricultural sector. Corruption and rent-seeking followed, and the most populous country in Africa has seen economic decline for several decades. Oil importers likewise went into long declines, often caused by macroeconomic mismanagement as they tried to use foreign exchange controls and foreign aid to avoid the necessary adjustments to the higher price of oil and stagflation of the industrial world. The poor policy responses to the oil price increases, global stagflation, higher interest rate charges on foreign debt, and worsening commodity terms of trade have been well documented (Collier and Gunning 1999; Fosu 1992; 1999; 2001; 2002; Montiel 1995; Sachs and Warner 1995; Savvides 1995; Wohlmuth 1998). Most of the population of African countries, as a result, now has *lower* income than during the 1970s.

Slow and negative growth is especially serious because of the low levels of income that African countries had at independence. A digression on issues of measuring incomes levels, as opposed to growth, is worthwhile here. First, for many African countries GDP is increasingly diverging from gross national income (GNI), which measures the income generated by nationals of a country. Many Africans earn very high incomes when they are abroad, and much income produced in Africa takes the form of mineral and oil extraction by multinationals. Since a significant share of income earned abroad is remitted, and since much income earned by multinationals is repatriated, GNI might be a more suitable measure of well-being. GDP might, however, still be a good indicator of the *future* earnings of Africans born in their countries. Another measure that might be considered is net national product, which subtracts the considerable depreciation of capital and infrastructure from the total product produced in a year. If depletion of natural resource assets were also subtracted, by the argument that sales of existing assets are not really "goods produced," then incomes go even lower (Winter-Nelson 1995).

A second issue arises when valuing GDP in a common currency such as the U.S. dollar. To compare incomes earned in different countries, the local cash value of incomes measured in local currencies must be converted into a common currency. There are two alternatives. The first is to use current market exchange rates. The second is to use purchasing power parity (PPP) exchange rates. Most economists favor the PPP rates. These are constructed by taking samples of the prices of goods and services that are purchased in most countries and calculating the exchange rate that would equalize the prices of a basket of these goods with the prices in the United States. Suppose it costs ten dollars in the United States to purchase a given amount of food and the same amount costs 20 rupees in India. It makes sense then to use a ratio of two rupees per dollar when comparing people's incomes. The problem with market exchange rates is that they need not equalize purchasing power. Large deviations occur and persist, and exchange rates often exhibit dramatic swings from one year to the next. Because of these swings, if market exchange rates were used to compare incomes in common currencies, then incomes also would appear subject to large swings. But income does not exhibit such large swings when measured in national currencies, so neither should it when using a common currency.

PPP rates are not necessarily superior when it comes to comparing African incomes with those of wealthy, industrial countries. When PPP rates are used, most African countries appear to have higher incomes. This is because many goods and services produced in African economies are labor-intensive, nontraded goods (such as housing, haircuts, guard services, and food processing). Wage rates in African countries are extremely low, sometimes amounting to no more than $0.25 per day in rural areas (using market exchange rates). So services are very, very cheap. When these services are priced at the same price as in industrial countries, they appear more valuable, and income appears higher.

Table 2.2 also presents per capita incomes for African countries. The income figures are calculated using both market exchange rates and PPP rates. The PPP figures are about four times higher than the market exchange rate figures. Most African nations are still very far from the income levels of the rest of the world. They are absurdly far from the income levels of the rich countries, currently on the order of $30,000 per capita. Such gross inequality cannot be less than an urgent problem.

For measuring well-being, income is not necessarily best. Perhaps Africans do not value material possessions and instead spend time talking with neighbors and enjoying the arts. Perhaps some other measure of well-being would reveal Africa to be less poorly off. Unfortunately, the evidence that African populations are disadvantaged comes through plainly using other indicators. Three are shown in Table 2.3. Mortality of infants and children is very high—91 per 1,000 for infants and 162 per 1,000 for children under five. The death rate is also two times higher than death rates for other low-income countries. Africans are suffering in ways that are practically incomprehensible to the rest of the world.

Causes of Economic Growth

Peace and freedom may be all that are required for rapid economic growth. Adam Smith pointed this out more than two hundred years ago, and thinkers such as Ibn Khaldun, writing in North Africa in the 1300s, knew as much. Even so, the citizens of a nation might want to think about how best to speed growth within an enabling environment of peace and freedom, and especially how to make economic growth equitable.

What causes growth in per capita income to rise in a sustained way? Saving and investing are certainly important. Without them nothing is possible. But what kind of investing generates growth? There is broad agreement on four important determinants of the speed of growth, in terms of what kinds of investments generate big payoffs. These are: innovation, technology-borrowing, solving coordination problems, and ensuring an equitable distribution of opportunities to participate in the growing economy. Social scientists disagree, of course, over the relative importance of each of these and over the importance of other factors.

There can be no doubt that invention, broadly speaking, is the major engine of economic growth. Invention takes many forms, and recent thinking in economics emphasizes the importance of "ideas" over "gadgets." Instead of inventors, we should more properly admire innovators. Ideas are crucial ingredients in economic growth because they are nonproprietary. When someone generates a practical idea, it spreads quickly. The idea of fast food, for example, where the production process of prepared foods is subject to careful scientific analysis (or extensive trial and error) and mechanization, led to a revolution in the restaurant business. Even poor countries

Table 2.3 Mortality Indicators

	Mortality rate, infant (per 1,000 live births)	Mortality rate, under five (per 1,000 live births)	Death rate, crude (per 1,000 people)
Sub-Saharan Africa	91	162	16.78
Angola	128	208	18.80
Benin	87	143	12.98
Botswana	58	99	19.90
Burkina Faso	104	206	19.22
Burundi	102	176	19.88
Cameroon	76	155	14.22
Central African Republic	96	152	19.52
Chad	101	188	16.32
Congo, Dem. Rep.	85	163	16.58
Congo, Rep.	68	106	14.10
Côte d'Ivoire	111	180	16.82
Djibouti	115	178	17.76
Equatorial Guinea	102	167	15.54
Eritrea	60	103	12.90
Ethiopia	98	179	20.06
Gabon	58	89	15.52
Gambia	73		13.16
Ghana	58	112	11.08
Guinea	95	161	16.94
Guinea-Bissau	126	211	20.04
Kenya	78	120	14.24
Lesotho	91	143	16.96
Liberia	111	185	17.22
Madagascar	88	144	12.06
Malawi	103	193	24.16
Mali	120	218	20.04
Mauritania	101	164	14.50
Mauritius	16	20	6.70
Mozambique	129	200	20.46
Namibia	62	112	17.06
Niger	114	248	19.26
Nigeria	84	153	16.20
Rwanda	123	203	21.56
Senegal	60	129	12.70
Seychelles	9	14	6.90
Sierra Leone	154	267	23.40
Somalia	117	195	17.48
South Africa	63	79	15.96
Sudan	81		11.48
Swaziland	89	119	14.92
Tanzania	93	149	17.16
Togo	75	142	14.98
Uganda	83	161	19.20
Zambia	115	186	21.42
Zimbabwe	69	116	17.74

Source: World Bank Development Indicators (2002).

in Africa now have fast food outlets. One might think of ideas as *combinations* of old ideas (Weitzman 1996). Two old ideas get combined, and that becomes a new idea. If ideas are a major source of growth, then the future of advanced countries looks bright indeed, as the enormous pace of technological and institutional change over the last century has generated a gigantic potential for combining ideas. Moreover, the "bionomic" revolution of advanced countries, where human lives are extended by decades through scientific advances in medicine and biology, may lead to even more new ideas, provided the old are more wise than foolish.

For poor countries, where people do not have the time or the opportunity to engage in much systematic thinking and creating, and where life expectancies are still short, growth happens through more prosaic means. Most obviously, by saving and investing, poor countries can borrow, buy, and rent ideas and inventions from the wealthy countries. This "latecomer" theory suggests that poor countries should be able to grow rapidly because they can import the stock of technology developed in the wealthy countries. Neither the toaster nor safety razor has to be reinvented. Computer and solar panel technology can be licensed from a multinational. Nonproprietary ideas such as fast food or corn cribs can be put to use. Almost every capital city in Africa now sports an extensive array of fast food choices. Why are these important? Fast food technology and organization enable just a few persons to provide hunger-sating food to large numbers of people in short periods of time. Those people then have more time to work on other activities. There are drawbacks: perhaps people's health is being impaired, as they fail to understand how the nutrition in fast food is different from "regular" food. But fast food outlets evolve, and veggie burgers and other low-fat entrees are increasingly common. McDonald's may be a symbol to many of a freakish fast-food culture of factory-engineered beef, potato, oil, and salt products, but the principle behind McDonald's is an idea that even an organic, whole-grain industry can use to increase productivity.

Other technology-borrowing is less controversial: calculators, radios, televisions, plows, automobiles, antimalaria drugs, pesticides to control riverblindness, tampons, the list goes on and on. "Less controversial" is somewhat tongue-in-cheek. There are always Luddites who prefer to imagine a bucolic world of farmers, carpenters, and blacksmiths, who have plenty of time to construct elaborate creation myths and celebrate intricate seasonal rituals. More seriously, every act of technology-borrowing destroys the incomes of those who lived producing the old technology. The healers who cured malaria and river blindness are displaced. The barbers who stropped razors on leather need to invent new, more elaborate, hairstyles for men or they will lose their livelihoods. Donkey breeders may need to become Subaru dealers.

The extent of technology-borrowing is greatly influenced by the institutions of society. The secret to growth is to create a propitious environment for transferring technology. In the early years of independence, many African governments assumed that government itself was the appropriate agent for doing the technology-borrowing. Unfortunately, they proved themselves spectacularly inefficient in this endeavor. First, they were unable to tax their populations, even to modest degrees, so they had few resources with which to acquire technology. Second, investments were poorly chosen and managed. The continent is littered with grandiose, showcase projects rusting from disuse. Third, in their zeal to assign to government the role of innovator, and in the high and arbitrary tax rates used to try to collect revenues, governments discouraged private economic activity, especially private technology-borrowing. This was particularly true for foreign involvement in African economies. Few African nations allowed a liberal, enabling environment for foreign investment. Those that did came to naught, as the actions of a few disreputable neighbors, such as Idi Amin with his eviction of Asian entrepreneurs from Uganda, scared away foreign investors.

The foreign front should not be looked at through rose-tinted glasses. Foreign aid could be used to effect technology transfers, as aid would be tied in any case to the purchase of technologies marketed by donor country firms. But the experience of foreign aid has been very disappointing, and much of the blame lies squarely on the shoulders of the donors (Easterly 2001; 2003). Foreign aid has been channeled through agencies such as the U.S. Agency for International Development and the German GTZ (Gesellschaft für Technische Zusammenarbeit), and through multilateral organizations such as the United Nations Development Program and the World Bank. These agencies are large bureaucracies with political mandates. The World Bank's board of directors, for example, is determined according to the share of capital contributed by its state members, and so is dominated by the United States and European governments. The political mandates impede the organizations from considering projects on their merits. They also are impeded from adopting long-term and egalitarian perspectives. The bureaucrat in the organization is rewarded by quick and trouble-free project implementation, not by project results. The revolving door from aid agency to private consulting agency stacks the deck in favor of technologies and projects that have organized lobbies. Large infrastructure and mining projects are perennial favorites of these organizations. Small may really be beautiful but not to Washington bureaucrats.

It should be pointed out that this donor culture is changing. The new trend in foreign assistance is toward decentralized approaches to finance and insurance, and it emphasizes the ability of poor people to locate and implement projects on their own, and on small scales. This is as it should be, and the approach holds much promise (Morduch 1999). Again, although some bureaucrats like to think that gigantic dams are how countries get rich, it may be more true that corner shops deliver the daily bread.

But bureaucrats do have a significant role to play. Technology-borrowing needs to be coordinated in order to ensure rapid growth. Economic theorists of development emphasize that private individuals may not undertake investments in new technologies if they have little confidence that a market exists for their products (Matsuyama 1992; Murphy, Shleifer, and Vishny 1989). There is a whole range of products that may be produced primarily for domestic markets. But if domestic incomes are low, there will be little demand. Incomes will be low, however, as long as entrepreneurs do not invest in new technologies that make people more productive. Even entrepreneurs thinking of making investments for the export market, where demand is not an issue, still need to be worried about coordinated investments. The profitability of their investment will be influenced by investments that other firms make in the human capital of their workers. The presence of a large pool of trained labor, able to adapt quickly to new machinery and production processes and mindful of factory discipline and reporting requirements, is required for success. Without the labor pool, entrepreneurs will be reluctant to invest. Without the investments, there will be no pool of trained labor. Both investments for domestic and export markets will depend on transport and legal infrastructure. There is a range of possibilities, therefore, for successful government guidance of a complex, industrializing economy.

Finally, growth is a good thing, but unless it is widely shared it will be problematic. All scenarios of technology-borrowing and investment mean that some people will suffer reductions in incomes. The adjustments that this suffering induces should be facilitated and the suffering eased. Rising disparities in incomes and life chances produce resentments and social conflict (Lichbach 1989; Moore, Lindstrom, and Oregan 1996). Poor people feel that a social contract has been broken; rich people hunker down to defend their property. Inefficient and wasteful redistribution will be inevitable, and the investments of a generation of entrepreneurs may be burned away in two weeks of urban rioting.

Far better, then, to take steps early on in the process to ensure equality of opportunity. For most countries this is not costly. Universal schooling has been easily achieved by nations that have tried. Universal primary health care and nutrition are likewise quite cost-effective. This is especially true, it might be added, for interventions that prevent maternal mortality, one of the major causes of death of adult women in developing countries. Prenatal examinations and supplemental nutrition for pregnant women are high-return interventions. Postnatal services, such as early treatment of sepsis and education about breastfeeding and weaning, are widely known to promote the wealth and welfare of all (Almroth and Greiner 1979; Liljestrand 1999; Mbaruku and Bergstrom 1995; Winikoff, et al. 1991).

Why No Growth in African Economies?

The discussion above made economic growth sound reasonably simple, once civil conflicts have been resolved. Unfortunately, the hopeful discussion neglects a serious negative feedback effect. Economic growth might indeed follow from borrowing of new technologies, investment, and trade in an atmosphere of peace and freedom. But the benefits of growth, especially that generated by the opening of trade in natural resources, might be highly concentrated in the hands of a small elite, which then ignores the imperative of more equitable distribution and prevents the broader population from reaping any reward from their greater potential (Ross 2001a; 2001b). New technologies can be used for repression and predation, and not just production. Foreign aid can divert critical human talent away from investments with positive value and towards investments that reward corruption and bureaucratic aggrandizement. Globalization of technology can facilitate the lack of accountability of dictators by enabling them to control new opportunities for plunder and squirrel their booty away in Switzerland. Old theories of growth assumed benevolent polities, even a benign neglect by people with the power to control societies through the use of violence. New theories recognize what Tornell and Lane (1999) call a "voracity effect," in which windfall economic gains from technology or assistance can exacerbate predatory politics, making the country worse off.

In much of Africa, the "night watchman" state of Adam Smith, ensuring peace and freedom for individuals to enter into contracts for the use of their property, has indeed mutated into a warlord state, an "open sore" on the African continent (Soyinka 1996).

African dictators have not been good for the economies of the countries they rule. This outcome was not necessary; in some parts of the world dictators have fostered decades of rapid economic growth. There is something different about African dictators, on the whole. Wintrobe (1998) presents a useful typology of dictatorships. Some dictators, the timocrats, might promote the institutions necessary for economic growth. They allow commerce to flourish. They do not overly tax commercial activity. Other dictators do less for economic growth. Totalitarian dictators usually ignore the common-sense prescriptions of Adam Smith in favor of visionary plans to transform societies through coercion. Tyrants actively use fear and terror to maintain their holds on power, and often think of terror as an end in itself; they enjoy the power of controlling terrified people. Tinpot dictators use less awful methods of divide-and-rule, corruption, random shifts of allegiances, and lengthy imprisonments to secure their hold on power while they plunder the wealth of the nation. Although no researcher has categorized African dictators along these lines, it is probably a safe bet that most of them fall into the tinpot category. Tyrants, though, have ruled over some of the largest and most populous countries. Others lie waiting in the hinterlands.

Tyrants and tinpot dictators have only a shaky hold on power; therefore, they are interested in plunder. Plunder sustains and even improves the dictator's position relative to his potential political opponents. The dictator gets richer and more powerful, and everyone else gets poorer. Policies that promote economic growth might make the dictator even better off, but they also make his opponents better off. Since control over political power depends on both absolute and relative standing of opponents, keeping them as far down as possible, and as far away from the dictator as possible, is the preferred strategy (Acemoglu and Robinson 2000a; 2000b).

Foreign powers have contributed to this bad outcome both directly and indirectly. Directly, foreign powers have often aided and abetted rulers who would serve their purposes. During the Cold War, numerous African leaders received financial and military assistance from the United States or the Soviet Union long after they abandoned any pretense of legitimate rule. The rivalry between Britain and France, as former colonial powers seeking to maintain commercial and diplomatic power, provided another source of support for illegitimate rule. Foreign powers rarely took any strong steps to limit the actions of African dictators, and offered little support to democratic opposition forces.

Developed nations did eventually begin to sanction countries with dictatorial regimes. Unfortunately, this often improved the position of the dictators. While the dictators might lose under sanctions, the citizenry often lost even more. There is a clear lesson from the Nash bargaining solution, to be examined in Chapter 7, that applies with much relevance to today's disputes over the effectiveness of sanctions against dictatorial regimes. If the sanctions hurt the citizenry more than the dictator, they are unlikely to be effective in changing the balance of power, even though they do hurt the dictator (Hufbauer, Schott, and Elliott 1990; Niblock 2001).

The preponderance of tyrants and tinpot dictators is straightforward to explain. African countries were forged in flawed crucibles, which is not surprising given the haste of the colonial blacksmiths to disembarrass themselves of their possessions. At independence, few democratic institutions checked the powers of the head of state. Colonialism was thus responsible for the African nightmare, though not in an obvious or intended way. Colonialism did not "extract" all the wealth of Africa, though it certainly did extract significant quantities from some countries, such as Congo (Hochschild 1998; Rodney 1982). In many countries the colonial experience left considerable infrastructure and opportunities for wealth creation. What colonialism did do was leave a legacy of illegitimacy to the nascent states (Englebert

2000a). This illegitimacy was both conceptual and geographical. African states were born unconstitutionally and their borders drawn arbitrarily.

In the contemporary world, polities are organized as states that monopolize violence within their borders, yet do not have to resort to violence because they are legitimate. States earn loyalty and acceptance when state actors respect self-imposed, constitutional rules of procedure. Citizens of states come to respect borders when these have emerged from long histories of compromise.

One problem African countries have is with the borders that define the rule of the states. The arbitrary borders created and bequeathed by European powers have borne little relation to the affordable infrastructure to "project" power over the entire state territory (Herbst 2000). The colonial powers had at their disposal the enormous resources of the metropole, the colonial army, and an ability to coordinate with neighboring states often controlled by the same empire. After independence the resources and possibilities for coordination were gone. This meant that huge swaths of territory lay effectively outside of the states' control; people in these hinterlands were subject to arbitrary policies, or even no policies. They had little ability or opportunity to act or be treated as citizens (Mamdani 1996). African states have been consumed by the low-intensity rebellions and civil wars that resulted from this problem. Few cities or other potential growth areas have been able to free themselves from the insecurity of disruption.

Recent evidence supports this view of the problem of borders, legitimacy, and ability to project power and so establish the rule of law, Englebert, Tarango, and Carter (2002) review the literature on borders: African boundaries contain more straight lines, more land-locked countries, and more partitioned ethnic groups than other borders on other continents. The authors conclude, after statistical analysis, that "arbitrary boundaries do magnify the likelihood of domestic and international conflicts, and reduce the quality of policies and institutions" (p. 3). The inability to control "the interior" exacerbated the problem of unconstitutional rule.

While newly independent states were left with paper constitutions, these reflected no real compromise among powerful entities. There was no constitution-making in the real sense of different and important actors in society sitting down, bargaining, and agreeing on "rules of the game" for how political power and legal authority is to be acquired and exercised. The colonial regimes quite often had delegated important powers to "indirect rulers." These chiefs and priests were given broad leeway to exercise authority, and their power could not be questioned by their constituents. (The colonial rulers, of course, kept the prerogative of appointing and dismissing these indirect rulers "at will.") The colonial constitutions bequeathed to the new states typically gave no role to these indirect rulers.

Chiefs and priests, powerful in "native" society, were excluded, and the Islamic societies of Sahelian Africa, with their extensive "brotherhood" organizations, were marginalized.

What was worse, armies created by the colonial authorities to suppress domestic rebellions, rather than secure borders against foreign invaders, were assumed to be under the control of civilians. These civilians had never exercised power before, and they had few institutional ties to the armies. It is no surprise that the constitutions were quickly seen by all as documents not even worth the paper they were written on. Deeds would be judged by results, not constitutionality. The rise of tinpot dictators and tyrants followed inevitably.

The emphasis here on the political vicious circle of civil unrest and economic decline is deliberate. Policies are bad, and polities are in turmoil. Careful studies of economic growth in African countries suggest that the problem is not so much one of low accumulation of investments in infrastructure, capital, and schooling but increasingly poor utilization of those investments. As the comprehensive investigation of O'Connell and Ndulu (2000) puts it: "Only about half of the growth difference between Africa and other developing countries is due to slower accumulation of physical and human capital; the remainder is accounted for by slower growth in the productivity residual. Factors behind slow productivity growth are thus an essential part of the story of slow African growth" (pp. 1–2). A study of growth in Burkina Faso reaches a similar conclusion (Savadogo, Coulibaly, and McCracken 2002).

Legitimacy, Civil Wars, and GDP Growth

There is growing evidence supporting the theory that the initial conditions of illegitimacy and consequent political instability and war explain much of the variation in growth rates across countries (Acemoglu, Johnson, and Robinson 2001; Englebert 2002), though there are some studies that cast doubt on the causality and robustness of the relationship (Campos and Nugent 2002). The experience of Botswana is instructive. There, GDP and per capita income have been growing at a very rapid rate for almost thirty years. In fact, Botswana by some measures has had the highest growth rate in the world (see Table 2.2). Because of its exceptional growth, Botswana has attracted a lot of scholarly attention. No smoking gun has been discovered to solve the mystery. Reality turns out to be prosaic and points directly at the issue of legitimacy. The country at independence in 1960 was very poor, certainly just as poor as any other African country. Fantastic diamond wealth was discovered, and that wealth was not squandered but rather wisely invested in infrastructure for cattle (the main economic activity of the population) and schooling. Macroeconomic policies have been good. There has been little inflation, and the central government has done a good job controlling fiscal deficits. The exchange rate has been kept in line with purchasing power in the major trading partners (chiefly by being kept formally pegged to South Africa, by far the largest market for Botswana's imports and exports). State-run enterprises, usually leading indicators of disastrous government policies of patronage, have been profitable and relatively uncorrupt.

Policies were reasonable, it seems, because Botswana at independence maintained a set of political institutions that were widely perceived as legitimate and the political actors in those "indigenous" institutions did not have to compete with a new class of political actors to occupy the emptying state apparatus set up by colonial administrators.

Samatar (1999) and Acemoglu, Johnson, and Robinson (2001) summarize the current thinking about Botswana, arguing that a constellation of good initial conditions enabled subsequent success. The most important of these initial conditions included:

1. An alignment of interests between political and economic elites (as Marx and Engels put it long ago, the state was simply a committee for managing the affairs of the bourgeoisie).
2. A lack of indirect rule, which meant that no separate dual authority was created.
3. Strong local institutions of accountability persisted.
4. A single economic activity (cattle) meant that different groups could not be exploited for the benefit of other groups.
5. Ethnic heterogeneity was not as obvious; no large number of exclusive groups were marked by identifiable physical and cultural characteristics.

Going through this list, one finds that many of these conditions have not been met in other countries.

Case studies are fine, but one can always find an exception that proves the rule. Another way to test this theory of the importance of state legitimacy is to run a regression explaining the variation in economic growth rates across countries. Some variable measuring state legitimacy might explain the variation in growth rates, and this would lend credence to the intuitive discussion above. A great many studies have been undertaken using regression analysis, with samples of all the countries of the world for the period since the decolonization of the third world during the 1960s. A regression enables the analyst to determine whether and to what degree a certain factor influences an outcome. The regression method measures the effect by controlling for the effects of other explanatory factors (see Appendix).

In this case, the regression is slightly more complicated than usual, taking advantage of the fact that countries are observed over time. For each country, the growth rate over a decade is calculated. This is the outcome variable, and there are four decadal growth periods since 1960 for each country. With the ninety or so countries of the world for which data are available, this yields just under four hundred observations. One group of explanatory variables represents characteristics of countries that do not change much over time. Included in this group is a variable constructed by Englebert (2000b) to classify countries according to state legitimacy at the beginning of the 1960s or at independence. Table 2.4 outlines how the variable is constructed. Also included are dummy variables indicating whether the country is landlocked and whether the country is an oil exporter, regional dummies (only the coefficients for the Africa region are reported), and the degree of ethnolinguistic fragmentation (the probability that any two persons picked randomly will be of the same ethnic group).

Another group of explanatory variables includes the values of certain key policies and economic characteristics of the country at the beginning of the decade. These explain subsequent performance. First and foremost are the initial, and squared initial, levels of GDP. Poorer countries might be expected to have higher growth rates than wealthier countries. They are expected to converge, for the reasons given above. Included also are measures of the extent of "democraticness" of the country's polity, as measured by a major research initiative in political science, the POLITY IV project,

Table 2.4 Construction of the State Legitimacy Dummy

	Legitimate (= 1)	Nonlegitimate (= 0)
1. Was the country colonized in modern times?	No	Yes (go to question 2)
2. When reaching independence, did the country recover its previous sovereignty, identity, or effective existence?	Yes	No (go to question 3)
3. If the country was created by colonialism, was there a human settlement predating colonization?	No	Yes (go to question 4)
4. Did the colonizers (and/or their imported slaves) reduce the preexisting societies to numerical insignificance (or assimilate them) and become the citizens of the new country?	Yes	No (go to question 5)
5. Does the postcolonial state do severe violence to preexisting political institutions?	No	Yes

Source: Reprinted from *World Development,* Vol. 28. Pierre Englebert, "Solving the Mystery of the AFRICA Dummy," p. 1828, Table 2, copyright 2000, with permission from Elsevier.

that codes every country in the world on a scale of –10 (very autocratic) to 10 (very democratic). In addition, two measures of trade policy are included. One is the black market premium, which captures how much the black market exchange rate diverges from the official exchange rate. It is an excellent measure of how much a government is allowing trade and investment to be determined by market forces as opposed to government fiat. A related measure is the real exchange rate. This index compares the domestic price level with foreign prices. The higher the real exchange rate, the more overvalued the country's currency is, and the more expensive its goods will be abroad. The country will presumably not be exporting as much, and so will grow more slowly. A measure of the terms of trade is also included, to capture adverse shocks to an economy that sees the world prices for its exports decline. Finally, included in the regression is a measure of the country's commitment to the human rights of women. This indicator codes ratification of the Convention for the Elimination of Discrimination Against Women and the strength of commitment to the gender rights regime that convention put in place. The higher the indicator, the more the country is a "good world citizen" when it comes to gender rights. Details are available in Kevane (2003).

Table 2.5 shows the results. The different specifications of the regression yield similar results. Three variables stand out. If the postcolonial state is legitimate, then growth rates are considerably higher, just a bit more than a full percentage point. The effect is even stronger in Africa. Civil wars have been very bad for growth, especially for African countries where spending the decade in war lowers annual growth by four percentage points. Finally, bad policies by governments, as captured in the real exchange rate overvaluation variable, negatively affect growth in a serious way, and in a magnified way for African countries.

The regression also affords an opportune moment to ask whether gender equity, broadly measured, is correlated with economic growth. A couple of recent papers suggest that is indeed the case (Dollar and Gatti 1999; Klasen 1999), and these papers were featured prominently in the World Bank's policy research report, *Engendering Development* (2001). The report suggested that one of the reasons for this supposed strong correlation may be that women are significantly less likely to be corrupt (Swamy et al. 2001), and less corruption is strongly associated with higher rates of economic growth (Mauro 1995). It should be noted that Seguino (2000) offers a counterhypothesis, arguing that in Asia gender inequality was, paradoxically, good for growth. She maintains that relatively low wages for women in nascent industrializing sectors were an important consideration for foreign direct investment. The results here suggest that more work on these hypotheses needs to be carried out. The estimated coefficient on the commitment to gender equity in Table 2.5 is sometimes negative, sometimes positive, but never statistically significant.

Table 2.5 Results of Regressions Explaining Growth in GDP per Capita, 1960–2000

	Mean of variable, 1970	Mean of variable, 1990	(1)	(2)	(3)	Sub-Saharan Africa only (4)
Real GDP per capita, USD[a]	4,851	6,097	0.039 (3.12)[b]	0.037 (2.58)[b]	−0.031 (1.29)	0.026 (0.47)
Square log real GDP p.c., USD			−0.003 (3.61)[b]	−0.003 (2.78)[b]	0.000 (0.00)	−0.002 (0.40)
Africa, 0–1			−0.031 (2.23)[c]	−0.020 (1.49)		
Englebert measure of state legitimacy	.62		0.013 (2.54)[c]	0.013 (2.26)[c]		0.032 (2.22)[c]
Ethnolinguistic fragmentation	.41		−0.002 (0.24)	0.003 (0.30)		0.040 (1.87)
Extent of democratic polity	−.13	1.36	0.028 (1.20)	0.004 (0.16)	−0.005 (0.17)	−0.038 (0.55)
Index of commitment to women's rights	5.05	13.05	−0.019 (1.08)	−0.008 (0.39)	0.043 (1.64)	−0.070 (1.44)
Percent of decade in civil war	.06	.12	−0.010 (1.99)[c]	−0.014 (2.67)[b]	−0.011 (1.77)	−0.044 (2.53)[c]
Black market premium	.02	.06		0.005 (0.48)	0.017 (1.24)	0.020 (0.34)
Real exchange rate overvaluation	1.01	1.18		−0.010 (3.20)[b]	−0.007 (2.11)[c]	−0.017 (2.82)[b]
Index of terms of trade	.12	.10		−0.007 (0.21)	−0.040 (1.04)	0.038 (0.54)
Landlocked country, 0–1	.19			−0.002 (0.47)		0.006 (0.66)
Oil exporting country, 0–1	.09			−0.005 (0.78)		0.006 (0.48)
Constant			−0.086 (1.81)	−0.095 (1.70)	0.264 (2.71)[b]	−0.106 (0.57)
Observations			387	270	272	71
Number of countries			115	89	90	30
R-squared			.23	.34	.30	.28

Sources: World Bank Development Indicators (2002); Easterly and Levine dataset available at http://www.worldbank.org/research/growth/ddeale.htm; Polity IV dataset available at http://www.cidcm.umd.edu/inscr/polity/; Gleditsch et al. (2002); Kevane (2003).

Notes: Absolute value of z-statistics in parentheses; a. In the regression this value is logged; b. significant at 1% level; c. significant at 5% level. Regressions (1) and (2) include regional dummies, of which only Latin America is consistently significant. Regression (3) includes country dummies, and so is a "fixed effects" regression looking at variation over time within countries. Each country can have up to four observations, one for each decade. Several variables (polity, women's rights, real overvaluation, black market premium, and terms of trade) are rescaled in the regression analysis by dividing by 100. The magnitudes of the coefficients, then, are actually much smaller than presented, in terms of economic significance.

Implications

This discussion of African decline has been an exercise in diagnosis. What remains is prescription and prognosis.

The discussion above suggests some specific steps that people of good-will living in foreign powers can encourage their governments to take. Foreign powers do have the ability to help reverse the decline of African economies and to encourage a return to economic growth. These powers must be pressured to end their support for undemocratic and corrupt regimes. They must be pressured to aggressively enforce their own laws prohibiting and penalizing corrupt behavior by their own nationals. There is little doubt that many of the large mining and oil companies that operate on the continent turn a blind eye to the diversion of funds into government coffers (Reno 1998). The definition of the criminality of bribes in industrial countries calls for extensive proactive measures and due diligence. These definitions should be broadened to include payments to organizations run by criminal regimes (such as state-owned petroleum companies), even when these regimes have the veneer of official recognition that comes from occupying a chair at the United Nations. A related measure is to establish an international body that would classify certain international lending to sovereign countries as "odious" and therefore not justiciable in domestic courts (Kremer and Jayachandran 2002).

Going beyond halting dealings with criminal dictatorships, there is also much that can be done to support semilegitimate regimes as they transform themselves into legitimate regimes. Those regimes need to be encouraged to follow the path of legitimacy and institution-building. The way to do that is to urge them to enter into binding international commitments. Future dictators will find it costly to escape or interfere with these international responsibilities. Preferential trade zones, for example, which guarantee the transparency of investment and public procurement processes, are one such example. Another example is cross-border infrastructure investment. Many countries have few road or rail links across borders. Burkina Faso and neighboring Ghana, for instance, have few paved roads and no common electricity grid linking the countries.

When more honest regimes are ready to receive increased foreign assistance, there is a new consensus on the efficacy of many public health interventions that were written off over the years. Projects to reduce parasites have been shown to provide very high returns, in terms of enabling people and children to invest more in their futures (Lengeler, Cattani, and De Savigny 1996; McMillan 1995; Miguel and Kremer 2001).

In 2002, the rock singer Bono and U.S. Treasury secretary Paul O'Neill took a much publicized trip across the continent (Hertzberg 2002). They listened to the eloquent voices of ordinary Africans and disagreed over how to interpret the projects and successes they saw. More aid, said Bono. More efficacy, said O'Neill. They ended their tour with a handshake and little else. It is a platitude, but change will only happen on the continent when Africans are engaged in the debate. It is important to acknowledge the grassroots work and courageous leadership by countless women and men across the continent who speak out against corruption and dictatorship. Many of these individuals are murdered as they struggle to form coalitions capable of overthrowing tyrants and building new foundations. Every country has its martyrs to the causes of justice and freedom from want. Someday they shall succeed and will be able to have open debates about economic and gender policy, followed by open elections, followed by honest implementation.

3

Gender and Development: Some Preliminaries

Zimbabwean Etta Dendere blamed the family structure for not empowering women. In the family hierarchy a boy is ranked higher than a girl, irrespective of their ages, she said. This hierarchical system is usually transferred to marriage. "A woman has no choice when it comes to having a baby." Dendere explained that the in-laws expect children as soon as the "bride price" has been paid.

—*Celeste Booysen, SABCnews.com, July 11, 2000*

The traditions of all the dead generations weigh like a nightmare on the brain of the living.

—*Karl Marx*

The grinding poverty of African countries falls heavily on the shoulders of women. Both the living and the dead share responsibility for this gendering of poverty. Men and women lead gendered lives because they make different choices, and they make different choices in part because they are presented with different opportunities. These opportunities are shaped by social structures. More than the traditions of dead generations, structures include legal rules, norms of behavior, ongoing institutions and hierarchies, patterns of competition in different markets, persisting prices of goods and services, shared expectations about the future, and mechanisms for nonmarket transfers of property, services, and resources.

Structures fix the space of feasible action that persons might take. Sometimes structures shape choices by bundling rights, obligations, contingencies, and commodities. Choices that respect the bundling are treated as legitimate by other actors in society, while choices that unbundle the package are considered illegitimate. Sexual acts, for example, are often bundled with rights and obligations to care for children.

It is not always easy to identify precisely what constitutes a structure in any given society. The forms of structures vary. In some cases, structures are monolithic entities, codified and crystal-clear. In other cases, multiple structures exist and people choose and negotiate among structures to secure their own advantage. For many African societies structures are not written down. Regimes and rules are transmitted across generations and social groups orally, through recitation and collective memory. This is why "elders" are often so important in many African societies. Their expertise, derived from experience, makes them repositories of structure.

Structures bound opportunities in a relational way. Each individual in a society occupies a different position in relation to a structure. Sometimes those positions are unique to each individual, as when a person contemplates who in his or her circle of friends might help in a time of need. In other settings the relational spaces are common: all women are excluded from the priesthood in the Catholic Church. Sen (1981), in stressing the role of market structures in perpetrating famines, introduced the notion of structures as shaping the *entitlement mappings* of individuals. Food entitlements, how much food a person or family might command, determine whether someone lives or dies. More broadly, entitlements, opportunities, budget constraints, and feasible actions are all different terms for expressing how people might reasonably consider their actions to be constrained.

The models that people construct to make sense of the world are themselves structures, if they are widely shared. If many people share the same model of how the economy or society works, then their behavior will be patterned in predictable ways. If everyone thinks the Catholic Church does not allow women into the priesthood, then no women apply, no male priests challenge the system, and the pope devotes little time to the issue. The structure persists, and people's models are confirmed. If everyone thinks the price of gasoline will be similar to what it was yesterday, then no one changes their purchasing and supplying behavior to any large degree, and the price indeed turns out to be the same.

In current thinking in evolutionary biology, applied both to humans and nonhumans, structure consists of the set of evolutionarily stable strategies. Because other genes are encoded to respond to social stimuli in certain ways, genes that are similarly encoded do better than other kinds of genes. This is one way of thinking about the persistence of altruistic and social behavior in many species.

Politics is the metastructure of society. Political actions are often geared toward changing structures, and political institutions are the structures that shape how structures can be changed. Political structures are also about the way violence is controlled; this is of paramount importance in many African societies, as so many swing from periods of horrific violence to periods of relative calm with low-intensity violence in the background.

Self-Ownership: A Critical Structure

A most basic structure is self-ownership. Does a person own her or his body, and have control over her or his actions? Is a person an inferior entity in the social order, a legal minor? When women do not own themselves, that structure clearly trumps any other structures of social life for women. Many societies around the world have denied to women the right of self-ownership. In the United States, the legal system whereby married women were considered to be minors was called *coverture* (after the French, *femme couverte*) and was in place in many states of the union until the early twentieth century. Hymowitz and Weissman described the system as follows:

> Under coverture married women had no property and no money of their own. Even a married woman's clothing and household goods belonged to her husband. A married woman's dowry and any inheritance she might receive also belonged to him. In most instances he could sell her property without her consent. Nor did a married woman control her own wages. She could work all day as a servant, and her husband was legally free to take her earnings and allow her to starve. A married woman could not buy or sell anything without her husband's permission. She could not make contracts, sue in court, or be sued. (1978, 23)

The most significant economic effect of coverture is likely to be the disincentive for women to carry out any extra effort at improving their livelihoods, if their husbands get to appropriate all of the benefit. Women are not the "residual claimants" of their efforts. A woman who wants to become an entrepreneur will think twice. Her husband will have first rights to all of her profits.

Many African societies in the past have also treated women as legal minors unable to make independent decisions. Many continue to deny to women the right of personhood. Lack of control over self has been most evident in cases of forced marriage and bridewealth used to purchase a wife. There has been much discussion in anthropology as to whether societies with bridewealth ought to be thought of as having men purchase rights over women. That is the case for some, but not all, societies with bridewealth. In a famous paper, Gray summarized the evidence from a good number of societies of Central Africa: ". . . certain defined rights in a woman are regularly sold and purchased for a price, and therefore it is not absurd to consider her as property" (1960, 36). Gray's interpretation is not at odds with other contemporary reports. Colson quotes a woman as saying: "When we were young there was no argument. If a woman told her parents that her husband beat her, her mother would say, 'you stay or we will beat you: we have already . . . accepted bridewealth for him. It is for you to return to him'" (1958, 183, cited in Chanock 1985, 19). As one male informant speaking about the colonial era in Tanzania put it to Lovett: "Once bridewealth was given for a woman, she was like a slave. She had no freedom because she could say nothing" (1996, 61).

Even in Ghana, with matrilineal societies that gave women considerably more rights and privileges than many other societies, women were offered up as "pawns" for loans between men (Austin 1993). The uncle or guardian of a woman would give her to a creditor as a kind of collateral. The creditor then had rights over the woman much as he might have rights over a piece of property. Sometimes the creditor could be her very own husband, lending money to the uncle (of his wife). In those cases, according to Grier's (1992, 311) reading of the available historical record, a man was said to have "bought" his wife. The evidence suggests to Grier that during the World War I cocoa boom it was very common for men to obtain land for plantations by pawning female relatives. Girls were reduced to the status of indentured servants.

Women could apparently buy themselves out of these sale marriages and indentureships. Gray's own analysis of Sonjo bridewealth practices suggests as much:

> In most respects a broken betrothal is dealt with by the Sonjo in the same manner as a divorce. If a young man does not wish to marry his fiancée he sends her a broken twig, which signifies his decision. The girl is then free to accept another suitor, who has only to pay the fiancé the original bride-price in order to marry the girl. The girl herself can also break the engagement if she can find an alternative suitor who is willing to pay back the bride-price. If the fiancé finds another man who is willing to buy his marriage rights, the girl is obliged to accept the change unless she can find someone more to her liking before the time set for marriage. Whoever finally marries the girl must make the regular payment of ten goats to her father before the marriage, and must also pay a fee of seven goats to the village council, which is customary at every divorce and remarriage. (1960, 41–42)

Cornwall (2001) offers a particularly poignant tale from southwestern Nigeria:

> Iya Safuratu was initially engaged to a man who turned out to be a thief. She needed a way to repay her dowry and had no means of her own. A wealthy man, an associate of her brother, approached her parents, who gladly accepted him as a husband for her. He repaid her dowry and they were married. He married a string of wives, but gave them nothing at all to feed themselves or their children. Each wife used her own business to keep her hearth-hold going. Iya Safuratu struggled to make ends meet. But she endured. At first she was the youngest of four wives, but her husband went on to marry another seven. She stuck it out. It was only when he told her one day that from then onward his latest wife would be doing everything that Iya Safuratu had been doing on the farm she decided she had to go. She went back to her parents and started trading, saving small amounts of money. And the day came, finally, when she could go to court and repay her dowry. All these years later, she proudly showed me a receipt dated 1963. (p. 76)

There is no shortage of evidence that forced marriage and household servitude remain common. In Coastal Kenya, women in Mijikenda communities are not allowed to visit their natal families (Ciekawy 1999). Hodgson (1996) offers a fascinating case study of a Maasai woman who resisted the authority of her biological father. The woman had been raised by her mother and stepfather since infancy. When she went to marry the man of her choosing, her father announced that he had already accepted bride-wealth from a friend. Maasai elders concurred and obliged the woman to break her current engagement. She fought her elders and took her case to the national court system. A judge reprimanded the elders, who continued to insist that the woman did not have the right to choose her marriage partner. Another Maasai woman, Agnes Siyiankoi, also made headlines in the late 1990s for taking her husband to court for beating her. When asked why she had agreed to marry the man who had beaten her for more than a decade, Siyiankoi responded that her father would have cursed her if she had not done as he willed (Mwangi 1997). These examples illustrate how a young woman becomes convinced that her marriage will be enforced against her will. She must either remain in the marriage or suffer physical punishment. Perhaps, over the years, she will resign herself to her situation, or rationalize it, and may in the end even participate in the same violent punishment of other young women who try to test the enforceability of these marriages.

Where Do Gender Structures Come From?

Before looking at contemporary gender structures and their dynamics in African societies, a digression is in order regarding theories of the origins of gendered structures that disfavor women. These theories are more in the nature of junk food than meat and potatoes, so a conscious decision has been made to make the discussion brief.

The problem is how to explain female subordination on a global scale. This book will document how most African societies are gendered in ways that are detrimental to women's quests for well-being and self-realization. The gendering of African societies is less male-centered compared with the typical South Asian society, but still significantly so. There seems to be little point to arguing that female subordination is not a universal reality. To be sure, an extensive literature that does debate the issue stresses the enormous variation in indicators of status and manifestations of gender (Bradley and Khor 1993; Quinn 1977; Whyte 1978). While many researchers give up on attempting to assign the characteristic "male-dominated" to a society, and there are always dimensions where women are indeed privileged, few researchers venture the argument that the situation is overall one of female dominance (James 1978). There is no need or even constituency for an international convention to eliminate discrimination against men. This, despite a tiny but vocal movement in the United States, frankly undeserving of publicity (Sommers 2000).

Theories of female subordination run the gamut from crackpot to stunning. Most do not stand up to the test of internal consistency. That is, they rarely follow the method elaborated in this book, of specifying assumptions and drawing logical inferences. What is worse, theories of origins of gender subordination are not really verifiable. A test of an explanation might look like this: Put human babies on different worlds or continents, have them be raised by robots or well-trained actors, and then watch them develop over many generations. Of course, the worlds or continents and robots or actors would have to vary enough along the lines proposed by the explanation so that some societies ended up having female dominance. Otherwise, every and any "experimental condition" would explain male dominance, and hence nothing would be explained.

The problems with verification using the variance of gender structures in actual human populations around the world are twofold. First, almost all societies would end up being classified as male-dominated under any reasonable classification scheme. Second, all societies in the world probably emerged from the same hunter-gatherer origins in Africa, and if gender structures are very persistent, then the initial conditions of life several hundred thousand years ago generated a gendered structure that may have reproduced itself over time for every human society that branched off from the original group of humans.

So the exercise of theory-building and verification has little nutritional value, to continue with the food metaphor, but is tasty nevertheless. Ordinary Africans themselves constantly debate the causes of gender inequality. Indeed, one is hard-pressed to pick up an African newspaper without reading an article on the subject. The topic is not exclusively African, and theories of female subordination are often impressively divorced from geographic specificity. There is, consequently, no "African" theory about gender subordination, and no general theory of subordination for Africa.

The typical place to start with theories of gender subordination is with hunter-gatherer societies. For at least 2 million years, humans and their ancestors probably lived in small groups that engaged in hunting and gathering. That long period involved considerable genetic change (Robson and Kaplan 2003). There is no reason to doubt that the two sexes, male and female, were subject to different evolutionary pressures during this period. Some men and women with particular genetic dispositions would have fared better than others, and their dispositions would have been successfully passed on to more offspring. Susceptibility to and mechanisms of hormone triggering, cognitive processes, and physical capacities might have become (or remained, from an earlier prehuman period) different (Balaban and Short 1994). These differences, genetically coded, might then explain differential behaviors even in the more socialized worlds that children found themselves in after the domestication of plants and animals that marked the Neolithic revolution. Propensity toward aggressive behavior on perceived provocation, for example, might be a genetic difference that has led to common patterns of male dominance in settled societies that no longer face dangers from wild animals.

Theories of gender dispositions emerging from evolutionary pressures are debated in the field of sociobiology, which also considers genetic predispositions more broadly. Early critics of the sociobiological approach objected to a perceived political agenda of the new discipline, especially when it came to the issue of gender. As Lowe put it: "The basic message is that our society is partly shaped by biological factors, that we must be wary about trying to change the status quo, since attempts to do so will go against our natural propensities" (1978, 124). Over the past two decades, however, the field has attracted considerable serious scholarship. Much experimental evidence in economics and anthropology, for example, suggests that humans are probably genetically disposed to calculate and evaluate choices in ways quite different from the supposed "rationality" predicted by game theory (Bowles and Gintis 2002; Bowles, Gintis, and Osborne 2001; Henrich et al. 2001). Recent interpretations also suggest that humans in general have genetic dispositions toward altruistic behavior (Field 2001). This disposition considerably complicates models of persons as self-interested maximizers. Better models have to take into account how individuals evaluate the effects of their actions on the welfare of others.

Genetic dispositions that evolved from the pressures of hunting and gathering only go so far in explaining the gendering of societies in the contemporary world. Indeed, there is considerable controversy over the gendering of Neolithic society (Anderson and Zinsser 2000; Claassen and Joyce 1997; Donald and Hurcombe 2000; Ehrenberg 1989; Kent 1998).

The feminist movement of the 1970s spawned a "goddess" revival that asserted that the agricultural communities of the Neolithic period were dominated by women. This hypothesis of prehistorical matriarchy had a patina of truth that resisted healthy skepticism for many years and from many quarters. At least until recently. Eller (2000; 2001), in particular, has called into question the empirical basis for the idea of a matriarchal prehistory. Her debunking of the myth of a glorious matriarchal past does not reveal a patriarchal past but rather the paucity of evidence for a assigning any "-archy" to Neolithic societies.

Some hunter-gatherer theories mix the genetic flavoring into a Darwinian soup of societal selection. These theories emphasize how societies with particular kinds of social organizations would have been more successful than other societies because they would have been more efficient at securing sustenance or in fighting off competitors. Successful gendered societies would have reproduced their form of social organization over more and more people. If successful hunter-gatherer societies typically exhibited male dominance, and these societies were the cradles of all human civilizations, and gender structures persisted over time through the "stickiness" of norms, then there is an explanation of gender inequality in the contemporary world. One reason for male dominance of the successful societies is a straightforward tool hypothesis. Men evolved with greater upper body strength. This strength was especially handy when hunting large animals with primitive tools. Hunting societies that divided tasks in a way that favored male control over weaponry were more successful than gender-neutral societies, where weaker women wielded weapons. As male control over weapons enabled success in struggles against other human groups, there was little impetus for change.

Other theories draw attention to how male dominance may have emerged from the social interaction of humans in increasingly stable social situations where language and communication skills evolved from generation to generation. Some of these draw a distinction between public and private domains. In this view, early humans stayed close to their nuclear families. Gradually, groups began gendering their activities to take advantage of male comparative advantage in hunting big game. Hunting big game was a cooperative activity, while gathering, the domain of women, remained relatively solitary. Men developed a culture and language for mediating cooperation among strangers. They created a public space, where strangers respected rules of behavior. Knowledge of and participation in that public space generated compound returns as human tools evolved into ever more sophisticated technologies. Other theories employ psychoanalytic concepts to explore the inner life of children and explain the original male dominance of the public space, which subsequently proved so important to societies. Chodorow (1978), for example, focuses on the differential resolution of the Oedipus complex by girls compared with boys. Girls continue to identify with the mothering roles of their mothers and want to mother as they become adults. Boys resolve their Oedipus complex by detaching themselves from roles involving affection for children. Almost guaranteed to raise a smile in its simple version, another early Freudian-inspired theory goes something like this: Girls and boys are raised by their mother, by the hearth. They both identify with the mother, source of nourishment. One day, the boy discovers he is not like his mother. Will he eventually become like her, losing his penis in the process? He does not want it cut off. He wanders out beyond the hearth. Other boys are there, similarly fearful and resentful. They gang together. *Voilà,* public space dominated by men.

Choices: The Maximization Model

As the theories discussed above imply, structures change over time, and the changes in structure must be viewed as the outcome of some process whereby people change their actions or their thoughts, or both. Structures may persist because people are like automata, mindlessly repeating decisions they have taken in the past. As the old saying goes, "History does not repeat itself, man does."

But to understand or predict changes in structure that result from changes in the *choices* that people make, a model of decisionmaking is needed. There are many such models. Some hyperrational models have humans applying the foresight of chess grandmasters to every action they might take, including how such actions might affect their own "future selves." This book settles for a simple model that is an industry standard in economics (often called neoclassical microeconomic theory) but is also used with increasing frequency in other disciplines. A simple model simplifies; that is why it is useful. But that also means it has plenty of drawbacks.

The simple model goes like this: People make choices to maximize their satisfaction or happiness, subject to the constraints they face. Social structures are terribly important in determining these constraints, but of course individual, personal characteristics also matter. Structures typically determine the resources available to a person, their budget constraint, and their available labor, a time constraint. The measure of satisfaction or happiness is often labeled the "utility" received by a person from consuming or doing something, following the usage of Jeremy Bentham, the nineteenth-century British philosopher who is credited with founding the school of thought known as utilitarianism. A utility function maps actions taken and goods and services consumed by an individual to an indicator of the individual's utility. The utility function can be thought of as representing a ranking of all possible outcomes of the conceivable actions. Budget and time constraints delimit the feasible range of utility. People choose the highest-ranking achievable outcome. Why, after all, would they ever choose a lower ranking achievable outcome?

A compact, mathematical notation can summarize the maximization model. (Mathematics helps the model sound more 'scientific' than it might actually be!) Suppose an individual has preferences over two goods. The quantity consumed of the first is measured by x and the quantity of the second measured by y.. The utility function is $U(x, y)$. Utility functions such as this one are assumed to exhibit two properties. More of both goods is preferred to less of both, but the extra utility from consuming more of x or y declines as one consumes more. This extra utility is known as the *marginal utility,* and it is assumed to be positive but declining. Introspection suggests this is generally true: for almost any product that is divisible, having some more of the product engenders more satisfaction, when starting from zero, than when adding to some positive amount already consumed or consumable. Products that are "lumpy" may violate this principle. Going from zero to half a refrigerator generates little extra utility, while going from half to a full refrigerator may be quite refreshing.

A person chooses quantities of x and y to maximize their utility, subject to the budget constraint that the value of their purchases (the price of x times the quantity x plus the price of y times the quantity y) has to be less than the money or income available for spending. In the mathematical formulation, $p_x x + p_y y \leq I$, where I is the person's income.

The optimal choice of x and y will have the property that the marginal utility of consuming x, represented by U_x, divided by the price of x is equal to the marginal utility of consuming y, represented by U_y, divided by the price of y. Or, equivalently,

$$\frac{U_x}{U_y} = \frac{p_x}{p_y}$$

The ratio of the marginal utilities has to be equal to the ratio of prices. The ratio of marginal utilities says how many units of y the person would need to be given to be induced to give up a unit of x. If the marginal utility of x were two and the marginal utility of y were four, then the person would be happy to receive anything more than half a unit of y for a unit of x. The ratio of prices likewise says how many units of y a person could get in the market if she sold a unit of x. If she sold x, she would get the price p_x, and she could then buy some y at the price p_y. The ratio of the prices is how many units of y they could have. Again, if the price of x were three, and the price of y were six, then the person selling one unit of x could get half a unit of y. Maximization subject to a budget constraint means that the person keeps buying and selling x and y until the ratio of marginal utilities equals the price ratio. It is easy to see why this must be so. If it were not, then a person could obtain higher utility by selling some fraction of the good with the relatively low marginal utility and using the money to buy the good with the relatively high marginal utility. This discussion is really a development of the idea of *opportunity cost*. Maximization models emphasize how a choice to do one thing, given a constraint, implies that something else cannot be done. Not doing the other thing is the opportunity cost of doing the chosen action. The opportunity cost of purchasing and consuming an extra unit of the good with low marginal utility, relative to its price, is not consuming the other good. The other good generates more utility per dollar spent. The model predicts that a person allocates his or her income so that the opportunity costs of different actions are equal.

Firms, farmers, and traders are often modeled as maximizing an even simpler function, their profit function. Profits are the difference between revenues and costs. Profits rise as more product is sold, usually at a decreasing rate. As a firm expands production, it uses the inputs less and less efficiently. Management may get top-heavy, or machines may wear out quicker. A profit function that describes a firm that produces a single output using a single input might look like:

$$\Pi = pF(l) - wl,$$

where Π stands for profits, p is the price of the product, $F(l)$ is a production function, describing how labor input, l, is transformed into product. The costs of production are simply the wage times the amount of labor hired. The optimal amount of labor to hire is where the extra revenue from producing and selling the additional units produced by another unit of labor input, which is the price of the product times the marginal product of using more inputs, is equal to the marginal cost of production, here simply the wage. The marginal product is the derivative of the production function, or $F'(l)$, and indicates how much a change in labor affects production. There will be only one level of labor that maximizes profits. This level may be represented by l^*, and is defined by the equation $pF'(l) = w$. Figure 3.1 illustrates the maximum profits obtainable when using the optimal level of inputs. The curved line represents the price of the product times the production function, and this is rising at a decreasing rate as more of the labor input is used in production. The straight line is represents the "wage bill," the total amount of wage paid for hiring different amounts of labor, and is the wage times the amount of labor input used. The distance between the lines is the profit at any level of input use. Maximum profits obtain when using labor l^*.

The utility and profit maximization models are useful for a number of reasons. As mentioned, the virtue of the model is that it can represent compactly what might often be very complicated problems, and it enables the

Figure 3.1 Illustration of Profit Maximization

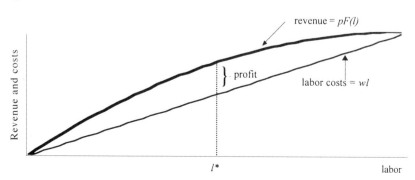

use of mathematical techniques to locate optimal actions. This may be very useful to decisionmakers. Many problems, such as determining the optimal allocation of a financial portfolio or the optimal mix of crops and planting strategies in high-risk environments, can benefit from careful specification of objectives and use of mathematical techniques to derive solutions. Indeed, application of these techniques has been one of the driving forces behind the increased productivity of agriculture around the world. More deliberate maximization may be very rewarding.

In addition, maximization models may help researchers explain people's decisions. The maximization model does not preclude ignorance, mistakes, and bad judgment. Nor does it preclude choices made under the influence of addictive necessity. It does emphasize how unlikely it is that an outside observer to a social situation, especially one involving economic decisions, will be able to easily identify choices that are making people worse off. The spirit of maximization models is that people are probably making the best choices they can given the information and possibilities that they have. If an outside observer sees a person doing something that seems strange, the person probably had a good reason for doing it. A classic case of the importance of this spirit concerns discussions about the future of peasant farmers (Schultz 1964). For many, peasants are tradition-bound, ignorant, and superstitious. There is little hope of bringing them into the world of "modern" agriculture, in this view. To put land to more productive use, peasants should be removed. The maximization approach suggests more careful investigation. Peasants are poor, but their behavior exhibits many of the traits predicted by simple maximization models. Give them more opportunities, this approach says, and you will be surprised.

Thinking about people as maximizers weeds out bad thinking and bad writing (the two grow together). Consider the following sentence, from an actual paper submitted to an academic journal, but typical of bad thinking: "Because farmers are poor, they are forced to grow cash crops, rather than food crops, and this makes them poorer." Interpretation of this sentence hinges on the sense of the much-abused word "forced." Was force actually used? The context makes clear it was not. Farmers had choices about whether to grow cash crops or food crops. In this case, the context makes clear that the sentence has little meaning. The choice to grow cash crops must make the farmer less poor. Otherwise, the farmer would be choosing to be poorer. The maximization model suggests caution when evaluating assertions about how choices have made people worse off. Circumstances make people find themselves in dire straits; choices make them better off.

Maximization models are also useful in figuring out and predicting complex responses to stimuli. For instance, the utility model enables us to see that most changes in economic environments have both "substitution effects" and "income effects." The substitution effect captures how a change alters the opportunity costs of different actions and consequently shifts behavior toward the action with the now lower opportunity cost. The income effect captures how changes make some people better off and others worse off. When the price of a product goes down, a consumer is conceptually wealthier; he or she can purchase everything he or she did before, with income left over. The income effect captures how people's spending changes.

These effects are much in evidence in gendered projects, where the interventions that change the circumstances of choices regarding girls and boys, or choices made by women or men, might have income and substitution effects that go in opposite directions. An example may clarify this idea. In the development economics literature, considerable attention has been devoted of late to the desirability of empowering women through micro-credit programs. The credit programs intend to lower the cost of capital for women and thus increase women's incomes and give them more bargaining power at home, and women then will be able to direct more household resources on their children. Using utility-maximization models (and some common sense) researchers quickly became alerted to the possibility that promoting women's microenterprises might have an unintended side effect. The income effect works in the right direction of helping children, but the substitution effect works in the wrong direction. The woman's time working is now more valuable since she has more capital and skills. The opportunity cost of her time at home with her children is higher (she now earns more outside the home than she did before). She may earn a higher income but spend less time at home caring for the children.

Finally, the maximization model also helps us see the two reasons why the choices that people and firms make might be gendered. First, men and women may see, interpret, and respond to stimuli and choices in different ways. Part of the difference may be biological. The brains of men and women may have evolved differently. Another part of the difference may be due to nurture. Human thinking is conditioned by the social setting in which a child is raised. Nurturing directly impacts individuals by shaping their thoughts and preferences. After years of wearing gendered clothes as a child, pants for boys and dresses for girls, an adult may retain preferences for those gendered clothes as an adult. Habit is rewarded by pleasure; breaking with habit punished with stress.

The second reason why choices might be gendered is that tradeoffs presented to a decisionmaker might be gendered. Structures determine the tradeoffs that people have to confront. Two kinds of tradeoffs may result from gendered social structures. The first is where men and women have to make similar decisions, but the specific choices and opportunities available to them are different. The second is where men or women have to make choices about the allocation of resources to other people, especially children, who are gendered. If some children are male and some female, then the decisionmaker must choose how to allocate resources across gender. The outcome of their resource allocations will depend on how social structures condition the status of the children.

Alternatives to Maximization

This book shall have little to say about how childhood socialization into gendered roles persists in the form of gendered adult preferences and ways of thinking. Stigler and Becker (1977) long ago suggested than a useful analytical approach for the social sciences (of economics and sociology, and as opposed to psychology) was to follow the maxim *de gustibus non est disputandum,* "of tastes we do not dispute." They argued that it was certainly true that much social behavior could be explained as a matter of tastes. But for analytical approaches outside psychology, a useful and complementary method has been to proceed as if tastes *were not* the issue and instead to seek explanations in other social variables (such as prices and technologies).

This position has been challenged by a new generation of "economic psychologists" (Camerer 1999; Rabin 1998; 2002). These researchers argue that the dispassionate disdain for tastes of the de gustibus approach has led many economists and sociologists astray. Too much research effort has been wasted trying to come up with tortured explanations of human behavior as resulting from something other than the "humanness" of humans. The classic example of this comes from predicting how humans respond to very simple strategic settings. For example, in the "ultimatum game," an experimenter offers two subjects the following proposition. They are offered twenty dollars, on condition that one propose a split of the twenty and the other agree. The experimenter chooses who gets to propose and who agrees. The subjects might be anonymous, and not even in the same room. The remorseless logic of maximization tells the proposer to offer $19.99, and the agreer to accept. A penny, after all, is more than no pennies. Nothing of the kind happens in experiments. Enormous fractions of populations all over the world agree on fifty-fifty splits. A better theory of human behavior is called for. Tastes for fairness or altruism have to be discussed and modeled. Especially since some of these tastes for fairness and altruism are demonstrably gendered (Eckel and Grossman 1998; Kamas, Baum, and Preston 2001).

Explaining these "puzzles" of departure from maximization behavior (narrowly defined) and gendering of behavior leads to a more general critique of maximization models. Perhaps people have no single organizing "rationality" to decisionmaking. Field (2001) suggests that humans have evolved with distinct kinds of hard-wired programs in their brains. One is the maximization program, which Field calls the "foraging" algorithm. The other kind is a set of programs that kick in and direct behavior as circumstances dictate. There are many examples of how these modular algorithms lead to behavior quite different from that predicted by a foraging algorithm. One discussed by Field is the "cheater detection module," whereby in many social situations people become obsessed with determining whether a social rule has been violated. To the outside observer, these people are irrational. And they are! Their brains cannot help it.

Quite possibly many of the gender differences observed in human behavior are due to these kind of modular responses to the same stimuli. We know too little about this, however, to abandon the clear thinking that comes from applying maximization models to human behavior. A more balanced approach will surely emerge as this exciting new area of research evolves.

Choices and Structures

Enduring debates in the social sciences address the relative weight to be placed on structure versus choice when analyzing any particular social phenomenon. Some academics see structures everywhere, predetermining any outcome. Others see people making choices, with structures little more than common patterns of choices. Bentham, an influential figure in the destructuralization of the economics discipline, was a firm believer in the importance of choice (Sweet 2001) and ushered in the concept of "methodological individualism," rejecting the idea that social outcomes or structures could be understood other than as the aggregation of individual decisions. Structures emerge from and are created by the choices of individuals. These choices might be intentionally geared to alter structures, or they may simply take the problem of the reproduction of structure as given and irrelevant. When choices are gendered, the outcomes of the choices reproduce gender structures.

These considerations are relevant in approaching the issue of change in gender structures. Some choices people make are about deliberately changing structures. Intentional, political acts involve voting for or enacting changes in law and national policy, but also of interest are the singular, sometimes heroic, acts of rebellion and defiance against the established order.

Important too are changes in the projects and policies encouraged by international donors. Multilateral financial institutions, such as the World Bank, the International Monetary Fund, and the United Nations Development Program, and smaller nongovernmental organizations in the development field influence national policy through their financial incentives in the form of grants and loans to countries. The Millenium Challenge is a major, coordinated commitment by many of these organizations to reduce world poverty by half and guarantee primary schooling for every child. The resources devoted to this effort are likely to be substantial, and gender aspects of the challenge are front and center.

Finally, the Convention for the Elimination of Discrimination Against Women (CEDAW) has been an important stimulus for change. Most African countries have ratified the convention, and some are rewriting national laws to conform with its provisions. The international women's movement has been influential in aiding local movements in African countries to secure rights guaranteed under CEDAW. These policy changes herald major changes on the ground in gender relations.

These kinds of policy changes from the top are not mere empty gestures. Doubters should be reminded of the overwhelming evidence on how colonial policy increased gender inequality in colonial Africa. Colonial authorities were quite biased toward men, delivering to them disproportionate shares of the benefits of technology transfer and formal education. Women were often explicitly excluded from sharing the benefits of colonial rule, and they typically bore an inordinate share of the costs. The policy pendulum is now swinging toward a more equitable treatment of men and women.

Many of the chapters that follow will illustrate how unintentional change in structure occurs, emphasizing how gender norms can quickly change as thresholds of practice are reached that induce many people to shift their behavior dramatically. Many structures consist of the shared expectations that people have about the behavior of other members of their society. As economic behavior becomes increasingly varied, new expectations take hold.

Because structural change can happen both intentionally and unintentionally, the interesting research question is whether to assign credit or blame for structural change to intentional or unintentional acts. Did a policy change cause a change in behavior or merely reflect or ratify the existing change in behavior? The pendulum swing toward more equitable policy may reflect changes that are happening on the ground rather than presaging future changes. A relatively underdeveloped area of research tries to address these questions, and determine the social origins of policy change. For example, coverture laws were overturned on a state-by-state basis in the United States beginning at the end of the nineteenth century. Were the legal changes a reflection of the reality of women asserting rights denied by coverture, or did the legal changes actually cause changes in behavior? In a fascinating study, Geddes and Lueck (2002) examine the determinants of state-level revocations of the laws of coverture. They argue that the changes were primarily responses to increasing value from self-ownership rather than recognition of the inherent injustice of inequality. That is, the efficiency costs of not letting women be residual claimants, and thus having incentives to make decisions for themselves, began to grow. Eventually, new alignments of power in state legislatures defeated rearguard bastions of male privilege.

Consider a final example, the case of marriage in the ancient Mossi kingdom of central West Africa, in what is now Burkina Faso. The kingdom has had a rigid hierarchy of local rulers, called *naba,* who have exercised considerable control over the local population. Part of this control used to be expressed in the institution known as *pugsuiré,* whereby the chief of a village would decide on the marriage partners of young girls (Englebert 1996; Labouret 1940, 100; Skinner 1964). Sometimes these politically arranged marriages would take place at two or three-year intervals, with all of the marriageable girls assigned to partners at the same time. The institution embodied notions of reciprocity and exchange, but it is clear that the actors were chiefs, while the objects were young girls. Skinner argued that during the colonial period: "Woman exchange stood at the core of a social, economic, and political nexus that held Mossi society together" (1964, 167).

Colonial authorities wavered in their stance toward this nexus. At times, they supported the *naba;* at other times they supported radical change. Policy toward women was often complicated by policy toward the Catholic mission. The White Fathers, as the Catholic missionaries in Upper Volta were known, wanted their converts to marry Christian women. They also wanted to recruit nuns. So they supported the "liberation" of women from the pugsuiré. Colonial policy toward women was conflated with policy toward the Catholic mission, which was problematic due to a prevailing anticlericalism among the bureaucratic elite. (It should also be recalled that France itself did not permit women to vote until the mid-1940s.) Meanwhile, women were increasingly applying to the mission, to colonial courts, and to the chiefs for redress against oppressive male structures. As women's labor became more valuable in the more commercialized and less violent region, they were able to assert more rights. Structures changed as men and women made political and economic choices.

4

The Land Tenure Rights
of African Women

During his inauguration ceremony as South Africa's first democratically elected president in 1994, Nelson Mandela expressed the value attached to land in Africa: "Each of us is intimately attached to the soil of this beautiful country. Each time one of us touches the soil of this land, we feel a sense of personal renewal." These words sound hollow to millions of African women who are forced to live off a land that they till but do not own.
—*Tania Ngima, LandWeb, April 2002*

If women mark the land and divide it, it will become "women's property," so that when the husband dies or divorces his wife, the wife will still retain the land, which is wrong. Women must not own land.
—*Village head of Genieri,*
Gambia, speaking at village meeting in 1949

A young man in Africa, growing up on the homestead of his father, might ask for a small field to cultivate on his own account. His father might give him a plot of land, but he might also refuse, saying that his son should continue to work on the family farm. The young man might then approach another villager, asking for a field. A neighbor might give him an abandoned field. The village chief, or perhaps an "earth priest," or a lineage elder, might give him a larger field, especially if the young man were married. This larger field may be out in the forest, and the young man might call upon his friends to help clear the trees and scrub. After harvest, the young man might give back a portion of the crop as compensation to the ancestors or as a token rent out of respect. Slowly, and depending on the social status of the young man, the field that he farms comes to be "his." He owns the land, though not in the Western sense of freehold tenure. He cannot sell the land. He may be enjoined from transferring the land to another person, even a villager. There may be restrictions on planting trees. He may have to allow pastoralists to graze their cattle, sheep, and camels on stubble. When the young man's father dies, the sons of the family might continue to cultivate the father's farm. After some time they will divide up the fields among themselves.

The man now has use rights over a substantial number of fields. As his life cycle progresses, he may take advantage of a nascent rental market and lease out his extra land to other villagers or new settlers. He might buck village rules and sell some land down by a stream for a town merchant to establish an irrigated garden. At some point in his life his rights over land will be challenged, and he will have to go to the chief, earth priest, or lineage head to have the matter resolved. He will call upon his friends and allies in the village for a show of solidarity. Elders friendly to his family will come forward to testify on his behalf. Magic might be summoned. He might consider approaching the district administrator. Very rarely, he might go to a town court. If the young man lives in Kenya, Uganda, or on an irrigation scheme, or in one of many official resettlement communities throughout the continent, he may possess a land title, issued by a government agency. The district office might have a land register, with his father's name listed as owner.

The stylized description of land tenure presented above covers a lot of the basics of land tenure in Africa (Bassett and Crummey 1993; Berry 1993; Downs and Reyna 1988; Shipton and Goheen 1992). Land is not usually titled, and only a few countries have conducted cadastres. Rental markets are common, though rental prices are more customary than market-determined. Sales markets are inactive, and often explicitly prohibited by both local and national laws. Africans gain, maintain, or lose access to land through multiple paths, as members in social groups or networks, through labor and investment, and sometimes through purchase.

Structures of Access to Land for Women

Deliberately, the emphasis in the preceding paragraphs was on men. A young woman in the typical African village has a very different story. Her father might give her a very small field to cultivate, and so might her husband when she marries. Nobody else will give her a field. Any field she farms never becomes "hers." She can neither rent nor sell the land she cultivates. As a pithy saying has it, "women are owners of crops and not owners of fields."

There is, of course, more complexity to the land tenure status of African women than this basic description. Most societies fall into one of six systems, detailed in the remainder of this section. The first two systems are ones in which women have rights to land that allow them to alienate (sell) or allocate land. These are the exceptions. More significant and widespread are systems where women have few rights. In these systems, women's access to land comes through their social ties to kin and husbands.

Areas Influenced by Islamic Inheritance Laws

In some regions, Islamic norms of inheritance have codified women's rights to inherit and transfer land. The usual Islamic inheritance is for daughters to inherit shares half the size of their brothers, the reasoning being that the daughter is provided for by her husband, while the son has to provide for his wife. Regions where Islamic norms hold sway include the Horn of Africa, coastal areas of East Africa, and the northern halves of Sudan, Chad, and many other Sahelian countries, extending all the way to Senegal. Northern Nigeria also has a strong tradition of applying Islamic law, known as *sharia,* to land matters.

Caplan's (1975) study of inheritance rights in a Swahili village on Mafia Island off the Tanzania coast is a good example of how Islamic law can provide women with strong rights. Women on the island have rights to both bush land and higher value coconut land. A large and dispersed descent group owns the land, but this ownership amounts to no more than an ability to exercise veto power over sales of land. Rights that are valuable are those held in coconut trees. On the death of her father, a daughter inherits a share of the plantation equal to one-half of her brother's. Husbands and wives also inherit from each other; a woman receives one-eighth of her husband's property, while a husband may receive a quarter of his wife's property. Women are more likely to inherit coconut trees from their husbands than vice versa because they tend to live longer and marry younger. Valuable coconut groves are also presented to women as marriage payment or compensation on divorce. Daughters retain rights to their groves even when they have married out of their kin group.

The power of Islamic norms of inheritance can also be seen in the Gezira area of Sudan, site of one of the largest irrigation schemes in the world. During the establishment of the scheme in the 1920s, and throughout subsequent extensions, land was confiscated under national domain laws. The scheme and extensions then redistributed land in the form of semipermanent tenancies (a right to cultivate the irrigated field for an indefinite period, revocable by the schemes). The schemes gave these tenancies only to men. Over time, though, women regained their access to land through Islamic inheritance rules (Barnett 1977). Bernal (1988) found that in one irrigation scheme, about 15 percent of tenancies had reverted to women in just a few decades.

Being Muslim, of course, does not mean that a society will adhere to either the spirit or the letter of orthodox Islamic inheritance laws. Most Muslim societies in West Africa do not follow principles of Islamic inheritance when allocating land. Hill (1970) found that among the Muslim Hausa, "when a father dies, then, his manured farms are usually divided between his sons. . . . Lip service only is paid to the rules of Muslim inheritance. . . . In so far as daughters receive shares, they often proceed to sell them to a brother" (p. 148). Holy (1974) describes how the Berti, a Muslim society in western Sudan, prevented women from inheriting valuable land planted with gum arabic trees.

Matrilineal Areas Sometimes Give Strong Rights to Women

There are many different family systems in Africa. When people say who their family is, they may refer to the blood relatives of their mother. Such a society is said to be matrilineal. If they speak of their family as being the blood relatives of their father, it is patrilineal. Most people in Western societies think of both sides as their family; they practice bilateral descent. Family and descent matter in part because families often own property collectively. Being a member of a family gives one rights to the land of the family. Even when property is not owned collectively, families matter because they may have rules of inheritance that specify how property is transmitted across the generations. Many societies prohibit property from being inherited outside of the family. Only members of the matrilineage, for example, may inherit the property of a deceased member of the matriline. Patrilineages often restrict land ownership to men in the patriline. Matrilineages sometimes have men inheriting, sometimes women.

Central Africa has a large number of matrilineal societies that privilege women as owners of land. These have been well described by anthropologists. Grundfest Schoepf (1985) writes that among the Lemba of Zaire, "Men say: we live at the homes of the women; the land here belongs to women; women have a say in everything we do; we listen to the opinions of women; and so on" (p. 5). Women live in their natal villages after marriage, allow their husbands to use their land, and pass the land on to their children. In nearby southern Malawi, Davison (1995) notes that, "The matrilineal *banja* household centers on the woman who has primary rights to land through her *mbumba* lineage." (p. 184). The residents of Zomba district in Malawi also have the same practice of women owning the land and husbands coming to live with them (Hirschmann and Vaughan 1984). Muntemba (1982) similarly finds that among the matrilineal Tonga and Lenje of Zambia, women who were married and lived in their husbands' villages retained access to land in their own matrikin villages. They could inherit and own property. Poewe (1981) describes the Luapula of Zambia where women had exceptional control over land. Keller, Phiri, and Milimo (1990) summarize the early anthropological literature for the Bemba, Tonga, and Lozi that illustrates how some of the women's land could be passed on to their heirs, while some was controlled by their husbands. Finally, van Donge (1993) finds that women on the Uluguru Mountains in Tanzania were just as likely as men to own land and participate in disputes over land—on their own behalf or on behalf of their matriline.

Similar rights are sometimes found outside of Central Africa. Women in West Africa often have strong customary claims on land they have cleared for low-lying rice swamps. In some parts of Gambia, women had the right to pass this land on to their daughters and considered themselves its owners

(Dey 1981). In southwestern Burkina Faso, Goin women owned and inherited rice swamps (Dacher and Lallemand 1992), and in Sierra Leone women could appeal to their natal kin for rice fields for their exclusive use (Leach 1992).

Sahelian West Africa

Although the Islamic system and some matrilineal societies give women strong rights, it is far more common to find that women's rights are limited and secondary, as described in the beginning of the chapter. In West Africa, where women usually have very limited rights to cultivate on their own account, growing land scarcity and concentration of ownership are shrinking their allotments (Roos and Gladwin 2000; Stone and Stone 2000). Women gain land chiefly through marriage. A newly married woman will be granted land from her husband's lineage. These use rights are precarious and contingent. On divorce, widowhood, or relocation, women generally lose these rights. Single younger women rarely have rights in land. Widows may have rights to small plots in their natal community.

To get a flavor of the inequality in inheritance and rights, the following three paragraphs report on interviews with Bwa women in southwestern Burkina Faso conducted in the winter of 2000. The transcriptions are deliberately kept rough to give the reader an idea of what "fieldwork notes" look like:

> *Elderly Bwa woman, December 2000:* In the olden times the family all worked together, so elders of the family took everything. Nowadays children take possessions. Girls have no rights to inherit cattle; no rights to inherit anything. They are destined for other families so they get nothing. When a woman dies everything is for the boys who will take the things for their own households, even the pots and pans. Older sons have more rights than younger sons. The older son will take the fields of the father. The youngest son will inherit the house according to Bwa custom. If the man had many sons, they may work cattle together, or they may sell and divide.
>
> *Middle-aged Bwa widow, December 2000:* At first she said that when a man dies his sons inherit his possessions, with the youngest son inheriting all. But then when pressed she suggested that the sons might cultivate the land together until they accumulated enough oxen that they could divide up things equally. Her husband built a house that they then rented. Since his death the money goes to her oldest son, who then gives it to an uncle. Her own house belongs to her eldest son. She did not get the house she lived in, but would get the pension. She did not get her husband's cattle that were in care of a Peul. A wife gets nothing. When a woman dies, her daughters-in-law would inherit her possessions, or her own sons, or else if she had no children it would go to the husband's family. The deceased woman's family gets nothing. Her daughters can come and ask for things but no obligation to give them anything.

Older Bwa woman, December 2000: If a man dies, someone from his lineage will take his possessions. If he has grown children, then his sons will inherit oxen and field; if lots of sons, they can cultivate together. Girls do not have right to anything; they must go and get married outside. The sons who inherit oxen should take care of the wives of the deceased man. Grown children will take the house, or maybe someone in the lineage will take it. If the house is rented, she does not know who would get the money, the children or the lineage. When a woman dies her husband will take everything, or else the sons will take her possessions. Unmarried daughters will take her cloth and personal effects. For a woman without children, the person in the lineage who handles her funeral will take her possessions. To her knowledge, there has never been a written will in the village, nor to her knowledge has any inheritance case ever gone to the authorities.

Unfortunately for women in Burkina Faso neither the ethnic, indigenous rules of tenure nor the state's rather unsystematic interventions give them standing as holders of rights to land. The major published interpretation of "customary law" of the majority ethnic group from the center of the country, the Mossi, states quite clearly that women never have a permanent land right (Pageard 1969, 230, 248, 256). For most ethnic groups of Burkina Faso, the only conceivable case of a woman having direct control over land is a widow who may assume responsibility for the land of her deceased husband on a temporary basis, while her own status is sorted out. She may be married to a male relative of her husband under the levirate system. To add insult to injury, most studies from Burkina Faso also find that personal fields granted to women by their husbands, as part of the marriage contract, are invariably small and often of low fertility (Kevane and Gray 1999).

East Africa: The House-Property System

Another frequently cited system in which a woman obtains use rights to land upon marriage is the East African "house-property complex." Some key references are Gluckman (1950), writing about the Zulu in South Africa, and Gray and Gulliver (1964), Moore (1986), Hakansson (1986), Davison (1988), Oboler (1985), von Bulow (1992), Okeyo (1980), and Karp (1978), writing on Kenya and Tanzania. A man allocates to each of his wives cattle, farmland, and homestead land. While cattle would invariably remain under the control of the husband, wives would frequently be the "managers" of the land allocated to them, with much control over day-to-day decisionmaking. In the house-property complex, a husband cannot alienate the land without the wife's permission. She would insist on her "veto" right, or at least on her right to subsequent compensation, since her children—and not the children of any co-wife or the members of any lineage—would inherit the land on the husband's (their father's) death. Her children would be providing her old-age security. Oboler (1986) observed that widows in Nandi society, though they had few options for remarriage, were better off than women from other Kenyan groups because of the house-property system. At the time of marriage a woman received a marriage settlement in the form of her husband's property that would belong to her descendants, even if she were subsequently divorced (as long as she had sons). Oboler (1986) further suggested that "House property means that a widow can have secure property rights without maintaining an ongoing relationship with any members of her husband's family."

These secure rights are temporary and contingent in an unusual way. Instead of depending on the goodwill of a husband, a woman depends on having sons, and then depends on the goodwill of her son. If a widow has no sons, then her deceased husband's patrilineal kin inherit his land and cattle (LeVine and LeVine 1966). As Glazier (1985) put it, "Inheritance is thus patrilineal, although rights to property are passed on through women who, paradoxically . . . cannot own productive property outright" (p. 111). Her sons will claim the land when they are older, and they will have the power to allocate land to their wives.

Not all groups in East Africa have even the limited rights of the house-property system. Moore (1986) found that women had no independent rights to land in the Chagga areas of Mt. Kilimanjaro in Tanzania. Smith and Stevens (1988) described another Tanzanian group, the Haya, located in a coffee-producing area near Mt. Kilimanjaro. Women appeared to be systematically excluded by local men and the state from independent access to land. For example, female household heads who were divorced could not use the land from the clan of their ex-husband, land they may have been farming and continued to farm, to plant coffee. Women seemed never to inherit land from their fathers, and their status when widowed was precarious.

Southern Africa

Southern Africa presents a complex picture in terms of tenure. Large-scale confiscation of land by settlers disrupted any "traditional" tenure systems that may have existed. Numerous legal scholars have shown how the traditional land laws codified during the colonial period were in fact products of collaborations between self-interested chiefs and administrators (Chanock 1985).

There have nevertheless been attempts to characterize the informal systems of customary tenure practiced in so-called communal areas of southern Africa. Fortmann and Nabane (1992), for example, present a picture of tenure in the Shona and Ndebele areas of Zimbabwe in which local authorities adjudicate according to local rather than national rules. The system they describe is much like the West African system. Women receive land through membership in patrilineages, according to their status as wives or as daughters. Daughters obtain land from male lineage heads who in turn obtain land from chiefs and headmen. Daughters' production on their fields would be exchanged for materials for marriage, their trousseau. Married women obtain land rights from their husbands. These rights are maintained as long as the marriage endures.

Cheater (1982) paints a different picture, highlighting the central role of female tenure in discussing the land question in Zimbabwe. She shows that a high proportion of women had usufruct rights, and argues that the "model" of traditional tenure in "communal" and "freehold" areas was falsified by on-the-ground reality. In the model, women have no direct rights, "only temporary usufruct within the lineage system through their husbands or male patrikin" (Cheater 1990, 191). In reality, Cheater argues, "women as affines would appear to be using their importance as farm workers to acquire . . . land in their own right" (1982, 84–85). Her data from the freehold area of Msengezi show that the number of women holding usufruct rights increased substantially from 1970 to 1980. Additionally, she contends that the rights of widows were considerably stronger than elsewhere. Though not recognized in either customary or formal law, in practice a widow was usually guaranteed rights to manage her husband's land until she chose to relinquish control to the heirs. Finally, Cheater presents a most interesting newspaper account of a land dispute between a man who had purchased land from a woman. The woman claimed she had not intended to sell, and that the land had been inherited from her mother-in-law. About this Cheater can only exclaim in wonder: "Legitimation of the rules, in the reported views of civil servants, comes from legislation, not tradition; the 'illegality' of purchasing land by men is trumped by the ownership of land by women, and its transmission—well beyond any rules of the family or matri-estate . . . between female affines" (1990, 195). In a system where women supposedly had little control over land, this example showed that they were not only owning land, they were selling it, and, even stranger, they were inheriting it from their mothers-in-law. Perhaps one should take a more humble attitude about the state of knowledge of women's land rights in southern Africa.

Cocoa Areas of West Africa

More than a century ago, farmers in Ghana, Côte-d'Ivoire, and Nigeria responded to the enormously lucrative opportunity to grow cocoa and coffee trees in the moist hillsides of the region. Vast areas of forest were transformed by migrant farmers into complex agro-forestry systems of cocoa and maize cropping. Land tenure arrangements governing these new fields were complex. Hill (1963) found that patrilineal migrants in Ghana organized land purchases through "companies" that were fronts for comparatively individualized ownership rights. Matrilineal migrants, on the other hand, more typically obtained land in the name of the matriarchy.

As for women in the company areas, Hill assessed the situation as follows:

> It is certainly clear that many of [the women] suffer from many disabilities in the extent of their individual control. It is unusual for a woman to be a company member in her own right, and it is usually only those fathers who have no sons who contemplate buying land for their daughters. A woman who possesses the status of an original farmer has as much control over her property as a man would have, and her children may inherit. But a great proportion of the women farmers in whose names company farms have been registered by the Ministry of Agriculture are daughters who are representing their non-resident brothers, or wives who have been granted usufructuary rights by their husband—the farms reverting to their husbands' sons on their deaths. Occasionally daughters as well as sons inherit on the death of their father, but is seems that such daughters are nearly always unmarried. (1963, 117)

For matrilineal areas there has been more disagreement. Berry, for instance, comments that "the proportion of tree-crop owners who are women is relatively low. . . . The chief exception is in areas of Ghana where descent is reckoned matrilineally. . . . In some communities, fifty percent or more of the women own tree crops" (1988, 6). Mikell, on the contrary, finds that despite the expectations that "matrilineal systems were more liberal in granting rights to females," there was little difference in practice between matrilineal and patrilineal groups in giving women access to land to engage in cocoa-farming (1984, 195). Women received few rights in both groups.

In all systems, women have owned considerably less area than men. Oppong, Okali, and Houghton (1975) found that in cocoa communities in southern Ghana in the early 1970s, women owned cocoa farms quite frequently, though men held double the area held by women. Mikell (1989) reported that women in the Sunyani district constituted approximately one-eighth of cocoa farmers, and again the sizes of women's cocoa farms were much smaller than those of men; the median size of women's farms was roughly eight acres, much smaller than men's median 160 acres.

Even these relatively insignificant and secondary rights have been eroded over time through an inexorable logic of male domination. In a synthesis of recent literature on bridewealth and marriage, Tambiah observed that "when 'permanent' cash crops like cocoa or tea have transformed the land on which they grow into patrimonial properties capable of being owned and transferred by owners by sale or inheritance, there too men have usually exercised the rights of ownership and excluded women (even where so-called matrilineal systems of kinship have prevailed)" (1989, 416). Asare

(1995) found that among the matrilineal Akan, the dominant ethnic group of the cocoa area in Ghana, women fared poorly. Male relatives in the matriliny were merciless in evicting women who had helped their husbands establish farms.

Mikell (1984) develops a careful analysis of this erosion of women's rights. Brong women in Ghana were successful cocoa farmers during the first half of the century, even though their farms were smaller than those of their male counterparts. But by the 1960s, women had retreated from the market, and during the 1970s the only women with cocoa farms were elderly women who had obtained their farms during the earlier period. Mikell observed that in Brong areas women were less interested in working on their own fields because their own matriline would prevent their daughters from inheriting. This loss of rights occurred even as men increasingly gained the right to designate an inheritor. Mikell's interpretation of this decline was that there was an apparent loss in a struggle over "meanings":

> Land did not exist as a sex-linked good before 1900, and the stool [symbol of chieftaincy] was the custodian of it. When land did begin to generate produce and raw materials intended for international markets, males tended to acquire it and pass it on to males. The females who began to acquire and control farm land after 1920 considered it their property (thus female property) and desired to pass it on to daughters and sisters . . . they did not list "brother" as the desired inheritor and seldom listed "son." Yet it is clear that the transmission of cocoa farms to female offspring was not taking place. (1984, 209)

Men increasingly were successful in defining land as "self-acquired" and outside the purview of the lineage. Matrilineages found unpersuasive the same argument when presented by women, that land they farmed was "female property." Men escaped the claims of the corporate body, while women found themselves more incorporated (Grier 1992). Men seemed to adopt the view that their old-age security was better served by having their sons inherit rather than their lineage group. Cocoa farms purchased by Brong males were inherited by their sons rather than going to the matrilineage, or *abusua*. Women likewise seemed to want to pass land on to their sisters or daughters. Instead of arguing that these farms were self-acquired, they argued that they were female property, like movable property such as cattle or money that had always been inherited by women from their mothers or sisters. The women failed. Women's farms increasingly went directly to the abusua and generally went to males.

Women, Mikell argued, became less likely to invest in cocoa farms because their farms were not "treated as female property but . . . as *abusua* property transferred to men following the death of their sisters" (1984, 212). Elsewhere, Mikell (1989, 125) has argued that in the late 1960s, "the court was silent on the issue of whether female generated property belongs to the lineage and therefore to *abusua*-controlled positions, or to individual female heirs." Okali (1983) confirmed this interpretation of the decline or erosion in the content of status of women's tenure. Court cases were favoring the rights of men to pass their farms on to their sons, and disfavoring the rights of women to exercise independent rights over their own land. Bukh's (1979) study suggests that the same process has been at work among patrilineal Ewe cocoa farmers. The patrilineage used to provide all women with a parcel of land to cultivate, but women were increasingly having to ask permission from men to use their fallow land, or go about "begging" land, borrowing land from men who did not belong to the women's lineage.

Change in Land Tenure Systems

The discussion of cocoa farms exemplifies how land tenure is constantly evolving, especially as population densities rise and the products of the soil become relatively more valuable. Two broad trends are clearly visible on the African tenure landscape. In some areas, property rights to land are becoming more individualized, and a market for land rental and sales is emerging (Kevane 1997; Lund 2001; Otsuka and Place 2001; Platteau 1996). Ironically, this is often not in areas that have seen expensive projects to develop cadastres and maintain title registers. Indeed, many researchers conclude that poorly run titling projects impede, rather than facilitate, the emergence of individual property rights. The titling process often seems to generate insecurity rather than tenure security (Dickerman and Barnes 1989; Firmin-Sellers 2000). Private landholding and individual transfer are instead surfacing in areas untouched by the heavy hand of centralized schemes to transform tenure. The spontaneous emergence of new tenure rights may be desirable, in that the process embeds the new property rights in the existing web of social relations, and thus carries more legitimacy. However, new privatization of land may involve stark expropriation of marginal or secondary holders of land rights.

The second broad trend is partly a reaction to the pressures toward individualization of tenure. In many areas, local jural groups are reasserting and strengthening their rights to communal ownership of land. Traditional chiefs and earth priests recognize their powerful positions as arbiters of land conflicts within and between groups, and so form an influential body of citizens interested in maintaining notions of collective ownership (Berry 2000; Toulmin and Quan 2000). If land becomes individualized, the role of chiefs and earth priests becomes an anachronism.

Within the push and play of these forces surrounding individualization and communalization, women as holders of land rights are subject to a different set of pressures and strategies. The discussion of change in the cocoa areas of West Africa suggested several processes by which structures of land tenure changed for women.

One process is that in which men and women negotiate definitions and meanings that are applied to land tenure. As the balance of power shifts from women to men, or as circumstances change, definitions and meanings are manipulated to favor one group over the other. Crops that previously "belonged" to women, are redefined as household (read, male) crops. Several authors have studied the effect of irrigated rice cultivation on women's access to land in Gambia, where this process of redefining tenure was particularly stark. In Gambia, farmers recognize both common and individual land rights. Women historically controlled rice fields that they cleared with their own labor. Their rights to this land were well defined: they controlled the production from this land, but more significantly they controlled the right to transfer land, which they generally did, to their daughters. The studies of different irrigation schemes illustrate how women's access to land changed when the irrigation projects changed the landscape. Brautigam (1992) argues that because the rice land was cleared and developed by male-centered development projects, local men were able to claim land as their personal plots. Some of these plots were categorized as household property that came under the control of male household heads. Inputs and mechanized services were allocated overwhelmingly to men. Carney (1988) describes how women's rights to irrigated rice land evolved in the Jahaly Pacharr irrigation project, which was targeted to benefit women farmers ignored by previous rice projects. About 13 percent of the irrigated rice land was registered in women's names, but Carney notes that "even though the land was registered in women's names, none of the pump-irrigated plots were considered their individual (*kamanyango*) fields. Irrigated plots throughout the project were designated by both men and women as *maruo,* or compound land" (1988, 71). Women's access to land was reshaped by redefining the meanings of the categories by which their access traditionally had been allocated. The new projects allocated land to women, but that did not mean that women had the power to control the land. Irrigated crops turned out to be different kinds of crops, and control over land was linked to the crop cultivated, rather than to a spatial concept of ownership.

A second process that alters the terms of access to land rights is one in which the terms of marriage contracts are changed (this section largely reproduces the discussion in Kevane [2000]). Consider a stylized model of marriage, introduced into the literature by Akerlof, Yellen, and Katz (1996), which may be adapted to a sub-Saharan setting. In this model, men and women decide whether or not to agree to marry. Assume that a woman can only marry once, but she can make offers of marriage to single men until an offer is accepted. She would like to marry a man who will promise to give her part of his land. Only men can own land, and husbands decide whether women can manage fields on their own. The woman is like a sharecropper, in some sense, and has only so many chances to find a landlord with whom to begin a long-term relationship. The problem is that some men would do much better if they farmed their fields on their own and did not give any land to their wives. So the woman may want to extract a promise from the potential husband that he will indeed give her a plot of land. The man, of course, would much rather not make such a promise: who knows whether his wife will turn out to be a good farmer or not? Perhaps the land will be wasted and lie underutilized. When asking for a promise to give land, the woman risks that the man will simply refuse, and go try his luck in the marriage "market" with another potential partner. Assume that promises are enforceable—the man cannot renege on the promise. The woman has to decide whether to request such a promise and risk refusal by the man.

The woman's best strategy depends on what she thinks other women are doing. If most other women demand promises to receive land, then the woman will also make such a demand. If the man considering the offer refuses and goes off to entertain offers from other women, he will find they are all making the same demand. He may as well have accepted the initial offer. Expecting this to be the case, he will indeed accept a demand for land at marriage. When many women do not demand promises, this undermines the willingness of men to make promises and marry, since they revise their expectations about the likelihood that they will meet other women who do not extract promises of receiving land.

Figure 4.1 shows the "decision tree" structure of the game that men and women play as they decide whether to marry a particular person. Combinations of decisions are represented as branches on the tree. The payoffs, to men and women, of any particular sequence of decisions are given at the end of each of the three branches. The net payoffs are assumed positive. The woman has the first decision of whether to insist that the man must give her land if they marry. If the woman insists that he give her land, and he agrees to be married under this condition, his payoff is $r_m - p_m - d_m$, where d_m is the cost of not allocating land optimally, but rather having the wife control some significant amount of the land. If the woman does not insist, the man of course marries (women are assumed identical in all other respects). He can do no better by waiting. His net payoff is given by $r_m - p_m$, with r_m the benefits and p_m the costs of marriage. He saves d_m. The woman gets a benefit r_f from marriage, but this comes at a cost. The cost of marriage is being tied down, as it were, as the wife (with children) is foregoing opportunities for entrepreneurship. Women have many income-generating activities, and some of the more lucrative activities involve travel, which may be proscribed after marriage and children. The cost of foregoing entrepreneurship is p_f. When the man gives the women land, part of this

Figure 4.1 Game Tree for Marriage Decision and Promise to Marry

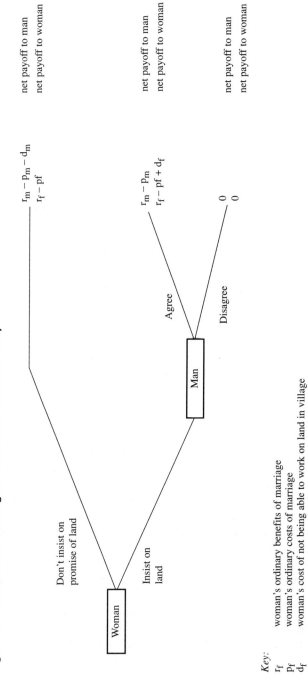

Key:

r_f woman's ordinary benefits of marriage
p_f woman's ordinary costs of marriage
d_f woman's cost of not being able to work on land in village

r_m man's ordinary benefit from marriage
$p_m + d_m$ man's ordinary cost of marriage
d_m part of the man's cost of marriage offset by not having to give woman land

cost is offset by the advantage of having an opportunity to farm independently, and this is represented by d_f. So the woman's net benefit when marrying with a promise from the man to give her land is $r_f - p_f + d_f$.

There are then three branches, representing the three possible sequences of actions. The question to ask is whether one of the branches is an equilibrium. That is, given that the actions of others determine the probability of getting married if a current "match" does not result in marriage, will men and women settle on a particular branch? The discussion above suggested the branch that has the women insisting on a promise of land, and the men granting the promise, can be an equilibrium in the marriage market. In this structure, a norm is an equilibrium in which people are observed following similar strategies because they assume that other people will follow the same strategy.

The equilibrium norm may change if any of the payoffs change. Suppose, for instance, that the initial equilibrium is the one where men and women marry with promises that men give out land. Suppose further that women have different p_f, different costs of foregoing entrepreneurship. Some women have no talent or interest in working outside the home; others do. It may then arise that increasing commercialization lowers, for entrepreneurial women, the opportunity cost of being married. They no longer have to travel to be entrepreneurs because there are increasing opportunities in their own villages or towns. This leads them to be willing to marry without promises of land. Other women, who may have no intentions of being entrepreneurs, find that if they continue to insist on promises of land, they are more often rejected in the marriage market. If the entrepreneurial women constitute a significant fraction of the population, then all women will be willing to marry without promises of land. A change that affects a fraction of women—those entrepreneurs who could take advantage of new commercial opportunities—potentially impoverishes all women.

This model is instructive for understanding the Gusii case in Kenya (Hakansson 1986). At one time a woman marrying was entitled to ownership or at least clear control over house property. Over the 1970s and 1980s, however, men increasingly refused to honor this right; they insisted on marrying outside the traditional customs. Men seemed able to negotiate more flexibility in the matter of disposing of their land. The new "elopement" marriage came with no implicit right to property. Elopement meant that until bridewealth was paid, the marriage had no legal status and women had no rights to remain and cultivate the land of their husbands. As the men said, women could be "chased away" if they did not work hard. As more and more men demanded this advantageous form of marriage, women either reluctantly agreed or else refused marriage propositions in the hopes of finally attracting a suitor willing to marry under the old terms. As more men demanded the advantageous marriage, the chance of finding other men fell, and women came to accept the new terms. This, of course, made men even less willing to offer the old terms; they knew they could easily find a woman willing to marry the new way. While in the 1960s only 26 percent of women eloped, in the 1980s Hakansson found that 87 percent had eloped.

Andre and Platteau found a similar process underway in a Rwandan village, where "roughly two-third of the couples in N. have been married without *inkwano* [customary payment], and the proportion is obviously much higher among young couples" (1998, 32–33). The effect was to give women little bargaining power in the marriage, and even less with respect to their own lineage should they divorce.

The model and experiences of Kenya and Rwanda suggest how processes can be self-reinforcing and can snowball. As many men begin to marry in more informal ways, without promising to give land, a "tipping point" may be reached. Even relatively unattractive men (in terms of marriage partners) can refuse to marry formally and grant their wives land. Unmarried women will accept these terms because their prospects of obtaining better terms in the marriage market are dimmed.

Policy

The dominant view of women's tenure status in Africa is that it is bad and getting worse (Davison 1988; Gray and Kevane 1999; Kevane and Gray 1999; Sawadogo and Stamm 2000). Numerous calls have been made for national governments to get involved and correct the situation. These calls have dovetailed with a greater interest in reforming tenure in general (Drylands Programme 1999; Gray and Kevane 2001; Lavigne Delville 2000; Toulmin and Quan 2000). These more general reforms are intended to redress a perceived lack of security in rural tenure. This insecurity deters investment directly, and also limits the use of land as collateral for loans. Insecurity also dampens the incentives that landowners have to rent out their land, or even sell their land, to more productive farm managers. The reforms are intended as measures to enhance efficiency.

Gender reform, however, is more of an equity than an efficiency issue (though efficiency considerations are certainly there). The policy challenge is to identify politically feasible and cost-effective interventions. There are a number of conceivable gendered interventions. In different countries, these might involve change in statutes and, perhaps more importantly, public awareness and enforcement. The following are some possible changes:

- Enforce new forms of joint conjugal ownership over land upon marriage, with provisions for spousal consent over land use and transfer, and provisions for division of land upon the termination of marriage through death or divorce.

- When moving toward individual, state-sponsored title, the first phase might involve giving title only to women.
- As village and associational recorporatization of land becomes an increasingly chosen tenure reform, more care may be devoted to nurturing gender-inclusive village authorities and female corporate institutions that would operate as counterweights to male-dominated lineage groups (Dei 1994; Schroeder 1999).
- Enable longer term security of rental transactions involving women as either landlords or tenants.
- Campaign for new obligations of kin and/or kin groups to women (for example, sons to their mothers).
- Require greater quotas for women in market-based or expropriation-based land reform, especially for public investments in irrigation projects.
- Create or expand the set of new assets for women (for instance, housing plots, trees, and village or urban retail space) and allow unequal rights to persist in agricultural land.
- Tax land differentially according to the gender of the registered owner, or tax progressively according to the size of individual holdings (so that men will have incentives to "distribute" title to wives and daughters to avoid higher tax rates).

These reforms are unabashedly discriminatory. They intend to redress decades of previous discriminatory treatment that favored men.

It goes without saying that these interventions will be meaningful only if complementary reforms are made in the institutions allocating agricultural inputs and outputs. Many extension agencies, credit programs, marketing boards, and fertilizer and other official state input programs are currently targeted exclusively toward men. Many contract farming schemes, crop marketing corporations, and other agribusiness firms in the private sector also target men as potential clients and refuse to enter into contractual partnerships with women. These structures need to be changed along with tenure reform.

All interventions involve gains and losses for different social groups. An intervention becomes more politically feasible if losers are compensated. An intervention becomes more cost-effective—has a smaller impact on the overall fiscal balance of the government or generates returns that enable the government to repay loans used to finance upfront costs—if the beneficiaries of the reform have some of their winnings taxed away. Reforming tenure rights to favor women, then, will be more feasible and cost-effective if female beneficiaries are taxed and male losers in the reform are compensated for their loss of rights.

Thinking of tenure reform this way has two obvious implications that are sometimes ignored. First, if losers are not powerful politically, then reform quickly degenerates into outright theft. The politically powerful use the reform as a pretext for abrogating previously recognized, respected, and enforced property rights. Early attempts to reform tenure in African countries are widely recognized to have degenerated into outright land grabs, by men against women, by well-connected urban merchants against weak rural communities, and by powerful lineage elders against their juniors (Fleuret 1988; Shipton 1988). The land grab inevitably leads to continued and costly political conflict. Second, if losers are indeed politically powerful, then either they have to receive the bulk of the efficiency benefits from the reform (or the outside funds supporting the reform), or they have to be divided, so that a fraction of losers will ally with the comparatively disenfranchised beneficiaries.

In the gender reform case, the natural line of fracture of the powerful male opponents of reform favoring women would be the urban-rural divide. Urban men have very different interests from rural men. The question then is how to package tenure changes in rural areas that favor women, with tenure changes in urban areas that favor urban men. Of course, the tenure changes in urban areas should not come at the expense of urban women. That is not necessarily a problem. There are many reforms in urban areas that have the effect of creating new assets. States around the world, by virtue of their monopoly over most resources and previous regulatory "takings," have plenty of largesse available, from urban zoning; to sidewalk, curb, and market space; to transport and occupational licensing. These are just a few of the assets that states can return to the private sector, and almost all of them will benefit men more than women, even if done on an equitable basis. The legacy of persisting inequalities between men and women is that men are often in better positions to profit from new opportunities. The one exception might be urban retail property, where in some cases women are more important actors than men. Building a viable political coalition is integral to reform. Of course, if outside donors are willing to fund the reform, and compensate losers directly, the domestic political constraint becomes less binding.

One area of actual reform is in laws of intestate succession, which determine who inherits the estate of a person who dies without leaving a will. Because married women in sub-Saharan Africa are on average considerably younger than their husbands, and live longer, when permitted they inherit and manage the land of their deceased husbands for long periods of time. Numerous land tenure reformers have called upon states to implement new laws of intestate succession that give widows strong ownership claims over the estates of their husbands. Sometimes these calls for intestate succession are treated as separate from land issues, to be dealt with under reform of personal law (Manji 1998). That is, marriage law and courts become the domain where women enforce their rights.

The skeptic immediately asks two questions of intestate succession reform, which straightforwardly changes the terms of marriage contracts. First, as marriage contracts are multidimensional (as shall be seen in Chapter 6), it might be expected that the gain of a property right is simply offset by a corresponding loss in some other dimension of the contract. Regulating one of the terms in a multidimensional contract might not alter the equilibrium in the marriage market; the welfare of women remains exactly as before, and improved tenure status masks a worsening status on another dimension. Second, because marriage contracts are voluntary, parties might simply opt out of official marriages and cohabit, or develop new, unofficial marriage contracts. There is already considerable variation in marriage rates and forms across and within African societies.

Also, rates of formal marriage have been declining over time. If a further decline in marriage is the response in the marriage market to legal reform, then the reform will have little effect. The incidence of the reform, then, depends on the substitutability of contract terms and the elasticity of response to changes in those terms. If contract terms are highly substitutable and alternatives to formal marriage are available, changing the laws of intestate succession will have few effects. To ensure significant effects, the state may find itself in the uncomfortable business of investigating the content of conjugal relationships, enforcing official marriages, and punishing unofficial marriages. There are high costs to creating marriage police.

This then raises the question of how to change marriage contracts in ways that enable stronger rights for women without encouraging evasion. That is, how can a new marriage contract be self-enforcing? Two things need to happen. The man's lineage must have a new, pecuniary interest in encouraging official marriage and enforcing the right of women to inherit the property of their husbands. In addition, men need to have incentives to get married in general, so that the terms of marriage do not turn against women and offset the new intestate succession rights. One way to do the first is to have a nonlineage person become the inheritor or administrator of land following the intestate death of a man not officially married. The lineage then has a strong incentive to make sure that lineage men are officially married. The woman becomes, in effect, a member of the lineage. There are many ways to give men more incentives to marry in general. One attractive change is giving women some right that will be valuable to her husband. Identity cards, for example, are valuable assets that governments can supply at low cost to women, who typically are much less likely than men to possess them. An identity card gives the holder considerable ease of passage, and access to formal financial institutions. The identity card holder will earn more money. The husband will be able to share in that new surplus. The general point is to bundle a change in intestate succession with incentives for self-enforcement and the transfer of assets from the state in order to maintain the attractiveness of marriage for men.

5

Control over Labor in African Villages

In the household, the woman cannot freely decide on where she allocates her labor power. She is *selero,* the one who offers her labor to others. The man—and here it is understood as the collection of all the men in the household . . . the producers of the household—is *seso,* the owner to the labor power of the woman.
—*Jean Capron,* Communautés villageoises Bwa

In our village, like the villages around here, the boys work with their fathers and the girls with their mothers. That is why each one learns the jobs of his or her sex. And the father tells his boys what to do, and a mother commands the girls. . . . Before, a woman only planted and harvested, and the man did the weeding and plowing. But now women do all the work except that at harvest they are told to step aside.
—*Elderly Bwa woman in village of Bereba in Burkina Faso, 1996*

In many parts of sub-Saharan Africa, men and women are restricted in the work they can do. The restrictions are not, however, as draconian as the gendering of land rights described in the previous chapter. Chiefs, earth priests, and other authority figures of village society have little to say on the gendering of work; neither, typically, does the state. Instead, the gendered structuring of work seems to be sustained by informal norms. These norms are enforced via internalization and sanctions. Children grow up learning the norms. Were they to violate the norms, they would feel uncomfortable because of the identities they had inherited from their childhoods. Moreover, they might be subject to ridicule, scorn, and ostracism. They might even be physically intimidated.

Anthropologists and other qualitatively oriented researchers have long been interested in this question, and there is an abundance of findings detailing the importance of restrictions in particular places and times. Only recently, however, has this become a question addressed by more quantitative and modeling-oriented methods. The maximization approach has proved very controversial here, ever since Becker (1981) famously argued that gender differences in the allocation of labor (in developed countries) were not explained by social norms restricting behavior but rather by men and women maximizing their incomes or utilities.

In fact, there are three alternative theories used to explain patterns of allocation of labor. The social norm approach emphasizes structure. People allocate their labor into certain activities because they have little choice. Social structures have already shaped the domain of choices. The maximization approach emphasizes choice, positing that men and women make different choices because of biological or learned differences acquired in childhood. (There is also a more psychological-oriented literature that argues that men and women have different preferences or modes of thinking, and this explains their different choices.) Finally, the "household bargaining" approach mixes choice and structure, arguing that men and women choose how to allocate their time within the constraints of household structures where men have considerable bargaining power.

Distinguishing between these three approaches has been a neglected topic. The last section of this chapter summarizes a study that tried to address this question in the context of labor allocation in Burkina Faso.

The arguments presented in this chapter are terribly important for policy. If social norms restrict the allocation of labor time, especially for women, in ways that favor men, then changing norms, through programs and activities that empower women as a broad social class, becomes a legitimate and high-payoff activity.

Social Norms Restricting the Allocation of Labor

Many studies of time allocation ask whether women work more than men, or vice versa. While casual observers often see sharp inequities in time allocation, many of the more careful studies find the extra work burden of women is on the order of an hour a day and that very often women and men are doing similar activities out in the fields (Ancey 1983; Stone, Stone, and Netting 1995). Housework, including the time-consuming tasks of cooking and fetching water, remain the exclusive obligation of women almost everywhere. The concern here is not so much the total hours of work, but rather the kinds of work done, and for whom.

Restrictions on work come in three varieties: restrictions on occupations, restrictions on the allocation of time, and restrictions on labor market transactions. Examples of these restrictions abound in African settings. For example, many societies sanction women who engage in intervillage, cross-border, or long-distance trade. Women engaging in this trade have been subject to verbal and even physical abuse. They have also been accused of being prostitutes (Hodgson 1996). The illegality of prostitution itself constitutes a norm restraining women's activities with economic implications.

Recent social histories of East Africa, following the lead of the seminal paper by Bujra (1977), have convincingly demonstrated the importance of prostitution in enabling women to accumulate capital and establish themselves in the informal economy (Barnes 1992; White 1990). Selling sexual favors to men proved more rewarding than being "owned" by a husband. This same literature traces the explosion of colonially mandated controls over women's occupations and mobility. These controls regulated both rural and urban areas. In colonial Mozambique, for example, virtually all garment workers were men. Well into independence, women constituted only a tiny fraction of the urban, industrial workforce (Sheldon 1991; 1988). Patterns of occupational segregation in the urban labor force continue (Kobou 2000).

Restrictions on the allocation of labor are certainly familiar to development economists who work in South Asia, where the prohibition of work outside the home is known as *purdah*. Cain, Khanam, and Nahar argue that these norms actually entail specific geographic restrictions: "The norms of *purdah* influence the distance a woman would be willing to travel to work, the distance a husband would permit his wife to travel, a woman's willingness to work for a stranger, and the receptivity of potential employers . . . the psychic and tangible costs of the job search rise quickly when a woman leaves the confines of her 'circle'" (1979, 428). Ramamurthy comments on how these norms are sustained among men of the Kamma ethnic group in India: "Patriarchal domination by the Kamma men limits women to work within the household. . . . Kamma men are highly critical of the local men and criticize them for being 'lazy' and letting their womenfolk work in the fields; they question the very manhood of these men" (1993, 198).

The seclusion of wives has also been studied in northern Nigeria and Niger, where the Hausa word *kulle* refers to the "locking" or "tying" of wives (Miles 1994, 260). The problem there is more complex than in the Indian case. Restricted women are often very active participants in local markets, using what Hill (1969) refers to as a "honeycomb" network of small children to carry out their trade. Thus, seclusion may be desired by both men and women and is sometimes characterized as a luxury good available only to the wealthy.

The experience of purdah suggests an application of the Nash equilibrium concept, as discussed in the appendix. For a norm to be constraining, it must mean that people would rather do other things. How are norms that constrain the allocation of labor sustained, if many people have an interest in violating the norm? Suppose the men of a village got together and acted like a cartel. They might all agree not to hire each other's wives. Then there would be no competitive labor market for women who wanted to work. Instead, each woman would have to bargain individually with her husband. Recall that men own all of the land, the most productive asset. Men are then in very strong bargaining positions vis-à-vis their wives and can offer them low wages. The collusive norm clearly favors the men at the expense of their wives.

But some of the husbands might want to break the norm. They can offer low wages to the oppressed wives of the other husbands and reap a windfall of low-cost labor. Some husbands may own more land than others and not be able to rent out the land because of tenure insecurity (they fear that the other men might claim the land as their own if they rent it for several years). They would like the wives of other men to be able to work for wages in their fields. Also, husbands who have little land might hope that their wives could go out into the labor market and earn higher wages, to supplement the family income. What constrains these potential "cheaters" of the norm from realizing their interests? The husbands are constrained by their fear of the consequences. If the situation is repeated over time, then each husband calculates his short-term benefit from cheating on the norm and weighs that against the long-term loss from the breakdown of the collusive equilibrium. If other men have strategies that tell them to also cheat on the norm whenever they detect cheating by one husband, then the one potential cheater might refrain from hiring the wives of other men. He fears the breakdown of the norm that favors men, and himself, in the long run more than he favors his short-term gain. The collusion is sustained.

A concrete example from the anthropological literature may illustrate how difficult it is to analyze collusive equilibria in the absence of a fully fleshed-out model. Stone, Stone, and Netting, writing about the Kofyar people of Nigeria, ask "why, given the high demands on labor among the Kofyar, are men not *further* monopolizing female labor for household production to the exclusion of women's ability to produce independently?" (1995, 181 [emphasis added]). That is, why do men not prevent their wives from working outside the household and then, once they have to work in the household, make them work for the men, rather than for themselves? Stone, Stone, and Netting answer the question by saying that men do not monopolize the labor of women because "women's labor and reproductive power are too valuable to the system as a whole, and to their households most particularly, for men to risk alienating them." They paint a picture of a dynamic and growing agricultural economy in the Kofyar region that is consistent with their claim that the labor of women is valuable. Apparently, a restrictive norm is too costly to sustain. The labor of women is valuable, and men would be tempted to hire female labor and break a collusive norm. One implication that might be explored is that in other less productive areas women are constrained to work for their husbands.

Monopolization of the labor of wives has been reported for many other African societies and takes the form of requirements that wives work on "family" fields controlled by men. Roberts surveys the literature and remarks that "the claims of a male head of household or husband over his wives' labor services are considerable and are not reciprocal. The extent of wives' obligations to provide labor to their husbands is a major constraint upon the development of their own-account enterprises" (1988, 104). Women in many societies are prohibited from working on the fields of other men. They cannot participate in an open, competitive labor market. Often, women are further prohibited from working on their own account as traders or processors of food to be sold in the marketplace. They are expected to minimize their involvement in market activities (Bernard 1966, 140; Broekhuyse and Allen 1988, 337).

Schroeder has more recently documented how women who work in personal small irrigated market gardens may be "demonized . . . as bad wives" (1996, 72). Jones (1986) and Carney and Watts (1991) likewise describe the pressures on women to work in their husbands' irrigated rice fields. Other researchers find that women are allowed to carry out market activities but not to hire labor. They are restricted to using their own labor, so their enterprises cannot expand. As Guyer puts it with regard to the West African Yoruba and Beti pre-cocoa economies, "women were ultimately subordinate to men in both systems in that men could mobilize women's labour but the reverse was not usually true. Women did not have the authority to recruit male labour for their own purposes except through their husbands" (1980, 364).

Unconstrained Maximization and Household Bargaining

Two other hypotheses regarding time allocation eschew discussion of social norms and constraints, focusing instead on common patterns of outcomes across similar households. These two hypotheses share the assumption that women's economic activity is being determined through a process of decisionmaking within the household. This decisionmaking takes place in the context of a gendered distribution of property (men own most of the assets) and a gendered biological and learned comparative advantage (girls are trained in home work). The decisionmaking may be amicable. Everyone in the household tries to do what is best for the household. This is the so-called unitary household. Or the decisionmaking might be acrimonious, with parents, children, and grandparents engaged in struggles over control of the resources of the household. They cooperate when it is their interest, and they do not cooperate when it is in their interest. This is the "bargaining" household. Other characterizations fall somewhere in between the unitary model, where the household can be treated as a single actor, and the bargaining model, where the household consists of individuals who selfishly come together to enjoy potentially shared benefits and who stay together because of the high cost of exit from the relationship. (There will be more discussion of alternative theories of the household in Chapter 7.)

A short digression on the concept of comparative advantage is in order. The concept is usually seen in the context of theories of international trade, where it is used to suggest that barriers to trade reduce the welfare of the citizens of a country. This is because barriers to trade block cheap imports from entering the country. Workers are then encouraged to move into the protected industry. But by definition, the extra domestic production of the protected good uses up more resources per unit of production than would have been used up if the previous production pattern had continued and the good had been imported. That is what it means for the foreign good to be cheaper, after all. The opportunity cost of encouraging domestic production in one sector is foregoing production of other goods and services in other sectors.

This same logic can be applied to the domestic situation of a husband and wife. The two partners in marriage have to determine an allocation of their time between home activities and income-generating activities. Suppose each has ten hours to work in the day, and the husband can earn $1 per hour outside the home while the wife can earn only half that, $0.50 per hour. In the home, the wife can make five units of home cooking, say, in an hour, while the man can only make four units of cooking. Confining ourselves to this simple problem of allocating time across activities, what is the efficient allocation? Clearly the man should work outside while the woman works at home. That generates $10 and fifty units of cooking. Any other allocation generates combinations of money and cooking that can be dominated by greater specialization. So the pattern of specialization in activities can be explained by a desire of men and women to produce the most stuff. They might share this stuff equally or unequally, but the wife (as the usual underdog) recognizes that an unequal share of more stuff is better than an unequal share of less stuff.

Regardless of whether the household is amicable or acrimonious, then, it may be the case that the resulting pattern of time allocation rarely has women working in the market. This outcome would be more likely the more efficient bargaining and market institutions were, according to this approach. If women's comparative advantage really were in home activities or as unskilled labor (and not as managers or entrepreneurs), then, with efficient mechanisms for bargaining, women's labor would be allocated to those activities. While some bargaining models contradict the oft-held presumption that social institutions lead to optimal allocations of resources, they are nevertheless firmly in a tradition that deemphasizes the importance of social norms and customs in explaining behavior. (For studies showing how "bargaining" breaks down, leaving the labor of women idle or leading men to physically beat their wives—surely an inefficient outcome—see Carney and Watts [1991] and von Bulow [1992])

To summarize, there are two alternatives to the hypothesis that male-biased social norms constrain women in their labor decisions. The first is that the allocation of women's labor is determined by unitary households operating in competitive labor markets. Husbands and wives are partners in a production and consumption enterprise. A woman's property, capital, outside income, or social standing has no particular bearing on outcomes or welfare. (Large enough changes in capital or outside income may, however, make the existing marriage inefficient and lead to its dissolution in favor of remarriage with more appropriate partners.) The household's property is pooled, and joint welfare is maximized; a marriage of a wealthy man and poor woman will be indistinguishable from a couple consisting of a poor man and rich woman, in terms of economic outcomes. The power that is derived from ownership over property is assumed to be uninteresting, since whoever has property acts benevolently rather than malevolently.

The second alternative is that women's economic activity is influenced by the distribution of economic power within the household, as well as the household's interaction with markets. Members of households, in this view, bargain among themselves for the fruits of their labors. Since some of the goods they consume are public within the household, and since some of the goods they produce require joint production, inefficient outcomes may result. More importantly, the distribution of property within the household will affect economic decisions and welfare. A poorer woman might be more likely to act in her husband's interest, for fear of the large reduction in welfare that might occur with divorce or with a breakdown in cooperation (Folbre 1986).

The spirit of these two different models, however, is firmly within the "neoclassical" paradigm, which deemphasizes the importance of social norms and customs in explaining behavior.

A Case Study for Distinguishing Hypotheses

Can data on time allocation shed light on these models? The alternative theories illustrate an important feature of much social science research: many social facts are consistent with different explanations. A finding that women's activities follow certain patterns, and that people articulate norms that prescribe these patterns, does not clinch the case that there are indeed norms that restrict behavior. Other processes may be at work. A structure that was thought to result from strong social norms may turn out to be no more than a pattern of activity common to many individuals.

More light may be shed on the difficult empirical question of distinguishing among various hypotheses by looking at the allocation of women's labor time in a medium-sized village of southwestern Burkina Faso. The evidence from this village suggests that ethnicity is a consistently significant determinant of variation in the allocation of time. One reason why ethnicity is so important may be that ethnic groups differ in the norms and attitudes regarding women's work. In particular, one ethnic group, the Mossi, appears to have women working less time at home and more time on the fields of their husbands, compared with another ethnic group, the Bwa. Mossi women also appear to be less responsive to incentives, a finding consistent with the proposition that they are more constrained. The anthropological literature also suggests that Mossi norms regarding gender and rights in marriage are less 'free' compared with those of other ethnic groups.

Mossi and Bwa in Burkina Faso

Men and women in Bwa and Mossi societies organize their lives in ways similar to other West African societies. Forced marriages are common. Polygyny is common. Men and women have separate budgets and activities. Men own most of the property and wealth; women often claim that they are poorly compensated for their contributions to household production.

But there is a widespread understanding in Burkina Faso that there are significant differences in gender relations between the Bwa and the Mossi. The two groups have very different histories. The Mossi are one of West Africa's more famous kingdoms, having survived repeated attacks and threats for over 500 years. The Mossi kingdom was rigidly hierarchical, with local rulers, called *naba,* having considerable control over the local population. Part of this control was expressed in the previously described pugsuiré, whereby the chief of a village would decide on the marriage partners of young girls for the village as a whole (Labouret 1940, 110; Skinner 1964). While the pugsuiré is now rare, a second institution of marriage in Mossi society, the *levirate,* where a son inherits "rights" to his father's wives (except for his own mother), remains quite prevalent. This form of the levirate can be contrasted with the more usual form, in which widows are inherited by the brothers of the deceased husband, rather than by his sons. The transfer of authority from deceased father to son is usually accompanied with a choice, for the widow, to remain alone, or sometimes to return to her natal village, so it is wrong to speak of it as forced (Lallemand 1977).

The Bwa, on the other hand, are famous as one of the premier examples of a "stateless" society. The major ethnographic work on the Bwa, by Capron (1973), and the classic "ethnographic novel" of Nazi Boni (1962), *Le crepuscule des temps anciens,* go to some length to emphasize the egalitarian and decentralized nature of village life. Boni is quite explicit in extending this notion to gender relations; the central plot of the novel is a love affair and marriage between a young man and young woman; the parents almost seem to be absent.

An institution that perhaps is most indicative of gender relations among the Bwa is the fairly prevalent practice of woman-woman marriage (Taraoré 1941). An older woman, typically with no children or whose children have left, may use her income generated from her own activities to marry a younger woman, known as a *yarohan*. The yarohan is free to sleep with men of her choosing, and the children belong to the older woman. While there is no study of the symbolic roles the yarohan plays in local society, it is conceivable that she, and her "husband-wife" stand as representations of a relative lack of dependence of women on men. A woman can acquire rights to children independently of her husband.

Divorce is one of the primary indicators of social norms regarding gender relations, and in this instance the two societies also seem to be quite different. Most commentators on Mossi marriage note that divorce is not readily granted to a wife wishing to leave her husband for another man. Skinner (1964, 84) observes that district chiefs would order a woman back to her first husband, except in the case of cruelty. Capron and Kohler (1978, 206) find that 90 percent of Mossi marriages are stable, only ending with the death of one of the partners. Their survey was administered to a large-scale sample in the Mossi-dominated areas, and they comment that this stability may be explicitly contrasted with the instability of neighboring ethnic groups.

Retel-Laurentin (1973, 294) confirms this marital instability of neighboring groups, finding that less than half the marriages in her sample of 545 Bwa women in the Hounde region were stable; the other half ended in de facto divorce, with the woman typically leaving her husband for another man. (The incidence of a woman returning to her natal family was low.) She presents overwhelming ethnographic evidence to support the notion that women were able to ignore the supposed indissolubility of the marriage alliance created between the husband and women's family through the performance of work and giving of other marriage prestations. Capron (1963, 85) argues that the Bwa social sanctions that might have previously enforced a marriage transaction—derived from the fact that a marriage was considered a transaction between two lineages inhabiting, almost always, different villages—have basically disappeared.

In some ways this situation is paradoxical. Mossi marriages are typically made with minimal gifts going from the husband's side to the bride's family, while Bwa marriages have more onerous demands on the groom to work in the fields of his bride's father. Social sanctions against leaving an arranged marriage (which most marriages were until recent decades) enforced this stability; the power of father and chief (whether village, patrilineage, or local "clan") was still strong. There is no doubt that these social sanctions are waning, under economic pressure from continued migration of young men to Côte d'Ivoire (who can then take escaped lovers with them) and under administrative pressure as successive regimes continue to push for explicit legal rules and rights for women in marriage.

By Bwa "tradition," according to Capron (1981, 98), women are not free to choose how to allocate their time and so must work for their husbands.

The word used to refer to women, *selero,* may be glossed as "who offers their work." The man is the "owner" of the work. Capron in a footnote further glosses selero as carrying with it the connotation of working "under constraint." He argues that in practice things were not always so rigid. At the time of his research, women did little work in agriculture, concentrating more on processing *karité* butter (a kind of vegetable oil). This processing and most other work was conducted in the household as a group under the direction of the senior woman of the household. Capron suggests that women exercised considerable freedom and control over their activities (p. 101). In fact, he argues, a man who calls his wife selero would find himself condemned by the public rumor of other villagers (p. 104).

Anthropological accounts of time allocation norms in Mossi villages are rare. Lallemand (1977, 61, 71) who spent considerable time on fieldwork in a Mossi village, is clear in using the word "constraint" to describe women's time allocation toward the "collective" fields of the household managed by the husband. Rohatynskyj observes that work burdens of Mossi women are very high and concludes, "The absolute nature of demands on the part of the husband's patrilineage and the tenuousness of the bond [to the husband and his lineage], as sensed by women, lead to the overemphasis on hard work and obedience as the basis of women's virtue" (1988, 538). She suggests that women who do not follow the wishes of their husbands risk becoming labeled witches and subject to ostracism.

It should be kept in mind that generalizing about marriage and divorce is an old question in West African studies, and a delicate one, for one of the primary areas of contention between the colonial authorities and their defeated "native subjects" was the institution of marriage (see Labouret [1940] for an excellent discussion cautioning against ethnocentric prejudice and Skinner [1964, 167–170]).

Mossi and Bwa Women in Bereba

The village of Bereba, roughly one hundred kilometers northeast of Bobo-Dioulasso (the regional capital and second-largest city in Burkina Faso), lies in the heart of the country's cotton zone, a dynamic and expanding sector of the national economy. The village is very well developed in terms of using animal traction, fertilizer, pesticides, and improved cotton and maize seed. There are few tractors, however, and many families still cultivate large areas by hand. Oxen are readily rented, though the price is high.

Bereba is a divided village, like so many others in the Sahel, with Bwa and Mossi vying for power and privilege. In 1996, two-thirds of the 121 households were Bwa, one-third Mossi. There was a scattering of Dafing, Djula, and Samogo. The great majority of the Bwa adhere to the local Do religion, while the overwhelming majority of Mossi and Dafing are Muslim. Only a small minority are Christian.

Women's economic activities in Bereba can be summarized in terms of three broad categories: working in their husbands' fields; working at a "personal" activity that generates income for themselves; and working at home. Table 5.1 presents the averages of the proportion of weekdays and market days (Fridays and Mondays) devoted to these activities, according to whether the period is an agricultural peak period of intense planting or weeding. The data comes from weekly interviews conducted fourteen times from July to December, recording the major two activities of each of the previous seven days.

The data reveal a relatively minor contribution of women to their husband's fields, but with significant differences across the two ethnic groups. Overall, women worked on the fields of their husbands slightly more than one day a week. This average varied over the season; when agricultural operations were at their peak times in terms of seasonal importance (plowing and planting during the initial early rains, and later during the harvest), women spent more time in their own and their husband's fields. Mossi women worked in their husbands' fields slightly more often on weekdays and much more so on off-peak market days. Bwa women were less likely to work in their husbands' fields, especially older Bwa women, whose work in husbands' fields drops by half compared with younger women. Many of the older Bwa women in the sample were widows, while there were only three widows in the Mossi sample, and this may explain their continued high participation. (Since the Mossi are a migrant community, widows were less likely to have migrated to Bereba in the first place, and if their husband died in Bereba they were likely to move back to their natal village.)

Men sometimes paid conventional payments for this work in their fields, in addition to meeting the wife's consumption requirements. For cotton fields the sums varied from 5,000 CFA to 20,000 CFA (the exchange rate was roughly 500 CFA per U.S. dollar). Grain was put into household

Table 5.1 Average Time Allocation of Women in Bereba, Burkina Faso

Mossi	Home	Husband	Income
Market day off-peak	0.35	0.11	0.55
Market day peak	0.33	0.14	0.53
Weekday off-peak	0.32	0.12	0.56
Weekday peak	0.29	0.35	0.35

Bwa	Home	Husband	Income
Market day off-peak	0.51	0.04	0.45
Market day peak	0.50	0.16	0.34
Weekday off-peak	0.46	0.10	0.44
Weekday peak	0.42	0.29	0.29

Source: Author survey, Burkina Faso, 1996, as described in Kevane and Wydick (2001).

granaries in most Mossi households. The Bwa conventionally divided the harvest into two parts: large cobs were put in the men's granaries, small cobs into the women's. Norms about rights to use and sell this grain varied from household to household.

In the past, women's time working in their husbands' fields was strongly conditioned by norms against women's use of the plow, and their labor being limited to planting and harvesting. People would still often speak as if women did not plow, but many did.

Women spent from one-third to one-half of their days on income-generating activities. This was divided among a number of activities. One was cultivating small groundnut, sorghum, or maize fields. The fields rarely exceeded one hectare, and most were one-quarter hectare. Most Mossi women had personal fields; only a few older Bwa cultivated on their own. In fact, the only Bwa woman to work a significant amount of time (about 30 percent of weekdays) on a personal field was an older woman whose husband was sick (and died) during the study period. Toward the end of the season, she spent most of the week helping relatives in their cotton harvests.

Another personal activity was selling home-processed foodstuffs, such as *soumbala* (a seed fermented to make a condiment for sauce) and karité, and by making deep-fried cowpea or flour fritters in the market. Two Mossi women illustrated this choice: they spent almost all of their time in the market, seven days a week. One, Oeudraogo Marie, sold sorghum fritters every day in the market, from morning to afternoon. The other, Sana Assiatou, operated a restaurant selling rice and sauce. Marie gave birth to a girl during the study, and Assiatou was breastfeeding her newborn daughter. Neither of their husbands cultivated. Marie's husband was a livestock trader and butcher; Assiatou's husband sold plastic dishware in Bereba and surrounding markets.

A third activity was brewing and selling sorghum beer, *dolo*. In Bereba, only Bwa women made dolo, though many Mossi women had made it in their natal villages, and two Mossi women were regular drinkers. Bwa women spent slightly more time on income-generating activities than did Mossi women during the week, but Mossi women were more likely to spend market days in the market selling processed foods.

Only one woman in the village worked for wages. She helped people in their fields, helped make karité butter, and helped with laundry. Several men in the village worked as day or contract laborers; the labor market was thin because land was easily accessible and income levels reasonably high so that people were not constrained, in general, to earn cash on a day-to-day basis.

Home time also varied from one-third to one-half of total time. This time was for cooking meals and drawing water, tending to sick children, assisting in childbirth, and carrying out the numerous other tasks associated with home life. Home time is a combination of this time with leisure and travel time; that is, it was "non-income generating" time. Age distribution of children, as will be seen below, was a partial determinant of time at home. Some young women stayed at home almost all the time. Among the Bwa, Kura Marie was a new bride and did not work in the small field her husband cultivated or in his father's field. Among the Mossi, several young women worked with or for their husbands on market days and spent weekdays at home, since their husbands did not farm. Another woman was pregnant, and her co-wives had many small children, so she stayed home to care for the infants while they worked. But many older women stayed at home for varying reasons. Mamboue Hadohoun, for instance, was a woman in her mid-forties whose husband, a griot balafon player, had secretly run off to Côte d'Ivoire with her co-wife, leaving her stranded. She spent much of her time trying to locate him (rumors were that he had only gone to Banfora) and to reestablish her living situation.

In terms of ethnic differences in the averages, Bwa women spent less time in their husband's fields, less time in the market, and almost no time in their own fields. They did spend more time at home.

Table 5.2 presents some statistics indicative of the status of women in the two groups (Kevane and Wydick 2001). While Bwa women had considerably more education than Mossi women, this reflected in part the much higher levels of education in general, for boys and girls, of the Bwa. Participation of women in women's associations, and the incidence of receiving training through income-generating training and literacy projects were comparable across the two groups. The table highlights other differences in the backgrounds and marriages of women in Bereba. Of note are the strong changes over time in whether a woman's father had visited Côte d'Ivoire for work, whether her father held a salaried position, and, for Mossi women, whether her father had spent time in the army. These changes, as well as the increase in education for fathers of Bwa women, were consistent with changes in the national and regional economy. The more advanced economy of Côte d'Ivoire continued to attract young Mossi men, many of whom were brothers of the women in the sample. Correlations among these and other variables—the father having traveled to Côte d'Ivoire, the number of brothers in cities within Burkina Faso and abroad, and whether the father received a salary—were fairly high, suggesting that they were reasonable proxy variables for the multidimensional "status" of the natal family.

Bwa families were somewhat wealthier than Mossi families. They cultivated larger areas and had more oxen. A per capita measure of the market value (using market prices, but not adjusting for quality) of assets listed in the census (oxen, pigs, sheep, goats, bicycles, and mobilettes) resulted in an average of 265,000 CFA per family (roughly $530).

Table 5.2 Descriptive Statistics for Mossi and Bwa Women, Burkina Faso

Variable	Young women (under 35) Bwa n=21	Young women (under 35) Mossi n=16	Older women (over 35) Bwa n=47	Older women (over 35) Mossi n=16
CHILDBF				
# of children 0–2	0.57	0.63	0.15	0.31
CHILD210				
# of children 2–10	0.9	1.24	0.83	1.31
OLDERG				
# of girls 11–20	0.14	0.12	0.53	0.63
OLDERB				
# of boys 11–20	0.17	0.16	0.93	1.21
BD				
year of birth	1971	1970	1946	1950
WID				
whether widow	0.00	0.00	0.36	0.19
MARRIED				
whether married	0.79	1.00	0.72	0.81
COWI				
fraction with more than one wife	0.24	0.47	0.55	0.31
SCHYR				
years schooling of woman	1.38	0.13	0.15	0.00
HOMETOT				
index of housing	1.29	0.94	0.85	1.25
OXEN				
# of husband's oxen	2.62	1.56	2.24	2.07
EDU				
years schooling of siblings	11.33	6.81	3.96	1.75
FCHIEF				
whether father was a chief	0.14	0.00	0.11	0.13
BROS				
# of brothers	2.19	5.59	1.66	6.81
SALAR				
whether father salaried	0.19	0.25	0.09	0.06
FARMEE				
whether father in army	0.24	0.06	0.13	0.13

Source: Reprinted with permission from Kevane and Wydick (2001, 125), Table 2, copyright 2001, by Blackwell Publishing.

Table 5.3 reports the results from a set of regressions, with the percent time devoted to home, income-generating activity, and husband's field as dependent variables. The explanatory variables included are a subset of the variables described above. There are a number of results to note. First, the presence of an older girl in the household greatly reduces the time a woman spends at home, enabling her to work in her husband's fields and on her own income-generating activities. Older boys make a woman spend more time at home; perhaps she had to spend more time cooking for the boy and his friends, and for the Mossi, a woman with an older boy was considerably

Table 5.3 Results of Estimations with Percentage Time Allocated to Activity as Dependent Variable, Burkina Faso

Variable	Time at home (OLS)		Time in market (OLS)		Time on husband's field (Tobit)	
	β	t-stat	β	t-stat	marginal effect	z-stat
Constant	0.26	3.22[c]	0.71	8.67[c]	−0.03	−0.47
CHILDBF	−0.05	−1.67[a]	0.02	0.84	0.02	1.29
CHILD210	0.01	0.62	−0.01	−0.56	0.00	0.28
OLDERG	−0.06	−4.07[c]	0.03	2.16[b]	0.02	2.28[b]
OLDERB	0.03	2.54[b]	−0.03	−1.97[b]	−0.01	−0.59
BD	0.00	0.77	0.00	−1.68[a]	0.00	1.06
WID	0.03	0.80	0.02	0.48	−0.06	−2.53[b]
COWI	0.02	0.66	−0.02	−0.64	0.00	0.00
SCHYR	0.01	0.38	0.01	0.44	−0.01	−1.01
HOMETOT	−0.02	−1.65[a]	0.02	2.00[b]	0.00	−0.30
OXEN	0.06	2.66[c]	−0.06	−2.59[c]	0.01	0.44
OXSQ	−0.01	−2.55[b]	0.01	2.15[b]	0.00	−0.07
BWA	0.25	5.73[c]	−0.14	−3.07[c]	−0.18	−6.03[c]
OXBWA	−0.10	−3.40[c]	0.03	0.87	0.11	5.44[c]
OXSQBWA	0.01	3.09[c]	0.00	−0.50	−0.02	−5.32[c]
EDU	0.00	0.47	0.00	0.25	0.00	−1.46
FCHIEF	−0.03	−0.67	0.03	0.69	0.00	0.00
BROS	0.00	0.23	0.00	0.67	−0.01	−1.52
SALAR	0.02	0.56	−0.06	−1.53	0.03	1.15
FARMEE	−0.09	−2.45[b]	0.03	0.72	0.06	2.27[b]
WKPEAK	−0.07	−2.26[b]	−0.19	−5.99[c]	0.24	11.42[c]
MKPEAK	0.00	−0.13	−0.09	−2.78[c]	0.11	5.24[c]
WKOFF	−0.04	−1.20	−0.01	−0.22	0.06	2.89[c]
R-square	0.21		0.22			
Log-likelihood					0.30	
n	380		380		380	

Source: Reprinted with permission from Kevane and Wydick (2001, 126), Table 3, copyright 2001, by Blackwell Publishing.

Notes: a. Significant at 10% level, b. significant at 5% level, c. significant at 1% level.

less likely to spend time in the market. Second, as might be expected, widows were less likely to work in the "family" field (of the male head of household with which they were affiliated). Third, none of the personal status variables of the woman (whether her father was a regular salaried employee, or in the army, or a chief, and whether she had many brothers) affected the allocation of time to any large degree. Fourth, the time of the season, whether peak or off-peak, and whether it was a market day or a regular weekday, mattered quite a lot. Women worked more in their husbands' fields during weekdays of the peak period (WKPEAK).

Fifth, and most important, the husband having more oxen seemed to influence the pattern of time allocation for the Bwa, but not for the Mossi.

The responsiveness of Bwa women to their husbands having more oxen was quite strong, but the same was almost negligible for the Mossi. This is consistent with the idea, developed above, that there are restrictions on the time allocation of Mossi women, compared with Bwa women. When an ethnic group places greater restrictions on a woman's ability to work as she pleases, the woman's decision to work in her husband's field varies less with his stock of oxen (or farm capital) than it would for women who were unrestricted. If both groups of women were equally free to choose their own activities, then the similarities in the economic environments confronting them (living in the same village) would suggest that their responsiveness to their husbands' capital should be the same. And yet they are clearly different.

There is a small literature that obtains similar findings. One that traces the very different gender relations in two groups subject to the same pressures of increased commercialization is Roos and Gladwin's (2000) study of farming in Cameroon. An interesting paper by Lilja and Sanders (1998) takes a different tack. They measured the returns to labor for women from working on their own personal plots compared with working in family fields controlled by their husbands. In their sample area of southern Mali, time in family fields increased as cotton cultivation was extended. The authors calculate that when women went to work in family fields, they were losing income. Presumably, women were not allowed to choose to remain in their higher-return activity.

Implications for Policy and Activism

This chapter has presented various approaches to thinking about how labor markets structure the allocation of women's time. One approach considers how men exercise extra-economic power over women. The hypothesis is that men have an extra source of economic power stemming from their implicit collusion embodied in social norms and custom. The theory of cartels and self-enforcing agreements suggests that men, as a group, may extract a surplus from women by turning the terms of trade against them or by restricting their participation in markets. This social norm approach contrasts with other approaches where gender matters at the individual level only. These approaches see labor market outcomes as resulting from biology (for example, specialization and build-up of human capital induced by childbearing roles, musculature, or psychological propensities) or historical contingencies (women own less property than men). Becker (1981), for example, argues that the gender division of labor between home and market was the result of specialization in sector-specific human capital brought about by the principle of comparative advantage and constructed on sexual lines because only women bear children.

Should enforcement, legislation, and promotion of women's empowerment be viewed as having high long-term payoffs because they undermine a cartel that distorts the price allocation mechanism and reallocates income in an unfair manner? Or should general poverty alleviation programs that have high economic returns be promoted in a gender-blind manner? Betty Freidan argued in a *Newsweek* article published in conjunction with the U.N. World Conference on Women in Beijing, that "sexual politics—reifying women's oppression and victimization by men—has come to dominate women's studies and feminist thought" (1995, 30). The rhetoric of sexual politics ought to have been toned down, according to Freidan, because it was drawing attention away from recognizing that bargaining among unequal household members was becoming more important than collusion. "The basis of women's empowerment is economic," Freidan wrote, reversing the causality of much previous feminist analysis, whereby a lack of empowerment made women poor. Indeed, empowerment used to be an end in itself. In developing countries, female literacy, consciousness-raising, group associations and, promotion of female solidarity were high on government and donor agendas. In Freidan's view, the resources and energy devoted to programs to empower women were reducing the more significant welfare gains to be had from gender-blind projects of poverty alleviation, such as work programs and asset redistribution.

An erosion of consensus around the existence and influence of discriminatory norms is not justified. There is no empirical basis for arguing that empowerment is secondary to economic improvements. It is possible that resources directed to empowerment programs may have larger effects on a sensitive local equilibrium of implicit male collusion, in terms of improving women's welfare, than do resources directed to marginally altering bargaining positions within the household. If male discrimination is recast in the light of cartels—that is, if it is also recast as an economic issue—then the case for working on the empowerment side is strengthened. The durability and strength of cartels depends on the ability of a cartel to clearly identify and sanction members. Identity enables groups to self-regulate their actions. The principle applies equally to a group suffering the effects of power. What is resisting and undermining a cartel through exercising countervailing power about, if not strengthening a sense of identity, of solidarity, of empowerment?

There is a real issue here. While all three approaches are valid and account for some part of how labor markets and time allocation work, policymakers have to decide what characterization is most appropriate for shaping public policy in a world of shrinking aid budgets. If there are social constraints on the actions of women, then programs to empower women may have welfare-improving effects for women even if they appear to imply very low individual net benefits from improved intrahousehold bargaining—or even imply individual net costs (such as being required to attend frequent group meetings). It is possible that programs that change norms generate externalities that escape individual cost-benefit analysis. The enforcement, legislation, and promotion of women's empowerment could be viewed as having high long-term payoffs because empowerment undermines social norms that distort the price-allocation mechanism and reallocate income in an unfair manner. If, on the other hand, norms have already been eroded by market mechanisms, then the general poverty-alleviation programs that have high economic returns should be promoted in a gender-blind manner.

Empirical studies of time allocation are vital in this regard. The typical study that finds that women's time allocation responds to market incentives can be misleading (Evenson 1978; Khandker 1988; Skoufias 1993; Tiefenthaler 1994). These findings are in line with Freidan's message that the gender problem is one of low endowments for women. The results are thus construed as casting doubt on the role of patriarchy or other discriminatory norms as explaining women's behavior. Though not usually the intent of the authors, these papers may be interpreted as lending an empirically based rationale to the twin forces of cultural relativism and antifeminist backlash, which have for some years now eroded the consensus around empowerment as policy and politics. Relativism says that programs of empowerment cannot be justified by appealing to norms about the roles and rights of women because there are no universal norms in this regard. The backlash approach says that, in practice, programs to empower generate considerable inefficiency and may even be paradoxically disempowering over the long run (because by privileging women they dull the incentives for women to invest in their own human capital). The backlash approach also objects to empowerment programs as affirmative remedies for past discrimination because these violate core ideals of gender-blind public policy. Much more empirical work is needed before commentators and policymakers can have serious debate about the magnitudes of these effects.

6

The Marriage Market

It is springtime in Zimbabwe, when hearts turn to romance and pockets
empty for "roora," the word for bride price in the local Shona language.
. . . Some people are requesting cellphones, second-hand cars or even can-
isters of gasoline, in this era of chronic fuel shortages and deepening
poverty, to sweeten the deal. . . . Local newspapers report that some
prominent families are charging thousands of dollars at a time when the
average private-sector employee earns only about $1,800 a year.
        —Rachel L. Swarns, New York Times, *October 3, 2001*

President Omar Hassan al-Bashir has urged Sudanese men to take more
than one wife in order to double the country's population of 30 million.
The Sudanese should ignore international family planning policies, Bashir
said in a speech to the ruling National Congress Party, shown on state television Tuesday night. He said Sudan needed more people for development, since it is Africa's biggest country and rich in resources. "We should
achieve this aim by having many wives," Bashir said.
        —Reuters, *August 15, 2001*

Marriage is like a groundnut: you have to crack it open to see what is
inside. So goes an Akan proverb; in this chapter, tools of supply and
demand analysis crack open some puzzling questions regarding marriage.
The chapter relies heavily on work by anthropologists. Anthropology has
maintained a consistent focus on the economics of marriage; indeed, much
anthropological work on marriage feels very much like economics in its
application of statistics to test the implications of models of individual
behavior. This approach competes with an alternative "symbolic" approach
that sees marriage as a structured ritual where cultural discourses are negotiated. This alternative asserts that the structures that shape marriage, and
payments such as bridewealth, are more like theaters than markets; marriage is a cultural event, a staging of ritual performances. There is no doubt
considerable truth in this assertion for many times and places. The brief
news item from Sudan exemplifies how states sometimes attempt to turn
marriage into political statement, in this case by linking polygyny with
"patriotic" outcomes. Both analytical points of view are worth exploring,

and in fact their divergence may be thought of as the difference between assuming perfect competition and assuming strategic interaction in the political-economy domain. The "economics" approach treats individuals as "structure-takers," bargaining for the best deal within a set structure. The "cultural" approach treats individuals as having considerable power over others, with every marriage act laden with meaning that affects other people's preferences and decisions, and hence marriage structures.

A wide variety of questions regarding marriage are amenable to social science analysis. Consider, for example, the forms of marriage. Why do some societies prohibit polygyny? Why prohibit same-sex marriage? Why do some villages mandate that residents marry partners from other villages? In explaining bans on certain forms of marriage, varied and changing moral standards regarding sexuality are often more relevant than changes in economic and social conditions, but there is still room for plausible explanations that have economic foundations.

Another set of questions focuses on the causes of changes in the incidence and terms of marriage forms that are socially permitted or enforced and the causes of cross-cultural variation in the terms and incidence of marriages. These are the more conventional questions of economics. What determines changes in the normal terms, or implicit price, of marriage? Why was bride price rising in Zimbabwe in 2001? What determines variation across groups?

Still another set of questions concerns variation in the terms and incidence of marriage across different categories of persons. Anthropological investigations of marriage are dominated by discussions of bridewealth and dowry, the major forms of monetary or kind transfers that take place upon marriage. Some marriages have large transfers, others small. Perhaps the characteristics of the parties involved determine the size of the transfers? Another major topic in the anthropology of marriage is the process of identity created and expanded through marriage. Marriages create social groups of affines (people related through marriage ties), and these groups may be important actors in controlling resources through political processes.

A final set of questions addresses government policy toward permitted marriages. Economists, more than anthropologists, are interested in the welfare effects of public policy regulating and setting the terms of marriages, or changing the incentives of parties to various kinds of marriages. For example, many African governments have recently moved to try to curb the incidence of polygyny by offering a "menu" of official marriages that includes an exclusively monogamous official marriage. Change in the content and enforcement of divorce laws presents another obvious avenue by which governments influence marriage.

Those are the questions. The problem in answering them, especially for African societies, is the necessity of imposing structure on what is clearly a multidimensional and constantly changing and contested set of rules and practices. Chanock (1985) remains a brilliant introduction to the pitfalls of assuming the existence of a coherent system that predictably responds over time to economic and political changes. Marriage contracts typically encompass multiple resource flows, which may begin even before the official marriage ceremony and may be contingent, and so never observed, and may also encompass difficult to observe behaviors, such as sexual practices. The characterization of payments made at marriages has caused sharp disagreements even among anthropology fieldworkers studying the same ethnic group. Experts and locals seem to disagree with startling frequency.

Another, and related, problem is that marriage practices vary greatly across societies and regions, as well as among people within a single region. Table 6.1 reports the findings of a careful study of actual marriage practices in Côte d'Ivoire. While close to a majority of marriages involved a standard ceremony and payments leading to cohabitation and sexual relations, the majority did not actually follow this standard procedure. Many couples simply cohabited, while others had ceremonies performed long after cohabitation and sexual relations.

These caveats not withstanding, a number of authors have found robust patterns in African marriage systems. Lesthaeghe, Kaufman, and Meekers (1989) and Kaufman and Meekers (1992) describe some of the different marriage zones in sub-Saharan Africa. Age differences are low and young women less likely to be married in southern Africa, while age differences are considerably higher, and almost all women marry young, in West

Table 6.1 Different Type of Marriage Sequences, Côte d'Ivoire

	Events that occurred in:				
Type	Phase 1	Phase 2	Phase 3	Number	Percent
1	Cohabitation, ceremony, and sexual relations			2,247	46.3
2	Ceremony	Cohabitation and sexual relations		468	9.3
3	Ceremony	Sexual relations	Cohabitation	40	0.8
4	Ceremony and sexual relations		Cohabitation	79	1.6
5	Sexual relations	Ceremony	Cohabitation	101	2.1
6	Sexual relations		Cohabitation	405	8.3
7	Cohabitation and sexual relations			673	13.9
8	Cohabitation and sexual relations	Ceremony		304	6.3
9	Sexual relations	Cohabitation	Ceremony	257	5.3
10	Sexual relations	Cohabitation and ceremony		281	5.8
Total				4,855	100.0

Source: Reproduced from Meekers (1992, 68), Table 2.

Africa. Central African countries are somewhat in between. Figures 6.1 and 6.2 show broad differences in such basic statistics as the difference between the mean age of men and mean age of women at marriage, the percent of women married by ages 20–24, and the marital status of the elderly. Chad, Niger, Mali, and Burkina Faso have very high rates of marriage of young women and among the highest age gaps. None of the high-marriage-rate countries have small age differences. All of the very low marriage countries are in southern Africa. Botswana has the lowest marriage rate but a fairly high age gap, suggesting that those few women marrying young (less than 30 percent) marry in more "traditional" marriages. There are many more widows than widowers, reflecting the common pattern that men die younger than women (leaving many widows) and women are not able to remarry (widows remains widows). Some countries, like Burkina Faso, have extensive incidence of levirate, where a widow "remarries" someone in the lineage of her husband.

Dimensions of Marriage

Around the world, marriage institutions typically contain both contractual and status dimensions (Carbone 2000; Cohen 1987). One way to think about the status dimension to marriage is to note a peculiar property of marriage as a transaction: the state or local jural group is a kind of participant to the marriage contract, along with the bride and groom and their families. (A "jural group" is a society that makes rules that are enforced internally; the rules are usually not written, and enforcement is not by the state but rather within the group.) Marriage is not just a private contract enforced by the state or jural group but rather an occasion during which persons enter into contracts with the state or jural group itself. Marriages that do not include this element of contracting with the state—marriages that are not "official"—are not achievable as private contracts. This can be seen most clearly when it comes to rights over children. In a common form of official marriage, for example, a man acquires rights over his wife's children. The rights are granted and guaranteed by the state, and the state often reserves some residual power to terminate those rights. Private contracts to acquire rights over children, however, are almost never enforceable; a private person cannot usually contract away rights over children. Without being married, men typically cannot have legal ownership rights to children, no matter how much they might be willing to pay.

On the contract side, marriages may specify actions that parties to the agreement can negotiate. The freedom of a woman to visit her relatives, for example, or the husband's obligation to give his wife a plot of land, may be negotiated. On the status side, marriages may specify a status for the husband

Figure 6.1 Percentage of Women Aged 20–24 Who Are Married and Average Difference in Age at First Marriage

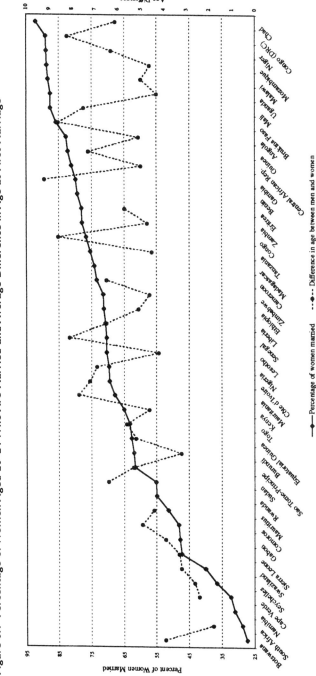

Source: Commission on Population and Development (2000).

Figure 6.2 Percentage of Persons Aged 60+ Who Are Married

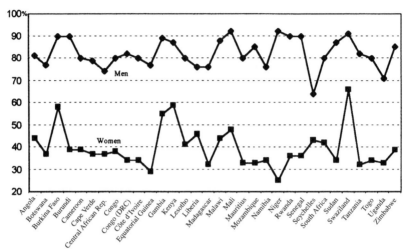

Source: Commission on Population and Development (2000).

or wife that cannot be contracted away. Bearing this distinction in mind, the marriage institutions of most societies bundle together in one transaction three separate transactions that various parties want to engage in: (1) the establishment of a household, with expectation of consequent benefits; (2) the creation and transfer of status-contingent rights; and (3) the creation of prestige.

Not every African society makes marriage so central. James noted that in eastern Sudan, "the Uduk practise an extremely 'free' system, in which it is individuals who make up their minds to marry, rather than their families who arrange the liaison; and no material or legal pledges are made between families in connection with marriage. . . . Either the man, or the woman, may decide to break off the relationship at any time; there is no formal divorce" (1970, 75). According to James's informants, children belonged to the matriline, and so it was untenable that legal rights to people, whether woman or potential children, could be the object of a transaction. Marriage simply acknowledged a sexual relationship and was accompanied by only "a few well-defined but short-term obligations." There was no elaborate marriage ceremony.

Marriage as an Enforceable Partnership Contract

A marriage contract is in many regards like a partnership agreement that facilitates establishing a household that makes investments, produces services, and generates children (Weiss 1997). Services range from the provision of housing to the provision of insurance. These services, produced in the household, are not like ordinary, private goods. They usually have moderate degrees of economies of scale; cooked food and shelter are more cheaply provided for persons living together than for persons living apart. Household services have moderate degrees of nonrivalry. Many people can enjoy them at the same time without infringing on the use or enjoyment of other household members. The household also serves as a kind of local, open-access storehouse for all kinds of goods. Pots and pans, books, lanterns, bedding for guests, toys, and educational materials for children; all are available to household members when they might need them. Sharing those items among a limited number of persons greatly enhances welfare, as any one person is unlikely to need them all the time, or at the same time as the other household members.

Marriage contracts commit parties to a continuing economic relationship, which enables investment in specialization and self-enforcing mutual insurance. Individuals are typically reluctant to specialize or insure others unless they are sure that the relationship will be long-lasting; an agreement to mutually insure each other against calamity would be of little use if you suspected that your partner might renege on his or her commitment whenever it suited. Marriage, then, is a more binding commitment to share the benefits of specialization and insurance.

Households are also efficient places to raise children. Child care is typically cheaper to provide in a group setting. As any parent knows, the marginal cost of a second child is considerably lower than the marginal cost of the first child. More importantly, long-term marriage minimizes the likelihood of the possible adverse effects on children of frequent change in adult caregivers. A parent wishing to ensure a large investment in his or her children will likely seek a partner willing to enter a long-term relationship.

So there is a straightforward economic reason to think of marriage as a contract for the establishment of a household. This view of marriage has much to commend it. For one thing, it explains the decline in marriage in advanced industrial economies. Modern appliances have reduced greatly the costs of single-person households. Daycare centers have emerged to provide economies of scale in child care, as wealthy societies can afford special controlled environments that are safer for children, with plenty of toys and play structures to keep them busy with less supervision.

More to Marriage than Household Production

But marriage is not only about the establishment of a household. If it were, there would not be so much uniformity in household structures. Around the world, households have seemed to consist disproportionately of monogamous, heterosexual couples (Laslett and Wall 1972). Marriage contracts among larger groups of men and women are rare. It is not difficult to imagine, even in a very poor country, many of the services mentioned earlier being provided by a variety of alternative groupings, ranging from communal kitchens to nunneries to dormitories. Moreover, marriage contracts almost always speak to the question of rights and obligations regarding sexual activity; most contracts are quite clear (explicitly or implicitly) about some degree of exclusivity. In many states of the United States partners had exclusive rights to one another's voluntary sexual activity (Cohen 1987, 271).

Two aspects of marriage in particular are *not* like a partnership contract. First, marriage is an occasion where prestige is garnered. Second, as noted above, marriage is a transaction involving the creation and transformation of status-contingent rights. The importance of rights is particularly salient in most African societies, for the simple reason that one of the parties to the marriage, the young girl, typically has few rights over her own actions. For the young woman, marriage is about creation and transfer of her rights, and less about her voluntary entry into a contract to create a household.

Creation and Transformation of Rights

Rights are properties of persons that are not easily alienable by the person to whom the right appertains. Status-contingent rights are rights that a polity does not see as universal but rather as appertaining to persons of well-defined social status. Marriage typically generates two sorts of rights for marriage partners: rights they will have over children and rights over the sexual services of each other. In addition, for most African societies, the rights of a father over his daughter are transformed into rights of a husband and his kin over the wife.

Besteman, writing on Somalia, observed: "Women's economic independence was thus controlled by early marriage and the denial of access to land. Women's labor was controlled by those who held land. Prior to marriage, a woman's labor was at the service of her father; following marriage, her labor was at the service of her husband. Between marriages, her labor may be her own, but she usually had to exchange it for access to land or food from her brothers" (1995, 202).

Finally, marriage also generates rights that children who emerge from the marriage will have over their mother and father and the families of their parents. An interesting example of this, though not from Africa, is the Hindu coparcenary system in India, whereby male children at birth become joint owners of the family estate.

For many commentators, African marriages are primarily geared toward establishing rights over children. This contrasts with the United States, where rights over children have only recently become the dominant element in marriages (Carbone 2000). Children are valuable both intrinsically and for the resources they generate when they are adults. There has been a long debate, it should be noted, over whether this latter value is in fact substantial in Africa. When children grow up, how much do they actually transfer to parents? Does the transfer value exceed the costs of rearing the child? The measurement exercise is complicated because if children are an important form of old-age "insurance," then many parents may not "need" their children (Hoddinott 1992). No transfer might be observed, even though there may have been an understanding that it would have been forthcoming.

Property rights over children are a central feature of the economic organization of any society. Marriage can be thought of as the social occasion where well-defined property rights over children are reassigned. (There is considerable variety among ethnic groups over who retains rights over children born out of wedlock, and how those are transformed at marriage.) Rights over fertility or children are often tied to bridewealth payments. When bridewealth is paid, the husband typically takes full control rights over children. Sometimes the rights over children are the primary purpose of bridewealth, in situations where a man has paid bridewealth and the wife then runs off with a lover, for instance. If the woman had children, they stay with the husband and the lover does not have to restitute the bridewealth paid by the husband. If the woman had no children, then the lover will have to restitute the husband for the bridewealth he paid.

Tauxier (1924, 170) describes this tradition for Bisa areas of what is now Burkina Faso. In parallel fashion, Père and Desroche (1973, 75) observe that in Bisa areas if a widow refused to accept the levirate after her husband died, the bridewealth had to be repaid; she could refuse to marry her husband's brother only if someone were willing to pay her bridewealth.

Parties to a marriage commit themselves to sharing in rights over children and to binding themselves not to alienate those rights. Three caveats should be mentioned. While children cannot be "sold," they can be "rented," and the issue of child fostering has been a perennial concern in the social science of African childhoods (Bledsoe 1990). Moreover, because children will grow up to become adults, a tension exists between rights of parents over children, and the ability of the child-cum-adult to exercise his or her will independently. It is hard even to imagine a society where parents maintained their strong rights over a child's behavior beyond adulthood. The reality of the transition from childhood to adulthood is that rights of parents over children diminish sharply at certain well-defined social occasions observed as rites of passage.

Woman-woman marriage, a common institutional arrangement involving from 5 to 10 percent of the female population in many regions, underscores the importance of rights transfer as an element of marriage. An older, perhaps wealthier, woman, marries a younger woman so that the older woman might own the children (Amadiume 1987; Cadigan 1998; Greene 1998; Herskovits 1937; Taraoré 1941). The older women becomes the "female husband," and has the same rights over children as a man might; indeed, she might be considered to have male gender. Hakansson describes another variant: "The Gusii practice a form of marriage where women with only daughters can take the bridewealth received for a daughter and use it to obtain a wife for a fictitious son. The children of such a wife become the paying woman's grand-children. This form of marriage is increasing in Gusii land due to the growth in the number of single mothers who see it as an alternative way of obtaining economic security and social acceptance" (1986, 16).

Marriages Change the Allocation of Prestige

If a norm determines which activities generate prestige, then people will respond strategically to that norm (Cole, Mailath, and Postlewaite 1992; Frank 1985). The basis for prestige varies from society to society, but it typically involves wealth, education, and social class or caste. In marriage, the party with higher prestige lends its prestige to the party with lower prestige, or the prestige of both parties may be reinforced.

Thinking about prestige may resolve a conundrum in the analysis of marriage: why is dowry—payments that the bride's family makes to the groom's family upon marriage —so prevalent in India, whereas bridewealth is so prevalent in Africa? If one thinks that the underlying economic conditions of peasant society in India are fairly similar to the underlying conditions of peasant life in many parts of Africa, one might wonder why the two areas should have such different patterns of marriage. One of three possibilities might be the case, if the underlying economic fundamental conditions are indeed similar: (1) either money and people are very fungible, so that the quality-adjusted prices are roughly comparable (i.e., dowry is accompanied by many more rights for the woman and obligations for men in India, that is the "net transaction" is the same); (2) somehow in a social situation where marriage payments signal information about family quality to others, societies can get "stuck" in equilibria where deviations from payment norms signal disadvantageous characteristics; therefore families continue to adhere to the norm; or (3) exogenous "culture" in India prescribes that to earn prestige for a family, a daughter must marry up the caste ladder.

This third possibility is analyzed by Anderson (2001), who focuses more narrowly on the question of dowry inflation. Anderson wants to explain why dowry has risen dramatically over the last decades in India and Pakistan. If anything, one might think the reverse should be happening if, as seems likely, men were the relative beneficiaries of the slow but steady growth in income. As men desire women in the marriage market, the higher their incomes the more women, or women's services, they might be willing to acquire. Anderson suggests that a contrary process might be at work, in which rising and more dispersed income levels lead successful families within each caste to more often pay dowries to buy into higher castes.

The ratcheting nature of prestige seems to dominate other effects in some African contexts. Masquelier (2001) describes for a town in Niger the common practice of indirect dowry, whereby grooms pay bridewealth to the mother of the bride, who then adds her own savings to endow her daughter with a large trousseau, with an expensive bed as centerpiece. Over the years the value of the dowry has risen rapidly, as the public display of bed, pots, pans, mattresses, and other household items leads to a competition over prestige. Most interestingly, the indirect dowry persisted despite a vigorous "reforming" Islamic movement led by males who tried to limit bridewealth and dowry displays.

Ensminger and Knight (1997) also follow this line of thinking, explaining how indirect dowry gradually replaced bridewealth in the Orma community of northeastern Kenya. According to them, wealthy fathers of daughters desisted from requesting bridewealth in order to make alliances with other wealthy families. Payments among the Orma elite declined relative to those of poorer classes.

A Supply-and-Demand Model for Marriage

To summarize, marriage is an occasion where rights, services, status, and prestige are transacted between bride and groom and their respective families. Marriage in many societies has numerous economic dimensions. The new couple often merges their previously separate finances. They move into a shared residence. They cook meals together and perhaps sleep in a shared bed. They raise children (and livestock and pets) jointly. The decision is not one to be taken lightly, and the rights and obligations of each partner to provide for and to cherish the partner are often spelled out by social norms, laws, and implicit understandings. A conjugal contract sets the terms, or price, of a marriage.

The task now is to develop a model of this complex and varied institution. A good place to begin is with the workhorse model of market transactions, the supply-and-demand model. This approach to marriage was pioneered by Becker (1981) in his famous *Treatise on the Family,* which stands out as a landmark in the changing perceptions of the appropriateness of an economics of marriage. Work by Grossbard (1976; 1980; Grossbard-Schechtman 1995), Friedman (1990), and Cherry (1998) has elaborated on and extended Becker's approach.

Following Friedman's (1990) formulation of the supply-and-demand marriage model, suppose that everyone in a society has some idea of the bundle of rights, services, status, and prestige transacted in a "standard" marriage contract. From the point of view of the woman, a monetary value can be assigned to deviations from the standard contract. (Not all deviations in the various dimensions to the contract will be fungible, in this sense, but for now the assumption is useful.) This monetary value of deviations from the standard contract is the "price" in the marriage market, and that price fluctuates so that the supply of brides available in the market is equal to the demand for brides. The price may be interpreted as the difference between the value, to a woman, of a marriage contract that implies a given bundle of rights, obligations, and payments, compared with the standard contract.

There is an analogy to be made with computers. For the past several decades, the price of a given amount of "computing power" falls every year, even though the price of "computers" may rise or stay the same. The commodity being transacted in the computer market is constantly changing. A contract that specifies that women should work longer than they are normally expected to implies a lower price for the woman; the man gets more of a woman in the marriage. If the contract specifies that a woman does less work, or is freer to do as she likes, compared with the ordinary contract, then the man is paying more than he would ordinarily. Following convention, a positive price is "bridewealth," which involves net payments from a groom to the bride or bride's family (Haanstad and Borgerhoff Mulder 1996). A negative payment is "dowry," which the bride's side pays the groom's side (always comparing payments to the standard contract). A positive price can then be interpreted as a situation in which the implicit contract is favorable to the woman (e.g., it may involve the man turning over assets to his wife, when he ordinarily might not be obligated to do that).

This view helps us understand that since marriage involves complicated transfers of rights, the money trading hands during the marriage ceremony may bear little relation to the true price of a marriage. For instance, if a larger sum of money is paid at the time of marriage, from the groom to the bride, but the man now has fewer obligations to his wife, the price of a wife may be falling rather than rising. For empirical work this poses a problem (especially if marriages involve payment flows from both bride to groom and groom to bride); in order to find out whether brides are really more expensive, researchers must collect a wide variety of data on marriage transactions and the provisions of the implicit contract.

A supply-and-demand model of marriage, represented in Figure 6.3, assumes three things: demand behavior of grooms is such that the quantity of wives demanded declines when the price rises; the quantity of brides supplied (by women) rises when the price rises; and the price adjusts in the marketplace until the supply offered is equal to the demand. The supply curve is described by $S(p, Z)$ and demand curve by $D(p, W)$, where Z and W are other independent factors that determine supply and demand, respectively. The independent or *exogenous* factors may overlap, and include such things as economic opportunities for women and men, opportunities from migration, and legal age at marriage. The equilibrium price p^* in the market must be such that the quantity supplied equals the quantity demanded, or $S(p^*, Z) = D(p^*, W)$. The price level is *endogenous;* it is determined by the other factors Z and W.

The first thing to do with Figure 6.3 is to understand the process whereby the price adjusts to clear the market. If the price were fixed at some arbitrary level (by a government, say), then there would be strong incentives to change behavior accordingly. Suppose the government prohibits all monetary payments at marriage, making the implicit price much lower than normal (say it was convention for men to pay a sum to women in exchange for rights over the woman's labor allocation). African governments have tried on numerous occasions to regulate bridewealth payments, including Niger in 1975 (Masquelier 2001), Cameroon during the early colonial period (Guyer 1986, 206), and Kenya during the colonial period (Shadle 2000, 168–174). The supply-and-demand model predicts that there

Figure 6.3 Supply and Demand in the Marriage Market

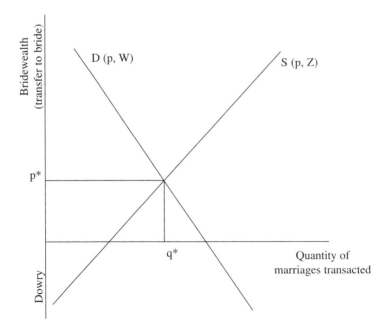

will then be an excess demand for brides (or, equivalently, an excess supply of men), and some mechanism will have to ration the men. The men who are rationed out of the market will be unhappy and will seek ways to pay women to choose them rather than other men. A black market for bridewealth payments might arise, with hidden gold jewelry exchanged at wedding ceremonies. The policy is unlikely to be successful.

James (1970) discusses an interesting policy innovation along these lines, mandated in 1963 in Uduk areas of eastern Sudan by the local *omda,* a kind of district commissioner in the "traditional" hierarchy of native administration. The omda ordered that marriages had to be validated by bridewealth. Marriages were too unstable. Presumably the omda was spending much time listening to marital disputes. Despite the very few conditions of the existing contract, noted above, there still seems to have been plenty to fight over. By making people pay to get married, the reasoning must have been that men would be less willing to forfeit the "bond" posted. The omda fixed some prices for bridewealth and told people they had to show him official receipts if they wanted him to hear cases of marriage disputes. James discusses how men and women rejected the policy and refused to pay, or when they did pay, the bridewealth would be returned some time later. The true price of marriage was zero, and fixing a high price simply led to "price evasion."

The second use of the model is to answer questions about what happens in the marriage market when there are changes in the exogenous variables. For example, suppose that population grows so that the younger cohorts become progressively larger than older cohorts. Further suppose that the society in question has a firm rule that men are only to marry younger women. Then, each year the cohort of women in the marriage market grows more rapidly than the cohort of men; the supply of wives shifts out. What happens? As illustrated in Figure 6.4, the supply curve of women shifts out (more women are available, at any price, than before) and the equilibrium price will fall, from p^* to p^{**}. This represents a decrease in bridewealth, or, if the price becomes negative, an increase in dowry. This "marriage squeeze" hypothesis is a leading contender for understanding the much-discussed problem of dowry inflation in India (Anderson 2000; Edlund 2000; Rao 1993; 2000).

Some commentators see increases in bridewealth in African societies. Why does the marriage squeeze logic not apply? Populations were growing rapidly in most African countries, at least until the AIDS crisis. African men also marry younger women, as a rule. So bridewealth should be falling, and even turning into dowry, by this model. Something else must be changing, increasing the demand for wives or reducing the supply of wives, or else the model is not right. Figures 6.5 and 6.6 suggest some of the difficulties of modeling marriage markets. Suppose the economy is changing,

Figure 6.4 Change to Dowry with Population Growth

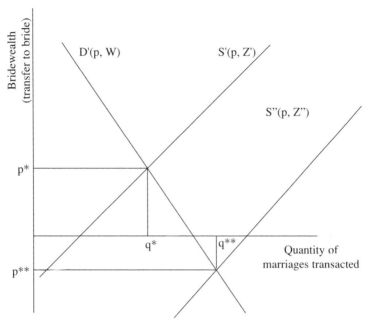

and incomes are rising. If the incomes of men were rising, then men might demand more wives, and in Figure 6.5 the demand curve shifts out and the price rises, from $p*$ to $p**$. But suppose the fathers' incomes were rising and their daughters were "normal goods." They might be less willing to part with their daughters. They might enjoy the company of their daughters or might want them to complete school. So the supply of brides falls, as in Figure 6.6. The price rises from $p*$ to $p**$. Both graphs display rising prices, but for different reasons. In each graph the change in the incidence of marriage (or, more likely, the age at marriage) would be quite different. In Figure 6.5 more women are married; in Figure 6.6 fewer women are married. The two possibilities (and there are still other complications, such as who "owns" the young women coming into the marriage market) highlight the limitations of the supply-and-demand approach.

The model is useful, however, as a first step. Marriage payments and the incidence of marriage do fluctuate over time in ways consistent with hypotheses from this supply-and-demand model. Borgerhoff Mulder (1996) is a good reference, suggesting that in Kenya, Kipsigi males' interest in paying bridewealth to secure wives diminished over time as the price of maize fell and the returns to child and female farm labor declined. Table 6.2 reports results from a study of marriages in Kenya by Hakannson (1986), previously discussed in Chapter 4. The percentage of marriages following

Figure 6.5 Men Willing to Pay More for Marriage When Male Income Rises or Female Productivity Rises

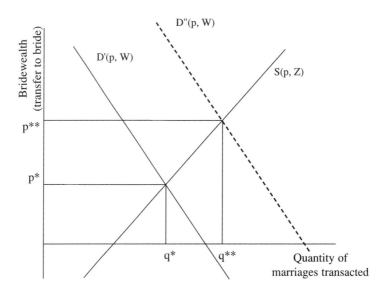

Figure 6.6 Men Less Willing to Supply Daughters When Male Income Rises or Female Productivity Rises

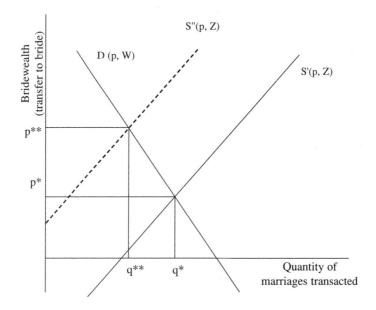

Table 6.2 Incidence of Bridewealth Payment and Elopement per Year Period, Kenya, 1957–1983

Years	0	1	2	3	4	N
1957–1962	64%	73%	91%	100%		30
1963–1968	72	79	93	93	100	28
1969–1974	55	64	68	74	78	35
1975–1980	46	50	52	66	66	48
1981–1983	14	26	28			50

Source: Reprinted by permission of the American Anthropological Association from Thomas Hakansson, "Detachable Women: Gender and Kinship in Process of Socioeconomic Change among the Gusii of Kenya," *American Ethnologist,* Vol. 21, 1994, p. 525.

Note: The horizontal row indicates percentage of all cohabitations that were paid immediately, then after one year, two years, and so on.

the norm of marriage payments before cohabitation declined dramatically over the decades, and the likelihood that a man would pay bridewealth within a few years after cohabitation also declined. Marriage as a publicly recognized institution was clearly on the decline. The implied price of marriage (the value to the women) was declining. Hakannson and others attribute this decline in the incidence of marriage to shifting opportunities for men and women as Kenyan society became more fluid and urbanized and as agricultural productivity growth stagnated. In particular, women's value in agricultural production declined rapidly during the period.

The supply-and-demand model is also useful for introducing Becker's (1981) pathbreaking analysis of polygyny. The incidence of polygyny is high, by world standards, in African countries (Adams and Mburugu 1994; Aryee 1997; Besteman 1995; Garenne and Van de Walle 1989; Jacoby 1995; Musisi 1991; Spiegel 1991). Southern African countries have rates of approximately 10 percent, eastern Africa is at around 30 percent, while the rates in West Africa can be as high as 50 percent. The incidence is lower for more-educated men and women, but even among this group it is common for men to have socially recognized mistresses, the informal equivalent of a polygamous union. Becker asked the question whether banning polygyny was in the interest of women, and he developed the paradoxical (for his American audience) proposition that polygyny would typically be good for women. African women are similarly ambivalent about polygyny (Meekers and Franklin 1995). But suppose for a moment that women do not care whether they are sharing a man with another woman, as long as the terms of the marriage are the same as if she were monogamous. In other words, the woman only cares about the income and benefits and duties that she herself receives or has to perform, and her welfare is not affected by what her husband does on his own time, as it were. It is most unreasonable, but it simplifies things to think that way for purposes of an introductory model.

The implicit assumption above was that men were demanding a single wife. Suppose now that men were allowed to marry more than once. What would be the effect? In terms of the model, there would be an increase in the demand for wives. If the price represents deviations from a standard monogamous contract, then the supply of women stays exactly the same (she only cares about what she gets in the marriage contract). The new equilibrium will have a higher price. Women who would have been happy to be married at the old price now receive a windfall (or perhaps their fathers do). Women who might not have gotten married because the price was too low now are willing to get married because the price is higher. As Friedman (1990) put it, there is nothing really different here from a rule that said people could only have one car. Relax the rule, and the suppliers of cars (or wives) are better off.

Given the heated political debates over banning polygyny, it is somewhat surprising that the economics literature has not yet developed any convincing arguments against polygyny. If polygyny is so favorable to women, why has it often been banned? There is no cross-country analysis for African countries or for tribes in terms of bans on polygyny, though there is a lively literature explaining the varying incidence of polygyny (see White [1988] and White and Burton [1988]). Hunt (1991) suggests that the 1950 colonial ban on polygamy in Belgian Congo arose from a conflict between the colonial authorities and educated elite; the ban was unusual in declaring polygyny illegal in urban areas only. For the United States, Anderson and Tollison (1998) argue that banning of polygyny in Utah by the Edmunds Act of 1882 was partly influenced by men's fear of women getting better terms out of marriages if they had the option of moving to Utah and entering polygynous marriage. As with other arguments justifying government regulation, there would have to be some nonpecuniary negative externality arising from polygyny. The state of being married (polygynously) or unmarried might have some effect that the person paying the price of getting married does not take into account. The assumption above that women's welfare did not depend on what their husbands were doing in their own time is unrealistic. The husband does not take into account the change in valuation of the first wife of the marriage to the second wife. One could imagine also that widespread polygyny entails either substantial increase in age at marriage for many men, or lowering of age at marriage for girls, or else entails positive and significant probability of nonmarriage for some men. If there are positive externalities from marriage, then "spreading women around" so that every male has a reasonable expectation of marriage after adolescence could increase overall welfare, even while making worse off some women who would have joined polygynous households.

This model represents the demands for and supplies of husbands as if husbands were homogeneous. Men and women differ greatly in many dimensions, from tastes to habits to looks; any marriage market will have implicit prices reflecting that variation in quality. The model could be amended to include some room for bargaining when men and women meet. The price in the supply-and-demand model is the normal price for a standard marriage with standard partners. A special person might command more than the normal price. This is analogous to modeling the labor market in terms of supply and demand, knowing that individual workers and employers bargain over many particulars of a labor relationship

Variation in marriage across individuals and households seems to be in accord with rather obvious economic hypotheses. Jacoby (1995) finds quite clearly that men with greater wealth have more wives and that, conditional on wealth, men with more productive farms have more wives as do taller men. Borgerhoff Mulder (1987; 1988; 1990) takes a more Darwinian perspective and finds much evidence consistent with the hypothesis that men in Kipsigi communities in Kenya treat marriage as a mechanism to maximize reproductive success (most tellingly, she finds that young age at menarche leads to earlier marriage and higher bridewealth). Cronk (1991) has an interesting discovery in this regard. He finds that wealthier men have more wives, but they also have fewer children per wife. This raises the interesting possibility that while women's maximum fertility was not being attained, male fertility in a given time frame might improve reproductive fitness. That is, perhaps reproductive fitness is maximized by having many children at the same time, rather than many children spaced over many years.

Thinking of the main feature of the marriage market as the variation in quality, or how bargaining determines prices because the transactions costs of "shopping" in the marriage market are very high, leads to different models of marriage, known as matching models. These models typically assume that people search for partners, make tentative contracts, break contracts, and search again, until everyone is satisfied with his or her partner, in the sense that no one prefers to reenter the marriage market, search for a partner, and convince that person to marry. Cigno's (1991) remarkable book on the economics of the family contains a very nice introduction to matching models.

Government Policy Toward Marriage

Marriage in Africa, as elsewhere, is political. Political processes do more than simply distribute property rights. They also restrict and encourage the form of economic transactions. For this reason there can be no presumption that marriage policy is neutral in affecting outcomes in terms of household division of labor and welfare. The Beckerian or Coasian view of marriage has tended toward this neutrality position. Fafchamps, for example, contended that marriage payments "at the onset of the union itself, [make] it difficult for an equity-minded policy maker to durably affect the intrahousehold distribution of welfare" (1997, 20). The argument is this: because only net bridewealth matters, and the components of bridewealth that are negotiated are fungible, a policy change that alters some aspect of the marriage transaction simply spills over into other dimensions. The net bridewealth will be the same. But this cannot be a general result, for by forbidding contracting on certain dimensions, the range of potential contracts that marriage partners might make changes, with consequent welfare effects. Changes in policy might unwittingly lead to opposite outcomes from those intended.

Much ink has been spilled in the United States and other industrial countries over whether the switch to no-fault, unilateral divorce changed behavior. Changing the divorce law implies a reallocation of property rights regarding who can decide when to terminate marriage. Under fault law, the spouse most wanting to leave has to buy out the other. Under no-fault, the spouse least wanting to leave has to pay the other to stay. Either way, divorce should only happen when efficient (when the sum of benefits in marriage is less than the sum of benefits if separate), and so a change in property rights should have no effect on divorce rates. All no-fault does is leave women (who more often want to stay, perhaps) with lower settlements; their husbands no longer have to buy them off. For the economics student, this is a variant of the Coase theorem (Acemoglu 2002; Coase 1988; Glaeser, Johnson, and Shleifer 2001; Usher 1998).

There is a lively controversy as to whether divorce patterns actually changed with changes in divorce rules in industrialized countries where data exist to carry out proper analyses (Allen 1992; Dnes 1998; 1999; Friedberg 1998; Peters 1992). Another, related, controversy is whether the switch led to different patterns of labor market participation. When divorce was contested in the United States, women had substantial negotiating power and could get remunerated for "investment" in marriage. Under no-fault divorce, courts decide settlements and do not consider compensation for investment. More importantly, Parkman (1992) suggests courts do not compensate for human capital foregone (i.e., opportunity cost, in addition to investment). Because of this, women, especially those with high opportunity costs to foregoing maintenance of market-oriented human capital, have more incentives to work outside the home to maintain marketability under no-fault.

Government intervention that forbids contracting on certain dimensions or that changes rights assigned as part of marriage may thus have effects on behavior. Assume that women have investment projects that yield returns in the future. Women contract for marriage in the present, and in marriage, money can be exchanged as bridewealth or dowry. But one thing cannot be negotiated: residual claimancy in the second period. Recall from Chapter 3 that residual claimancy determines who gets the surplus or product from some effort, above and beyond contractually stipulated payments. A worker who receives a wage is not the residual claimant to any discovery or extra effort that she might put in; her employer is the residual claimant. Under systems like that of coverture, the husband, through marriage, becomes the residual claimant for all the wife's activities. The state enforces this rule; it says it will not enforce contracts between husband and wife.

The woman will not make the investment if the husband has no ability to assure her that she will reap the benefits from her investment. How can he promise not to take the money away when she does earn more? What is his "commitment device"? Without some enforcement mechanism, she will not make the investment. Changing the policy, then, affects the investment behavior; the policy is not neutral. The problem is two-fold: men cannot commit to compensating their wives on the basis of investments wives made before their marriage, and women upon marriage cease to own their activities. The neutrality-of-government-policy proposition assumes that activities in marriage are not subject to moral hazard (where the husband promises something but then acts in a different way later on). But there is moral hazard in conjugal interaction, so marriage contracts need multiple dimensions to reduce inefficiencies of moral hazard. This perspective bears some similarity to the discussion by Geddes and Zak (2000) on the "rule of one-third," whereby a widow inherits one-third of the husband's estate should he die intestate. Geddes and Zak interpret the rule as an informal institution (enforced by the grandfather paterfamilias) having the effect of ensuring investment in children.

Another example of government action having effects is in the area of remedy for breach of promise. For many societies, sexual relations outside marriage remain a legally enforceable breach of the marriage contract. In some places adultery is a criminal offense. Chanock notes that in 1944 in Zambia the Ngoni Native Authority established a "right to damages in the event of adultery," and this "new payment grew in both value and significance" (1985, 179). Lovett (1996) reports how the colonial authorities sided with male elders in western Tanzania, imposing fines and even imprisonment for women committing adultery. Finally, in an interesting study, Brinig (1990) discusses how the elimination of breach of promise as an actionable tort offense in the United States encouraged the diamond engagement ring to emerge as a commitment device. There may be similar commitment devices in many African societies, but this remains an understudied area.

Marriage, Economics, and Rationality

Cheung (1972) was one of the first to approach the "rationality" of strange marriage institutions. The paper is somewhat chilling in the ruthlessness of its application of the principle that institutions in society are "efficient." Cheung argued that in "traditional" China, men had comparative advantage in farming, and women in weaving. He assumed that the problem of marriage was how to ensure that a couple would remain married and reap the benefits from a household, when one of the parties might want to leave. People and state officials had incentives, he thought, to develop institutions that would make marriage more lasting. (Recall the omda of the Uduk, in Sudan.) In China, according to Cheung's reasoning, the cost of "taming" women was lower, since they were more productive at home, and so women were transferred to men in marriage. To ensure their "domesticity," two practices emerged: foot-binding and raising from childhood of future daughters-in-law by the groom's family. Cheung's argument was not that these were good, but rather that marriage practices and social institutions result from the intentional choices of individuals and seem often to conform to a view of persons as basically self-interested maximizers and of structures as sometimes turning individuals into property. Marriage in Africa is not at all like marriage in traditional China, but, as there, can be understood in part as an economic phenomenon.

7

Bargaining Power at Home

When I first arrived at no. 23's home she was dressed up as a man "for a joke" as it was Easter Day, and the charade pungently emphasised the unusual nature of their marital relationship. She drank beer, sat and joked with us in a quite uncustomary manner. . . . There were separate bank accounts, separate sectors of the firm in the management of each, and a sense of independence rather than interdependence.

—A. F. Robertson, "Bugerere—A County Case History"

Once men and women get married, they may have little scope for making choices. Their actions may be determined by the contract they signed at the time of their marriage, as described in the previous chapter. In that regard, a marriage contract might be like a labor contract that determines the actions and wages of an employee. But this seems to not be the case. There is room for plenty of choices.

There are three reasons why so many choices remain to be made within the married relationship. First, many of the terms of a marital relationship are not specified in the marriage contract. The usual contract, whether explicit or implicit, typically lays down no more than a few general principles and a couple of explicit actions to be taken. Second, many implicit terms to the marriage contract are unlitigable because of high transactions costs associated with disputes. A wife who comes to complain before a judge or local authority that her husband is spending household money on drink will be dismissed. Can a judge involve himself in every petty dispute of the household? Third, initial terms of a marriage often do not include provisions for periodic renegotiation and possible exit, and the transactions costs of exit are often high.

If the contracts that emerge from the marriage market do not specify the choices or actions of members of households, then what does? The answer lies in understanding the choices that people make within households after marriage deals have been struck. These choices may reveal something about the patterns of behavior of households. If these patterns are common to most households in a given society, they may be attributable to a particular structure of households. While the structure of households is itself more in the nature of a "frequent outcome," it does have characteristics akin to the structures described earlier. To the extent that people assume that the frequent outcome is a structure, then deviations from the usual outcome may be perceived in particular ways—as violations of structures rather than as eccentricities. The departures from the norm demonstrate more than just the tastes of those involved.

Social scientists of all disciplines and all world regions have been debating appropriate characterizations of households. Generalizing about households is important for a number of reasons. To predict the effects of any change that affects households, analysts need to have a reasonable model of how households operate on average. This is especially true for the economic analysis of policies that are designed to affect men or women in different ways. Second, and somewhat more selfishly, we might want to understand households in order to test whether our own experience in households is the norm. Everyone grows up in a household of some form or the other, is exposed to other households of friends and neighbors, and absorbs the rhetoric and iconography of households from various media. Are these experiences and images shared? Are there other "models" of the household besides the one we know?

Characterizing the Household: The Unitary Model

In economics, the problem of how to characterize households emerged from a specific problem. Survey researchers were collecting data on household expenditure patterns, rather than individual expenditure patterns. So many expenditures are at the level of the household—from housing to cars to food—that it was often convenient to ask about all purchases at the level of the household. Measurement of expenditure patterns is important in economics for the purpose of estimating elasticities of demand. When the prices of goods and services change, the demand for them will change according to the elasticity of demand. When incomes rise or fall, so too will the demands for good and services. (Interestingly enough, this is one of the few activities that economists perform "for the market." Corporations have an enormous interest in getting estimates of demand elasticities as they plan investment decisions. Estimating demand functions remain one of the major activities of economists, both in research and teaching.)

The economists estimating price and income elasticities of demand realized early on that they had a problem. All their data were at the household level, yet clearly the decisions were being made by individuals. How could they be sure that the estimated elasticities would have predictive value, since different changes in prices and incomes might lead to changes in the relationships among the individuals within the household?

The elasticities would have predictive value if households were like "superindividuals." This might happen if household members had homothetic preferences (Samuelson 1956). Having homothetic preferences means that consumption expenditures represent a fixed share of the budget available, and the share of total expenditures on a particular item does not depend on the size of the budget. If the household consists of a group of people with different budgets, who also have homothetic preferences, then the expenditure effects of changes in prices or income will not depend on the distribution of resources within the household. The household acts as if it were a single individual. Obviously, as individual budgets shift within the household, individuals get more or fewer goods and services. This artificial model of household behavior simply underscored how *unlikely* it would be that household behavior resembled individual behavior. New tools of analysis were required.

Despite this admonition by Samuelson, economics research on households perhaps unwisely followed Becker's (1981) lead in developing a "unitary" model of the household. There are now many versions of this model. Some simply assume that the household members act together, as one, because they are linked together by ties of love and altruism. Everyone sits around and discusses what is best for the household, much as an individual decides whether it is better to satisfy the cravings of his tongue or the warnings of his digestive tract. Other versions of the unitary model are more elaborate, and offer more explicit justification of the altruism link among family members

In Becker's (1981) version, the household contains an altruist who is much wealthier than the other household members. Becker's assumption leads to the interesting "rotten kid" theorem. Suppose a two-person household has one member (the man, say) who is comparatively more wealthy than the other member (the child), and the man's utility depends on consumption of some amount of household goods, and also on the child's level of utility. Higher utility for the child means higher utility for the man. The man's altruism is effective if the equilibrium levels of consumption for household commodities are different than they would be if the utility of his child did not enter into his utility function. If the father were effectively altruistic and spent some of his income on his child, then he would be making a transfer to his child. We might then imagine the father choosing the size of the transfer to maximize his utility, which depends on the child's utility. When deciding on a transfer, he will take the child's income into account, so the relevant budget constraint is the family budget constraint, not just his own. If his child's earnings are relatively high, he does not have to make as big a transfer. The upshot of this is that if the child knows that the man will be redistributing income to her, she will nevertheless have incentives to maximize the family income. If she did not, she would still receive a share of the man's income, but now from a smaller "pie." The "rotten kid" would not take an action that raised her own income if it lowered total family income, because the altruistic *chef de famille* would just redistribute away her gain by giving her a lower transfer. The members of the family, then, even if self-interested, act as if they care about joint family well-being.

Characterizing the Household: Bargaining Models

The main alternative to the unitary model is known as the bargaining model. The study of bargaining goes beyond its applications to households and is worth developing more generally.

The supply-and-demand model of market interaction considered in the previous chapter and in the appendix is applicable to situations where there are large numbers of basically anonymous people transacting in marketplaces where prices are posted and fixed for everyone. Many other interactions take place in strategic situations, in the sense that the actions one person takes depend on his or her expectation of the actions of others. When a star soccer player sits down with the team owner to negotiate over her salary, the two do not simply look at a posted price for a player of her caliber. Instead, the player and owner bargain. Offers and counter-offers are made, and a salary is finally agreed on. Sometime the bargaining may go on for a long time, to the extent that the player misses some games. Clearly, supply-and-demand analysis will yield only partial insight into the outcomes that might result from such interactions.

Nash (1950; 1953) derived one of the most elegant and useful models of this two-person interaction. He supposed that any predicted outcome of a bargaining situation should satisfy certain properties. For instance, the outcome of their bargaining should not be inefficient, in the sense that the bargainers should not agree to do something if there were an alternative available that made one of them better off without making the other worse off. That latter alternative is clearly preferable (by definition) and should be the outcome of the bargaining. Another property Nash assumed was that the utility functions of the bargainers should not matter (i.e., only their rankings over alternatives mattered, not some unknown cardinal measure of how much people actually valued the alternatives). Nash also assumed that bargaining "ability" should be the same for the two bargainers. The last, and most controversial, assumption was that the outcome should be independent of irrelevant alternatives. Outcomes that would not be chosen by the bargainers should not affect the bargaining outcome. That is, in a situation where two people were bargaining, if an alternative that they did not choose in the first instance were changed, then, if they also do not choose that alternative in the second instance, the outcome that they do choose should be the same as in the first instance. In other words, suppose alternatives that will not be chosen are added to a bargaining situation; then again the resulting choice should still be the same as before.

With these assumptions, Nash proved that the resulting choice would be such that the product of the gains of the two players would be maximized. The gains represent the increase in utility over a fallback position, or threat point, that describes the utility of each person should bargaining fail. (Just how to think about threat points and fallback positions is specified very clearly in Chiu and Yang [1999].) Consider, for example, the simple problem of bargaining over the distribution of a cake. If the bargainers agree, they each receive a share of the cake. If they disagree they each receive nothing. So their fallback positions are zero. Then, the Nash bargaining solution is a share of the cake, s, that maximizes the product of the gains: $(s - 0)$ $(1 - s - 0)$, or (s) $(1 - s)$. Clearly, the share that maximizes this expression is 1/2: the bargainers would split the cake evenly. Suppose one bargainer had a fallback position, such as a being able to get a cupcake worth 1/4 of a cake should the bargaining fail. Then the share that maximizes the product of the gains would be the share that maximized $(s - 1/4)$ $(1 - s - 0)$. This share would be 5/8; the person with the cupcake fallback now gets more than 1/2.

This model can be applied to the context of the household. Suppose a husband and wife are bargaining over how much money the wife should get if she works on the husband's farm. The husband owns the land, which has a production function that depends on the labor supplied by his wife. That is, the husband gets zero if the wife does not work, and gets $F(l)$ if she agrees to work. If working, she must work a fixed amount of time, l. If she does not work, she can go off and work elsewhere and earn an amount of money I^f. If the wife does not work for the husband, then the husband gets income I^m. The husband values income according to the utility function $V()$, while the wife has utility function $U()$. So the Nash bargaining solution is a value for w, the wage paid to the wife by the husband, that maximizes:

$$[U(w) - U(I^f)] \, [(V(F(l) - w) - V(I^m)].$$

The solution, w^*, depends on the levels of the threat points. The higher I^f is, the higher w^* will be, and the higher I^m is, the lower w^* will be. Measuring these threat points will be a major issue in empirical applications of bargaining models.

Distinguishing Models:
Looking at Household Expenditures

Suppose men typically care less about children's nutritional status. They tend to spend more of their income on luxury items for themselves (such as cigarettes and alcohol). Women, on the other hand, care about their children and spend their income on good food and health care. This certainly sounds like a plausible characterization of men and women in many societies in many countries over much of history. How would the characterization be verified, if men and women always live in households and expenditures of people are recorded as household aggregates rather than at the level of the individual? Moreover, for every anecdote that a historian or anthropologist produced about some society, another anecdote could be found singing the praises of a wonderful man who cared about his children while his wife drank and cursed in the local tavern.

This is the empirical problem of characterizing households, in a nutshell. Over the years, there have been many assertions about what empirical investigation would find. Guyer, for instance, affirmed that "The assumption that the domestic group is a tightly functional unity of the kind put forward in Becker's recent theoretical work (1981) is untenable, even at the straightforwardly descriptive level. It matters who gains control of output because men and women have different spending preferences, not necessarily because they hold different values but because they are in structurally different situations" (1988, 160). Whitehead concludes her comparative study of household budgeting in England and Ghana with the admonition to recall that "the conjugal contract implies specific material conflicts of interest between husbands and wives" (1981, 110).

The Nash bargaining approach to interactions between two persons suggests that threat points, or fallback positions, influence the outcomes of the bargaining. The discussion above suggested that households are good places to think about two-person bargaining, since they are usually composed of husband and wife who have responsibility over a large range of economic actions. The model suggests that expenditures on male-oriented luxury items (cigarettes, say) should rise when the man's income or assets increase by more than when the woman's income or assets increase. Likewise, expenditures on nutrition for children might be more influenced by increases in women's income or assets. When looking at the income effects on expenditures, then, the regression estimates using data from a household survey might show that the partial derivatives of how income of men and women affect expenditures vary according to:

$$\frac{\partial x_c}{\partial Y_m} > \frac{\partial x_c}{\partial Y_f} \ while, \ \frac{\partial x_n}{\partial Y_m} < \frac{\partial x_n}{\partial Y_f}$$

where x_c represents expenditures on cigarettes, x_n are expenditures on nutrition for children, and Y_m and Y_f represent male and female income, respectively.

By contrast, the unitary model implies that the identity of the recipient of income in the household is irrelevant in explaining the pattern of expenditures. Who receives income in the family should not affect expenditures. If a woman receives the income, and she likes lipstick, the husband will just reduce his own expenditures on lipstick for his wife. All income effects will be identical:

$$\frac{\partial x_c}{\partial Y_m} = \frac{\partial x_c}{\partial Y_f} \; while, \; \frac{\partial x_n}{\partial Y_m} = \frac{\partial x_n}{\partial Y_f}$$

So in the unitary model, the effect on consumption of cigarettes or nutrition should be the same for a change in exogenous female income as for a change in exogenous male income.

An alternative, halfway between the unitary model and the bargaining model, has also been proposed (Browning et al. 1994; Browning and Chiappori 1998; Chiappori 1997). In this model, known as the "collective model," households are assumed to be efficient, though not necessarily unitary. The collective model turns out to have some interesting implications. For instance, the collective model implies that the ratio of the expenditure effect for child healthcare as the income of the man changes, over the effect for child healthcare as the woman's income changes should be equal to the ratio of male over female income effects for food:

$$\frac{\partial x_c / \partial Y_m}{\partial x_c / \partial Y_f} = \frac{\partial x_f / \partial Y_m}{\partial x_f / \partial Y_f}$$

The reasoning behind this condition is tricky. Holding overall household income constant, the effect of increasing a person's income can be broken down into two subeffects. First, the changed income affects the weight or importance given to the person's preferences in determining intrahousehold allocations. Second, the changed weight leads to shifts in purchases of goods and services. Since the effect of the changed weight on purchases of goods is the same regardless of the cause of the changed weight, the ratio of the income effects for any given good will be equal to the ratio of the effects of changed income on the weight. This means the ratio of income effects will be equal across all goods. The effect of a change in the weight on purchases of the good does not depend on why the weight changed.

Many researchers have used data on household expenditures to test these various models of the household, in countries around the world (Hoddinott, Alderman, and Haddad 1997). They rather conclusively reject the unitary model and its implication that the identity of the income earner does not matter in determining expenditure patterns. Many of the studies also confirm the implicit assumption of the bargaining models, that women's income and bargaining power matter quite a bit in bringing about expenditure patterns more favorable to children.

The findings are replicated in studies using African datasets. Hoddinott and Haddad (1995), for example, use data from the 1986–1987 round of the Côte d'Ivoire Living Standards Survey. The survey measured the sources of income, whether male or female, coming into the household and the household expenditures. The results of regressions, estimated simultaneously to explain budget shares allocated to different categories of goods, decisively refute the unitary model. Female share of income affects expenditure shares for six of ten expenditure categories. Increased female income leads to declines in budget shares for meals eaten out, alcohol, cigarettes, and both child and adult clothing. Lachaud (1998) replicates Hoddinott and Haddad's analysis using a large data set of 8,700 households collected in 1994–1995 in Burkina Faso. The survey was intended to be nationally representative. The shares of female income increase the budget shares on food, energy, and alcohol (a major consumption good in much of Burkina Faso, in the form of brewed sorghum beer) and decrease the shares of tobacco and transport items (such as bicycles and mopeds). The data also show that a higher proportion of income earned by females in the household is correlated with a large and significant reduction in child malnutrition. Both studies recognize that incomes earned are themselves the results of choices, sometimes taken simultaneously with consumption decisions. They use the statistical technique of instrumental variables to control for this problem.

Hopkins, Levin, and Haddad (1994) conduct a slightly different test, using data from 135 households in fifteen villages in western Niger. The households were visited for more than a year, and every two weeks information on income and expenditures was recorded. Food accounted for almost three-quarters of the annual budget of the households. The authors find that the gender of income earner does matter in determining total expenditures and food expenditures, when the seasonality of income and expenditures is controlled for. Table 7.1 reproduces the results of two of their regression equations. The dependent variables are the log of total expenditures and the log of food expenditures. Income earned by both men and women increased expenditures, though the effect was larger for female income. More importantly, the seasonality of female income had significant effects on expenditures, while the seasonality of male income did not. If the household were pooling male and female incomes together, as implied by the unitary model, then this differential effect should not be observed.

Finally, Doss (1997) uses the Ghana Living Standards Survey of 1991–1992 to construct measures of the share of household assets that are controlled by women. Measures on expenditures were taken at 14-day intervals for rural households and three-day intervals for urban households. The expenditure data is used to calculate the budget shares allocated to eight

Table 7.1 Determinants of Expenditures for Households, Niger, 1989–1990

Variable	Mean	Standard Deviation	Log Total Exp (FCFA/ household)	Log Food Exp (FCFA/ household)
			Estimation Results	
Predicted annual male income (FCFA)	149,336	148,113	4.47E-07[a]	5.72E-07[a]
Estimated seasonal share of male income in season *s*	71.82	368.62	−2.11E-05	−4.85E-06
Predicted annual female income (FCFA)	57,720	49,382	1.89E-06[a]	8.64E-07[a]
Estimated seasonal share of female income in season *s*	20.18	30.17	0.0019[a]	0.0014[a]
Age household head	43.08	12.53	−0.0007	0.0009
Household size	8.26	3.56	0.0391[a]	0.0383[a]
Share adult males in household (> 15 years)	0.28	0.10	−0.1222	−0.0452
Share adult females in household (> 15 years)	0.27	0.13	−0.2752	−0.4887[a]
Share child females in household	0.17	0.14	−0.2202	−0.2185[b]
Share infants in household (≤ 2 years)	0.12	0.10	−0.3354	−0.0843
Cold season dummy			0.1132[b]	0.0717
Hot season dummy			0.2460[a]	0.1394[a]
Rainy season dummy			0.1803[a]	0.2505[a]
Agro-ecological zone dummy	0.59	0.49	−0.1227	−0.1778
Constant			10.74[a]	10.38[a]
N			452	452
Adj. R-square			0.34	0.41

Source: Reprinted with permission from Hopkins, Levin, and Haddad (1994, 1222–1223), Tables 1 and 2. Copyright 1994, by American Association of Agricultural Economics.
Notes: a. Indicates significance at the 0.01 level; b. indicates significance at the 0.05 level.

categories of goods. Then a system of equations explaining the eight shares is estimated. The regression equations include a great many variables, but the interest here is only on the coefficients of the shares of assets controlled by women. In the unitary model of the household, these shares should not influence expenditure patterns. Table 7.2 shows that, on the contrary, the asset shares are unambiguously important in determining the budget shares for three important expenditure categories. In particular, a higher share of assets controlled by women results in a higher budget share of food and lower budget shares of alcohol, tobacco, and recreation. In addition, the budget shares for clothing increase when rural women control more assets, and household expenditures increase in urban areas when women control more assets. The magnitudes of the effects are not large, but neither are they negligible; a one percentage point increase in the share of assets controlled

Table 7.2 Effect of the Share of Women's Asset Holdings and Land Holdings on Household Expenditure Patterns and Health and Education Outcomes, Ghana

Budget Shares	Urban Women's Share of Assets	Rural Women's Share of Assets	Women's Share of Farmland
Food	0.029[a]	0.019[b]	0.036[a]
	(0.009)	(0.007)	(0.010)
Alcohol & tobacco	−0.018[a]	−0.029[a]	−0.042[a]
	(0.004)	(0.003)	(0.004)
Education	0.003	0.006[b]	0.011[a]
	(0.003)	(0.002)	(0.003)
Medical	0.0009	−0.003	0.004
	(0.003)	(0.003)	(0.004)
Recreation	−0.007[b]	−0.012[a]	−0.011[a]
	(0.001)	(0.002)	(0.003)
Clothing	0.003	−0.003	0.007
	(0.004)	(0.003)	(0.005)
Housing & durables	0.004	0.018[a]	−0.002[a]
	(0.004)	(0.004)	0.005
Household	0.01[a]	−0.004	−0.007
	(0.004)	(0.003)	(0.004)

Source: Reprinted with permission from Doss (1997), Table 4. Copyright by Cheryl Doss.

Notes: Standard errors are in parentheses; a. indicates significance at .01; b. indicates significance at .05. Budget shares are estimated using a system of equations.
Number of obs. = 4,179.

by women might result in an increase in food expenditures equivalent to one day's consumption per month.

These tests reject the unitary model. A growing number of other researchers are finding similar results, using ever-more sophisticated statistical methods (Kimhi and Sosner 2000; Quisumbing and Maluccio 2000), though there have been few tests of the collective model and its presumption of efficiency within the household using African or even developing country data (Agüero 2002, Dauphin, Fortin, and Lacroix 2002). Other researchers are developing tests of the intrahousehold allocation of resources for health (Dercon and Krishnan 2000; Doss 2001; Goldstein, De Janvry, and Sadoulet 2002). These show that even when it comes to health, men and women within households are not pooling their resources. Rather, the woman typically bears the burden of adjustment to shocks that confront the household.

Distinguishing Models: Looking at Agricultural Production

Perhaps the best way to think about the issue of bargaining within the household is with a problem from Burkina Faso. There, as in many parts of

Africa, men and women in farm households control separate plots. That is, men control the cropping decisions and input use of some fields (often called the "family fields") while women make decisions about smaller plots under their control (often called "personal fields"). These men and women live in households. The marriages between men and women are regulated to some degree by the terms of the marriage contracts. Surely any marriage contract worth its salt would have a provision calling for efficient household production so that the marginal product of inputs would be equal across the fields of the men and the women. This is just common sense; if the marginal products were different, then profit (the difference between revenue and cost) could be increased for the household by taking inputs from where they have low marginal product and putting them on fields where the inputs have high marginal product. All that is required for this efficiency condition is that men and women in households agree to split a bigger pie that leaves them both better off. If the partners are altruistic, this will be even more likely.

So one way to test the propositions that marriages are altruistic or that marriage markets work well (or that both are true at the same time) is to measure the extent of inefficiency of this kind. Is it large or small? To repeat, imagine two fields, side by side, farmed by people from the same household. On the first field, labor is applied abundantly and in a timely fashion. Manure is brought by the cartload and spread all around. The second field, by contrast, is farmed desultorily, with little labor and no manure. Reallocating labor and manure to the second field would generate higher income for the family. The marginal product of manure and labor is low on the first field and high on the second. Why not reallocate the inputs and share the extra production?

Finding out whether the marginal product of inputs is the same across the fields of the household is not an easy research task. Simply observing that the marginal products of inputs are different is not itself evidence of inefficiency. Farm managers perhaps applied different amounts of labor because the fields had different soil qualities or differed in some other property. A stony field is not the same as a field with rich topsoil. So, at a minimum, controls are needed for all indicators of soil quality before making an assessment. Another problem might be that there are "start-up" costs to getting out to the different fields. A field that is far away requires a long walk out in the morning and long walk back in the evening; less labor will be applied to it. So controls are needed for the distance of the field from the village. If the fields are the same in all quality dimensions and distance from village, then efficiency suggests that input use and yields should be the same.

The evidence from one careful study casts doubt on the hypothesis that households are of the unitary variety and that marriage market contracts work perfectly in ensuring efficiency. Udry (1996) finds that yields on women's plots in six villages of Burkina Faso surveyed by the International Crops Research Institute for the Semi-Arid Tropics (ICRISAT) were much lower than yields on their husband's plots. Table 7.3 reproduces summary statistics from the data, collected over three years, monitoring fields cultivated by household members. Measures were taken on each field of the amount of output (the weight or volume of the crop produced) and its value in CFA francs, the local currency. One fact to notice immediately is the extreme poverty of farmers in Burkina Faso at the time. The table gives the average value of output per hectare. This can be thought of as the return to the labor and farm management effort (assuming that costs of purchased inputs and retained seed are negligible; fair enough for grains and oilseeds, but not true for cotton). If the value per hectare is divided by the average of roughly 1,000 labor hours applied to each hectare, the result is something close to 70 CFA per hour. For a ten-hour day, of hard work in 100-degree temperatures, people earned approximately 700 CFA. At the then current exchange rate, this amounted to $0.20 per hour in the early 1980s when the data was collected. Agriculture is considered to be the most lucrative activity, but the rainy season only lasts approximately six months. Wages are lower during the other six months of the year. Sadly, wages and incomes have not changed much since that time (Savadogo, Coulibaly, and McCracken 2002).

Some of the fields were controlled by men, others by women. For each field the size, quality of soil, topography, and distance from village are known. So for each crop, year, and household, one can ask whether there were differences by gender of the farm manager. Imagine the following table: for each crop, year, and household, compute the difference between the average yields per hectare on the men's fields and the women's fields.

Table 7.3 Mean Yield, Area, and Labor Inputs per Plot by Gender of Cultivator, Burkina Faso

	Crop Output per Hectare (1,000 FCFA)[a]	Area (Hectare)	Male Labor (Hours/ Hectare)	Female Labor (Hours/ Hectare)	Manure Weight (kg/ Hectare)
Men's plots	79.9	0.74	593	248	2,993
	(186)	(1.19)	(1,065)	(501)	(11,155)
Women's plots	105.4	0.10	128	859	764
	(286)	(0.16)	(324)	(1,106)	(5,237)
T-statistic	−3.27	29.03	22.16	−21.31	7.68

Source: Reprinted with permission from Udry (1996, 1019), Table 1. "Gender, Agricultural Productivity and the Theory of the Household," *Journal of Political Economy* 105(5) Published by the University of Chicago Press. Copyright 1996 by University of Chicago.

Notes: N = 4,655. Standard deviations are in parentheses. a. In 1982, the exchange rate was approximately U.S.$1 = FCFA 325.

One problem is that for most households, the fields were of different quality. A different table could be constructed for each broad class of field quality. Such a table would show that the yields were higher on the men's fields. A better method would be to use regression techniques. Table 7.4 reports the results of Udry's regressions (which use estimation techniques somewhat more complex than ordinary least squares regressions). Yield per hectare is the dependent variable, and the regressions include dummy variables for each household and year. The inclusion of household dummy variables means that the regression is explaining the variation across fields within each household and seeing whether that is due to gender. The test of household efficiency is whether the estimated coefficient on the dummy variable of the gender of the farm manager matters in explaining yields.

The coefficients on the gender variable are significant and negative for the different specifications, indicating that women did indeed have lower yields than men, after controlling for crop and field quality. Udry goes on to show that the reason for lower yields was that the fields of women used

Table 7.4 Estimates of the Determinants of Plot Output, Burkina Faso

| | Household-Year-Crop-Effects: All Crops (1) | | Household-Year Effects | | | |
| | | | Millet Only (2) | | White Sorghum (3) | |
	coefficient	t-statistic	coefficient	t-statistic	coefficient	t-statistic
Mean of dependent variable	89		31		41	
Gender: (1 = female)	−27.70	−4.61	−10.36	−2.53	−19.38	−4.43
Plot Size:						
1st decile	133.99	3.50	−28.35	−2.67	−17.90	−1.92
2d decile	69.10	4.38	8.64	0.82	52.30	3.16
3d decile	63.45	5.52	16.95	1.81	47.68	4.77
4th decile	34.08	2.88	9.79	1.12	26.73	3.12
6th decile	−2.04	−0.29	−0.99	−0.11	−6.38	−1.16
7th decile	−13.44	−1.78	−13.01	−1.73	−11.31	−1.69
8th decile	−17.23	−2.59	−12.97	−1.34	−28.58	−4.82
9th decile	−26.68	−3.81	−21.50	−2.65	−28.65	−4.98
10th decile	−31.52	−4.49	−20.56	−2.55	−37.70	−6.03
Location:						
Compound	1.54	0.19	9.69	2.67	−4.98	−1.04
Village	−1.82	−0.40	6.07	1.45	−1.68	−0.62

Source: Reprinted with permission from Udry (1996, 1022–1023), Table 3. "Gender, Agricultural Productivity and the Theory of the Household," *Journal of Political Economy* 105(5). Published by the University of Chicago Press. Copyright 1996 by University of Chicago.

Notes: t-statistics are based on heteroskadastic-consistent estimates of the variance-covariance matrix. Household fixed effects, toposequence, and soil type variables were included but not reported here. The dependent variable in column (1) is *ln* (value of plot output/hectare); the dependent variable in columns (2) and (3) is *ln* (kg/hectare).

lower inputs of labor, fertilizer, and manure. Again, these findings control for the different qualities of the fields, so they show that there was a real misallocation of resources. Households with similar fields applied different inputs to those fields, according to whether the field manager was a man or woman. In a separate paper, Udry, Hoddinott, Alderman and Haddad (1995) estimate that reallocating factors of production across the plots of men and women could increase the value of household output by 10–15 percent.

Udry cleverly tests for one possible refutation of his result. Maybe the result is due to some important but unobserved variation in plot characteristics? That is certainly possible. But Udry runs regressions where he does not include the observed plot quality characteristics. If women had fields of lower quality, then the gender effect should now be even larger in magnitude; without controlling for plot quality, women's yields might be expected to be even lower. But when plot characteristics are dropped from the equation, the gender coefficient gets smaller in magnitude, though it remains negative. This can only mean one thing: women on average must have had *better* plot characteristics than men, for those that were observed. Why then would they have worse characteristics for those unobserved?

Another interpretation of the finding is that yields on the women's fields are lower because women are busy with child care on their fields. Indeed, perhaps the fields of women are like schools, where the children learn to farm. Since they are children, and learning, they do not farm very well. A nice hypothesis, but the data show that most of the labor of children was applied to the fields of the male household head. Women usually farmed their own fields alone, after the children had already returned home.

There are some other possible alternative explanations that are consistent with household efficiency and yet unequal allocations of inputs. These alternatives have not, however, been tested using the data from ICRISAT or other sources. One alternative is that the sample of male and female farmers is not a random sample of possible farm managers. Husbands own most of the land and control, to varying degrees, the land that women farm and the time that they can work. It is not hard to imagine that husbands make decisions about whether women in the household are to farm on their own or on the family farm. The decisions may be in the form of incentives to farm with the family. For instance, imagine a household with two women, one a young, healthy wife, the other an elderly widow, the aunt of the household head. The household head offers a kind of sharecropping contract to his young wife, where she will have control of part of the output from the family field. To the widow, he offers a small plot to farm on her own account. The point is that the marginal product of the widow, elderly and infirm, would be low no matter where she worked. If personal fields are farmed, on average, by elderly women with low marginal products, then the apparent inefficiency of resource allocation is explained by the sample selection mechanism. A true test would have to take women at random and assign some of them to work exclusively with their husbands and others to work on personal fields.

A second alternative is that gendering of fields is a convenient way to organize the timing of application of labor onto fields. When labor is productive, everyone works on the family fields. Later in the season, when labor is less productive because the timing of operations is no longer optimal, women farm their personal fields while men go off and do other low-return activities. Inputs are low on the fields of the women, but this does not mean that marginal products are high. The timing of operations determines the marginal products as much as the amount of input applied.

A third alternative hypothesis is that many households are land constrained, and in a situation of tenure insecurity landowners are reluctant to lend or rent land to people who may claim rights through use. So they lend land to women, who may be prohibited from acquiring more permanent rights. The husband is fully in favor of this: the marginal product of his wife's labor on his own land may be very low. But the condition of the rental is that he cannot help his wife on her little farm. Productivity differences arise, but it is the differential status of men and women in land tenure that matters.

Although these and other alternative explanations can be suggested, the most plausible interpretation is that individuals within households are bargaining over how to allocate their labor. This is Udry's preferred explanation, and he suggests that the conjugal unit in Burkina Faso more closely resembled a contractual, bargained relationship than a "loving family" maximizing common welfare, as the unitary model predicts. In a bargaining framework, one expects that men and women allocate their resources in ways that raise their threat points, or options in the event of disagreement. If a woman ceded control of her land and labor to her husband, she would have no credible threat to make if he failed to compensate her. Women maintained flexibility within the conjugal unit by reserving part of their labor for their own land.

There is evidence from other countries that strengthens the conclusion that inefficiency in household production reflects bargaining and self-interest within the household. The discussion above concentrated on the work of Udry because it offers an especially clear test of the hypothesis that households are efficient. Goldstein and Udry (2002) recently conducted similar tests, with similar results, using data collected in Ghana. They were further able to narrow down the actual differential productive practices, attributing the gender variation to shortened fallow periods on the women's fields. Von Braun and Webb (1989) found that gross margins (value minus variable input costs except for unpaid land and labor, per day of unpaid labor) on male-controlled communal plots were typically double those of "private" female plots in Gambia. A more recent study of pastoralists in Kenya found that household bargaining was important in determining where herders located their herds (McPeak and Doss 2002).

Finally, two important studies of irrigation schemes and household negotiation over labor allocation also cast considerable doubt on the hypothesis of the unitary household. Jones (1986) found that in Cameroon there was less use of labor and input-intensive production practices following the introduction of irrigation that permitted rice growing. The division of the increased surplus could not always be negotiated. Some women acquiesced to the increased demands for labor from their husbands, but many simply refused to devote large amounts of time to rice production. These women withdrew from household production activities and concentrated on their own, separate, sorghum plots, or worked as wage laborers. Carney and Watts (1990) are more explicit in addressing the process of creating norms about the uses and relations of household labor. They argue that a Gambian irrigation project, the latest in a series of interventions designed to reduce rice imports, provoked unexpected kinds of conflicts. The particular external production relations were "inflected inward" to the conjugal unit, rather than expressed "outward" as in earlier instances of peasant resistance. Struggles over meaning permeated household relations: "As a consequence women have withdrawn their labor from the rice fields, an explosive tactic with far-reaching impact on the social organization of household production" (p. 228). Comparatively low yields and increases in wage labor were the explicit manifestations of these struggles over cultural representations. Their analysis suggests that the changes in forms and representations of social structure were likely to make future interventions (perhaps mechanization) even more problematic.

Implications

The evidence presented in this chapter shows, rather conclusively, that bargaining within households is of considerable importance. Moreover, the bargaining results in inefficient allocations of productive resources. Is there room for public policy to improve the situation? There are two considerations that argue against a gung-ho approach to social reengineering of the household. First, the evidence shows that households are not unitary. This does not mean that there is no altruism within the household. Plainly there is, for many households. The next step in household research is to explore the degree to which, or dimensions over which, altruism matters more or less than bargaining. It may well be the case that households act altruistically when confronted with some situations and act as a collection of self-interested agents when confronted with other situations. Self-interest is tempered by altruism in many contexts. One paper that begins this effort to understand the relative importance of altruism and self-interest is Smith and Chavas (1999). They simulate the solution to the Nash bargaining problem with a household model calibrated to the same data from Burkina Faso used by Udry. They then ask how variation in the bargaining power and hetero-geneity of preferences between men and women change responses to changes in cotton prices. (Recall the beginning of the chapter: they are esti-mating price elasticities of supply.) Not surprisingly, the more bargaining power women have, and the more their preferences diverge from those of men, the less responsive they are in allocating their labor to cotton fields. Since they do not control cotton incomes, they only work on cotton fields if compelled to or given incentive to, by men. Smith and Chavas suggest that diverging preferences could make households 25 percent less respon-sive to changes in cotton prices than they might be.

A second important flag for caution is that there remains much work to be done in understanding how bargaining takes place in the context of contracts determined in the marriage market. These marriage contracts specify, perhaps, conditions and payoffs after divorce, as well as welfare for parties who continue to live together even though they no longer cooperate to any important degree. Lundberg and Pollak (1994) have noted that the effects of public policy on households will depend crucially on whether the threat points in the bargaining are those that follow from divorce or those that follow from reverting to a household where each person takes respon-sibility for his or her "separate sphere." Suppose a government wants to help children by giving parents a transfer (and, in the event of divorce, giv-ing custody of the child and the transfer to women). Will giving the trans-fer to the man or the woman have different effects? Suppose the outcome of concern is the provision of public goods within the household (e.g., child-care services such as ensuring good nutrition, hygiene, and cognitive skills). Both parents benefit from a child that is brought up well. One model of household bargaining says it does not matter who gets the transfer because the outcome within a marriage depends only on the threat point outside of marriage. Since the woman always gets the transfer in the event of divorce, it does not matter who gets it within the marriage. That policy is irrelevant in determining the outcome. If the relevant threat points are "within" the marriage, where a failure to agree results in each household member retreating to a separate sphere, carrying out assigned responsibili-ties as married men and women but not cooperating, then each person decides on a "voluntary" provision of the relevant gendered public good. In this separate spheres model, the outcome of the provision of the public good may depend on the child allowance scheme. The woman's income matters, so if the transfer is given to the woman, the outcome may be bet-ter for the children.

8

The Gendered Treatment of Girls and Boys

Petrus intervenes. "The baby is coming in October. We hope he will be a boy."

"Oh. What have you got against girls?"

"We are praying for a boy," says Petrus. "Always it is best if the first one is a boy. Then he can show his sisters—show them how to behave. Yes." He pauses. "A girl is very expensive."

— *J. M. Coetzee,* Disgrace

In many parts of the world, particularly in northern India and China, the first expression of gender is horrible to contemplate. Census figures show that there are far fewer girls and women that there should be. Girls and women are "missing." Parents and families are making life and death decisions about whether baby girls are to be born and survive. According to numerous accounts, abortions are now common following prenatal identification of fetuses as girls (Coale and Banister 1996). In earlier times female infanticide was common. Other "missing girls" die in early childhood through neglect. One estimate has girls aged one to five being 25 percent more likely to die than boys of similar ages, in parts of South Asia. Normally, boys would be more likely to die than girls. The mechanism for these excess deaths in early childhood appears to be inadequate health care rather than unequal nutrition. Boys are often more likely to be treated when sick, more likely to get other kinds of special care, and more likely to be immunized. There may be other, subtle mechanisms at work. In regions with large numbers of missing girls, parents are also more likely to have a child after a shorter interval if the previous child were a girl. Families with girls born first are more likely to be larger, as parents continue past their desired family size in order to have sons. So very young girls are more likely to compete for parental attention and resources than very young boys (Jensen 2002).

The result of this neglect of girls (and also poor treatment of elderly widows) is that an estimated 80–100 million fewer girls and women are alive in Asia than should be (Bardhan and Klasen 1998; Coale and Banister 1994; Miller 1997; Sen 1990). This number is a most dramatic expression of gender preference and inequality, and the problem of missing girls has justly been on the front pages of newspapers around the world.

Are There More Boys than Girls in African Countries?

At a gross level, there is no large problem of missing girls in Africa. The evidence is strong that sex ratios are roughly where they should be in a nondiscriminatory setting, which is roughly 95 girls per 100 boys at birth, moving toward 97 girls per 100 boys in early childhood, reflecting boys' higher rates of mortality, and then often having more older women than older men, as women's longer life expectancies increase the number of older women alive at any point in time. Table 8.1 computes the overall sex ratios for most of the countries in Africa. None of the African countries have fewer than 97 young girls per 100 boys. This contrasts sharply with India and China, with 93 and 90 girls per 100 boys, respectively. Brazil, Mexico, and Indonesia have 97 girls per 100 boys. Among young adults and the elderly, India and China barely differ from the childhood ratios, while the African countries exhibit the usual pattern of better female survival under equal conditions of access to nutrition and health care. Côte d'Ivoire stands out as an African exception; for decades men from all over West Africa have migrated there in search of work. Many settle permanently in the country, skewing the sex ratios. Figure 8.1 shows how sex ratios have changed for low- and middle-income countries in various world regions. South Asia has seen improvement in sex ratios, while African sex ratios have declined, a worrisome trend given that wars and civil disturbances normally raise the sex ratio by reducing the numbers of primarily male combatants.

On initial examination, the aggregate data does not indicate any strong preference for sons leading to differential life chances. But studies using more precise methods do find some evidence that son preference exists and matters for life and death. Consider, for example, the careful work of Hill and Upchurch (1995). They note that a rigorous determination of whether girls are at greater risk of dying than boys should take into account the fact that girls have lower biological chances of dying than boys do. So equal rates of death would imply that girls are actually being somewhat neglected. With neutral treatment, girls should be dying less often than boys. Evidence for this comes from statistics from countries that might be used as a standard because there is little reason to suppose that they have exhibited discrimination against girls. The countries that form the standard-setting group used by Hill and Upchurch are England and Wales, France, the Netherlands, New Zealand, and Sweden. Life statistics on mortality for

Table 8.1 Sex Ratios, Life Expectancy Ratios, and Mortality Ratios, 2000

	Girls Aged 0–4 (per 100 Boys)	Women Aged 15–64 (per 100 Men)	Women Aged 65 and Above (per 100 Men)	Female-to-Male-Life Expectancy at Birth	Female-to-Male-Mortality Rate (for Adults)
Sub-Saharan Africa	98	101	124	104	91
Angola	100	103	124	107	88
Benin	99	106	103	107	86
Botswana	99	106	178	99	94
Burkina Faso	99	114	145	103	94
Burundi	100	109	167	103	94
Cameroon	99	101	122	104	88
Central African Republic	100	107	135	104	92
Chad	100	103	126	107	88
Congo, Dem. Rep.	99	103	135	103	94
Congo, Rep.	101	106	131	108	85
Côte d'Ivoire	99	92	94	102	95
Djibouti	99	123	148	102	
Equatorial Guinea	99	104	124	107	
Eritrea	99	102	125	105	89
Ethiopia	97	100	117	105	92
Gabon	99	103	120	105	89
Gambia	100	103	114	107	89
Ghana	99	101	119	104	88
Guinea	97	99	117	102	99
Guinea-Bissau	100	104	124	107	89
Kenya	99	102	113	102	93
Lesotho	98	102	133	102	94
Liberia	99	97	124	105	92
Madagascar	100	101	119	106	87
Malawi	98	103	127	101	97
Mali	99	103	130	106	89
Mauritania	99	102	131	106	85
Mauritius	97	99	139	111	51
Mozambique	100	103	126	106	89
Namibia	99	104	129	101	92
Niger	97	99	121	108	82
Nigeria	97	99	116	103	89
Rwanda	100	102	134	102	95
Senegal	98	102	128	107	76
Seychelles				111	
Sierra Leone	101	104	129	107	91
Somalia	99	103	118	107	86
South Africa	99	103	164	105	89
Sudan	96	100	118	105	88
Swaziland	100	104	126	102	93
Tanzania	99	103	125	103	93
Togo	99	102	124	105	91
Uganda	99	101	122	101	98
Zambia	98	99	124	102	97
Zimbabwe	99	99	119	98	94

Source: World Bank Development Indicators (2002).

Figure 8.1 Percentage of Population That Is Female, Various World Regions

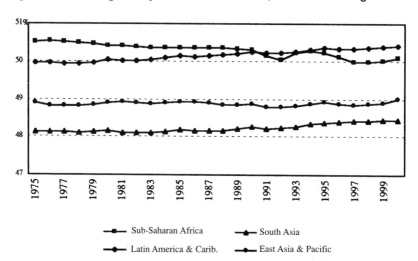

Sub-Saharan Africa   South Asia

Latin America & Carib.   East Asia & Pacific

Source: World Bank Development Indicators (2002). Low- and middle-income countries only.

these countries go back to 1820 and thus include periods of high mortality that might be comparable to contemporary mortality rates in developing countries. The data may be used to evaluate the differential mortality of girls and boys in contemporary developing countries.

For the standard-setting countries, female advantage in mortality ranged from 10 percent to 18 percent, with the higher relative advantage coming with improvements in overall mortality. For any level of overall mortality in an African country, the data can be used to benchmark differential mortality between girls and boys. The question is whether mortality of girls and boys in African countries is close or far from the northwest European standard. The following statistic may be calculated:

$$I_{(x,x + n)} = (_nq_x^f / {_nq_x^m}) - (_nq_x^f / {_nq_x^m})_S \mid (_5q_0^m)$$

In the equation, $_5q_0^m$ stands for the mortality rate of males aged zero to five, while $_nq_x^f$ stands for the female mortality rate for a particular age range of $x - n$. The statistic computes the difference between the female to male ratio of under-five mortality for a given country compared with the northwest European experience, controlling for the overall level of under-five male mortality. Every country considered has its own overall child mortality rate, so comparing them against a single standard would bias the results if mortality rates for males and females decline at different rates as overall mortality rates decline.

As Table 8.2 shows, African countries mostly have positive indices for infants aged zero to one, for young children aged one to five, and for children under five overall. With the lone exception of Botswana, girls are relatively more prone to die than boys. Therefore, more precise measurement of the neglect of daughters finds evidence of female disadvantage. These findings hinge on the appropriate choice of baseline boy and girl mortality figures (Svedberg 1996). Perhaps intrinsic mortality rates are different for girls and boys of African descent, compared with girls and boys of northwest European descent, even at similar overall levels of mortality. A number of authors have examined alternative normalizations, and their findings are consistent with the pattern of some female disadvantage. Klasen (1996) concluded from a review of 14 demographic and health surveys that nine showed females to suffer from excess mortality in infancy and nine also showed excess female mortality for children aged one to five.

Other demographic measures more related to the sex ratio of adults include the ratios of female-to-male life expectancy and female-to-male adult mortality. Because life expectancy in African countries has been declining, and mortality rising, the usual large female advantage is becoming increasingly muted in Africa (Table 8.1). Only Seychelles and Mauritius

Table 8.2 Index of Female Mortality Disadvantage

Country	Index of Female Mortality Disadvantage (positive indicates female disadvantage)		
	Infant	Young	Under 5
Botswana	−0.123	−0.004	−0.085
Burundi	−0.054	0.190	0.090
Cameroon	0.055	0.258	0.150
Ghana	0.015	0.090	0.067
Kenya	0.070	0.044	0.070
Liberia	−0.025	0.089	0.013
Madagascar	0.168	0.027	0.116
Malawi	0.088	−0.049	0.037
Mali	0.062	0.083	0.090
Niger	0.133	0.131	0.148
Nigeria	0.128	−0.078	0.040
Senegal	0.026	0.043	0.063
Sudan (North)	0.040	0.097	0.077
Tanzania	0.104	−0.021	0.064
Togo	0.083	0.280	0.186
Uganda	0.094	−0.056	0.040
Zambia	0.030	−0.004	0.032
Zimbabwe	−0.024	0.187	0.046

Source: Reprinted with the permission of the Population Council, from Kenneth Hill and Dawn Upchurch, "Gender Differences in Child Health: Evidence from the Demographic and Health Surveys," *Population and Development Review* 21, no. 1 (March 1995), p. 149.

continue to have ratios comparable to those of other large developing countries such as Brazil and Mexico, around 110 for life expectancy and 50 for mortality. As Figures 8.2 and 8.3 show, female life expectancy and mortality rates are worsening, relative to men, in African countries. This a quite a departure from other world regions.

Figure 8.2 Life Expectancy at Birth, Female-to-Male Ratio (Years), Various World Regions

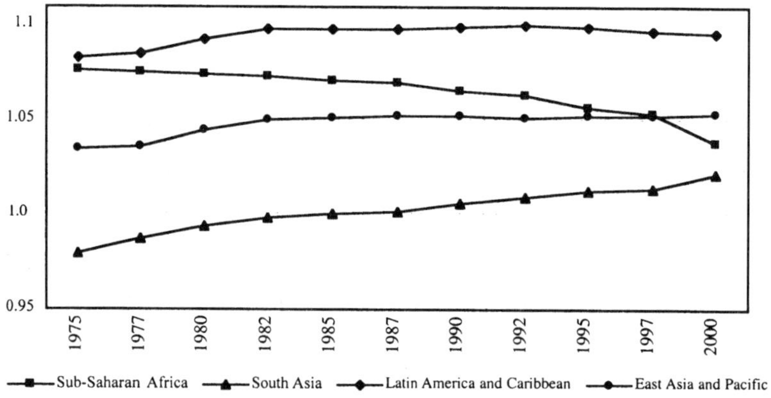

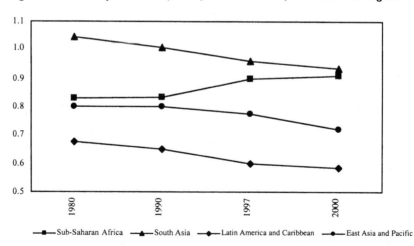

Source: World Bank Development Indicators (2002). Low- and middle-income countries only.

Figure 8.3 Mortality Rate Ratio, Adult, Female-to-Male, Various World Regions

Source: World Bank Development Indicators (2002). Low- and middle-income countries only.

Evidence of Son Preference in Fertility Behavior

Parents in Africa do not seem to deliberately kill or neglect girl children to the extent that they do (on average) in northern India and China. Still, parents may prefer or "value" boys, even though when girls are born they suffer little bias. This might be evident in patterns of the sex composition of families that follow what demographers call "optimal stopping" strategies for fertility. A family that has two sons may decide they have no need for further children since they do not really value girls. A family with two girls may however decide to go on having children in the hopes of having a boy. Parents who prefer boys are more likely to stop having children once they reach their desired number of boys. This behavior has three implications: (1) the youngest children in families that have completed their fertility are more likely to be boys; (2) girls are more likely to belong to larger families; (3) the birth intervals between children will be longer after boys, as parents who have a girl, if they desire sons, are more likely to have another child quickly.

An interesting recent study from South Africa investigates the birth interval manifestation of son preference (Gangadharan and Maitra 2002). The authors use observations of births from approximately 9,000 households interviewed in the South African Integrated Household Survey of 1993. The survey is representative of the population of the entire country and includes all the major "skin color" groups of South Africa as classified under the old apartheid system. The estimates, from what is known as a "hazard model" regression, confirm that son preference exists for the Indian households, descendants of indentured servants, but not for any of the other groups. As Table 8.3 indicates, the average interval between the first and second child was much higher for first boys than for first girls for Indian parents. For parents with two children, the average interval if the first child was a boy was 51.7 months, while if the first child was a girl it was 41.7 months, almost a full year sooner. These parents hurried to have a second child when their first was a girl.

Theories of Variation in Son Preference

A digression on theories of sex ratios is worthwhile. Many demographic studies find significant (but usually small) variation in sex ratios across different socioeconomic categories. Smokers have fewer boys, and younger parents have slightly more boys, for instance. Finding that sex ratios vary across socioeconomic groups suggests the need for theories about why some social groups may prefer sons or may have physical processes going on in their bodies that lead to higher propensities for sons, while others are

Table 8.3 Average Duration in Months Between Children by Race and Sex of Children, South Africa

Number of Children	Sex of Existing Children	Black	Coloured	Indian	White
1	1 daughter	53.8	46.6	35.7	38.5
	1 son	53.2	47.5	47.2	39.3
	t-value for difference in duration	0.6	−0.3	−2.51[a]	−0.4
2	No boy	48.4	43.4	41.7	44.4
	At least one boy	45.7	47.7	51.7	44.1
	t-value for difference in duration	1.84[b]	−1.1	−1.72[b]	0.1
3	No boy	46.0	49.8	33.6	30.0
	At least one boy	43.8	47.3	42.4	48.0
	t-value for difference in duration	1.0	0.3	−0.7	−1.4
	n	6,981	756	262	840

Source: Reprinted with permission from Gangadharan and Maitra (2002), Table 3. Copyright 2002 by Lata Gangadharan and Pushkar Maitra.
Notes: a. Significance using the 95% confidence interval; b. significance using the 90% confidence interval.

neutral or prefer daughters. Work along these lines focuses on behavior induced by physical processes selected for by natural selection, Darwinian "deliberate" maximization of genetic fitness, or utility maximizing choices. The physical processes are poorly understood; there are no good natural selection stories for how or why hormone changes in humans cause the sex ratio to change (Sieff 1990). In famine situations, however, there is evidence that boy embryos are much more frequently terminated in the womb, as predicted by natural selection (Gibson and Mace 2003).

In Darwinian theories of human behavior, people act to maximize their genetic reproductive success rather than to maximize their utility. These theories are usually not troubled by whether choices are conscious or unconscious. Evidence that behavior favors one sex over the other, for a person's children, is taken to be evidence that such a choice maximizes genetic fitness (otherwise why would the action be taken?). The art in these theories is to come up with a plausible explanation for why favoring one sex might be an equilibrium for a large fraction of the population. One interesting theory is that the sex ratio might exhibit differences across economic class. First presented by Trivers and Willard (1973), it goes as follows: Parents want to maximize their genetic fitness by ensuring as many grandchildren as possible. Assume that the marriage market exhibits assortative mating; rich parents want their children to mate with offspring of other rich parents. Children of wealthy parents are more likely to thrive and reproduce because they have better access to nutrition and mating "plumage," so to speak, that also influences mating outcomes. This is especially true for sons, whose capacity to reproduce their genetic material is high, compared with daughters, who are limited to the approximately ten births per lifetime that seems to be the practical upper bound for female fertility. It follows that wealthy parents will have preferences for sons because they can enable successful mating for their sons, while poorer parents might prefer daughters, as their sons are unlikely to be successful in the mating market. Perhaps, then, humans have evolved with a genetic impulse to favor sons when external signals tell the human organism that they are high status.

Finally, some social scientists suggest that the variation in sex ratios across regions in India is due to different social systems in those different regions. In different regions people want sons or daughters according to how much sons or daughters will contribute to their future livelihoods or social status. Parents all over the developing world lack old-age insurance from the state or private pension funds. They rely on their children for financial support. Quite reasonably, they invest in their children with this support in mind. These transfers might depend on gendered norms that determine the "remittances" that children send back to their parents and that determine the gender of the child that moves away. Anthropologists study these norms and have even invented a special vocabulary to describe norms of movement after marriage (Adam 1947). "Virilocality" means that daughters move away from their families. "Uxorilocality" means that daughters stay at home and their husbands move. "Ambilocality" means that either child might move, and "neolocality" means that bride and groom move out of the homes of their parents into a new home. A perfectly reasonable hypothesis is that parents in virilocal areas prefer sons (who will stay in the village) while parents in uxorilocal areas prefer girls. There are few studies testing this and other hypotheses of variation in sex ratios for Africa, but a small literature does examine the data for other countries, with varying degrees of confirmation of the theory (Dube 1997; Dyson and Moore 1983; Levine and Kevane 2003).

Son Preference in Health and Nutrition

A second set of indicators of quality of life for children includes measures of health and nutrition. Some of the widely accepted indicators are height-for-age, weight-for-age, and weight-for-height. These are calculated as "z-scores," meaning the number of standard deviations a child's height or weight is away from a reference mean. The most widely used reference means and standard deviations for different ages are those published by the

U.S. National Center for Health Statistics (NCHS) and Centers for Disease Control, and adopted by the World Health Organization (WHO). The data originate in part with a sample of bottle-fed children in the Midwestern United States. Heights and weights for boys and girls in this reference sample are very comparable through age ten. The standard reference population exhibits no strong gender differences in growth charts.

To calculate the height-for-age z-score for a child, and then to average these scores for a population, a given child's height h_i is compared with the appropriate entry in the table, and the z-score calculated as:

$$z\text{-}score = (h_i - h) / s_h$$

where h is the mean height for the age and gender of the child, and s_h is the standard deviation of heights for children in that age and sex category. Falling two standard deviations below the mean height-for-age is usually considered a sign of "stunting." Nutritionists agree that height is determined very much by nutrition in early childhood. Children who do not get adequate nutrition do not grow as tall as well-nourished children. But stunting need not necessarily be associated with lower quality of life. Stunting does indicate a reduced allocation of nutrients to the child, and may be associated with longer term effects on brain development, but there is no definitive scientific evidence on this question (Drewett et al. 2001; Pollitt 1996). Weight-for-age z-scores that are significantly below the mean indicate "being underweight" and are thought to measure the incidence of recent illness and malnourishment. Weight-for-height is interpreted as indicating "wasting" over a longer period of time.

There is of course controversy over whether the assumption that children around the world have the genetic potential to follow a single growth path, or whether differences in genetic codes of children in Africa or Asia, say, imply different growth paths for well-nourished children. These debates have yet to be resolved satisfactorily (Klasen 2000). Studies do find that children from wealthier households are considerably closer to the reference mean, in most societies, and this finding reinforces the view of a single standard growth path for children.

African children seem to begin life with weights and heights close to the reference standards, but they drop fairly smoothly over the first three years of life in height-for-age and weight-for-age, ending at between one and two standard deviations away from the reference mean (Madise, Matthews, and Margetts 1999). Weight-for-height, however, is much closer to the reference mean, lending some truth to Klasen's (2000) suggestion that the reference standards are not appropriate for all human groups. Boys seem to be further from the reference means than girls. Madise, Matthews, and Margetts (1999) find that all of the coefficients on sex in regressions explaining the cross-sectional variation of z-scores show girls doing better than boys, for six African countries. Two analyses from Côte d'Ivoire found the same pattern; the coefficient on sex (equal to one for boys) was always negative, though not significantly different from zero (Haddad and Hoddinott 1994; Thomas, Lavy, and Strauss 1996). Garg and Morduch (1998) also find for children under age eleven that boys were further below the reference standards than girls, in the 1988–1989 Ghana Living Standards Survey.

These findings of little significant antigirl bias are confirmed with "metastudies" of anthropometric differentials between girls and boys. These metastudies collate the findings of many different surveys over many different countries. Svedberg (1991; 1996) and Klasen (1996) are two examples. (Their lively exchange in 1996 nicely illustrates the interesting methodological issues that persist in the field and, indeed, argues for caution in reaching firm conclusions.) Svedberg found that out of 121 data sets covering most African countries, about two-thirds showed no statistically significant difference in anthropometric status of girls and boys. One-third of the data sets showed antimale bias, while only one showed antifemale bias. Klasen, on the other hand, suggested that then recent demographic and health surveys from twelve countries showed antigirl bias in indicators of wasting for six countries. The same surveys, however, showed much clearer patterns of stunting and insufficient weight-for-age for boys than for girls.

The study by Garg and Morduch (1998) complicates the picture somewhat. Their main result is reproduced in Table 8.4. The average z-scores for height-for-age are presented in the top panel, and weight-for-height in the bottom panel. In each panel, averages are computed according to the number of siblings, and also the number of sisters. The table shows that z-scores decline in families that are larger; children have to compete for the scarce resources of the household. More interesting is the fact that the z-scores improve as the percentage of siblings shifts from all brothers to all sisters. For any given child, it is better to have sisters than brothers. This is clearly consistent with a pro-male bias in the household. One explanation would be that parents allocate a fixed amount to the children but give larger shares to boys. Thus, a child with many sisters obtains relatively more calories and micronutrients. As the authors put it, "shifting from having four siblings, all of which are brothers, to having one brother and three sisters leads to a 23 percent improvement in height-for-age" (1998, 479). The improvements in weight-for-height are somewhat smaller.

Another indicator of relative treatment in the household is access to health care. In northern India and China, the higher mortality of girls seems to be mostly caused by unequal patterns of access to modern medicine. Girls are simply not taken to doctors, are not provided with antibiotics or other curative drugs, and are not vaccinated as often as boys. This unequal access seems to be absent from most African countries. Table 8.5, for example,

Table 8.4 How the Number of Sisters Affects Nutritional Status, Ghana

	Number of Siblings							
	One	Two	Three	Four	Five	Six	Seven	Eight
Height-for-age								
average z-score								
Sisters								
None	−1.28	−1.44	−1.32	−1.74	−1.60	−1.85	−2.40	−2.12
One	−1.22	−1.49	−1.52	−1.62	−1.58	−1.65	−1.91	−1.75
Two		−1.31	−1.44	−1.28	−1.50	−1.68	−1.90	−1.50
Three			−1.39	−1.34	−1.27	−1.59	−1.94	−1.73
Four					−1.22	−1.25	−1.97	−0.66
Five						−1.09	−1.86	−1.54
Six								
Mean	−1.24	−1.43	−1.44	−1.53	−1.49	−1.52	−1.74	−1.72
Observations	401	595	681	535	330	237	161	112
Weight-for-height								
average z-score								
Sisters								
None	−0.68	−0.63	−0.67	−0.67		−0.52	−0.55	
One	−0.69	−0.64	−0.72	−0.64	−0.77	−0.68	−1.02	
Two		−0.69	−0.66	−0.63	−0.75	−0.65	−0.78	
Three			−0.57	−0.59	−0.75	−0.64	−0.72	
Four				−0.59	−0.71	−0.63	−0.68	
Five					−0.59	−0.60		
Six							−0.35	
Mean	−0.69	−0.64	−0.66	−0.64	−0.73	−0.65	−0.79	
Observations	239	354	397	269	159	116	87	

Notes: Height-for-age is calculated for all children age 15 years and below. Weight-for-height is calculated for all children age 10 years and below.

Source: Reproduced from Garg and Morduch (1996, 479), Table 1.

reproduces a table prepared by Doss (1997), who uses data from the Ghana Living Standards Survey of 1991–92 that measures preventative health care. The numbers are sadly low—most children were not getting complete vaccinations, nor were their mothers going to clinics after birth. Quite clearly, there are no differences in access to vaccinations between girls and boys, even when controlling for urban versus rural areas. Hill and Upchurch's (1995) analysis of Demographic and Health Surveys (DHS) for 18 African countries finds a similar pattern. Table 8.6 shows the differences between the percentage of girls with a particular health condition or treatment and the percentage of boys. Positive signs mean female disadvantage. The numbers suggest that girls do better than boys on most ailments—they are less stunted, less wasted, and have less diarrhea and fewer acute respiratory infections (ARI). On the other hand, they are not treated differently from boys for ARI; the signs are just as likely to be negative as positive.

Table 8.5 Percentage of Children Who Have Received Preventive Health Care, Ghana, 1991–1992

	Urban		Rural		Total	
	Boys	Girls	Boys	Girls	Boys	Girls
Some vaccinations[a]	69.1	67.0	51.2	54.0	56.5	57.9
Complete vaccinations[a]	54.2	54.1	38.3	39.1	43.0	43.6
Postnatal clinic visit[b]	48.6	50.7	36.9	38.5	40.4	41.9

Source: Reproduced from Doss (1997), Table 6.
Notes: a. N=5,280; b. N=3,435.

Table 8.6 Differences Between Girls and Boys in Health Indicators from DHS Surveys (Female Percentage Minus Male Percentage)

Country	Immunized	Stunted	Wasted	With Diarrhea	With ARI	Treated for Diarrhea	Treated for ARI
Botswana	−0.2			−0.1	−0.9	−1.9	0.4
Burundi		−0.5	−1.1	−0.7	2.6	−0.7	2.1
Cameroon	3.0	−2.0	−0.3	−2.9	−0.3	−1.3	9.2
Ghana	−9.4	−0.4	−2.1	−0.9	−0.4	−4.8	−3.4
Kenya	−5.9			−0.3	0.5	0.4	−6.6
Liberia	0.4			−1.7	−1.5		
Madagascar	2.0	−4.7	−0.9	−2.4	−1.4	−2.4	−5.2
Malawi	−0.2	−4.4	−1.1	−3.4	0.7	8.0	−3.4
Mali		1.1	−2.2	−2.7	−0.1	0.1	6.5
Niger	−2.4	−1.4	−1.5	−1.3	0.3	−0.3	4.9
Nigeria	2.4	−0.7	−1.5	−3.0	−1.1	−3.2	−4.2
Senegal		−4.2	−3.5	−2.0		0.0	
Sudan	2.7			−0.5	−1.7	−0.1	12.4
Tanzania	−4.0	−2.8	−1.1	0.3	−1.0	−5.4	0.9
Togo		−5.3	−1.8	−0.4	−1.8	−2.5	−1.6
Uganda	5.2	−5.7	0.1	−2.2	−0.2	−2.0	2.3
Zambia	−0.6	−2.7	0.3	−2.9	−0.3	2.5	−1.6
Zimbabwe	−2.0	−1.9	−0.1	−1.5	−4.0	0.3	−4.2

Source: Reprinted with the permission of the Population Council, from Kenneth Hill and Dawn Upchurch, "Gender Differences in Child Health: Evidence from the Demographic and Health Surveys," *Population and Development Review* 21, no. 1 (March 1995), p. 149.
Note: The numbers are female percentage of sample having condition indicated minus male percentage having condition indicated.

Son Preference in Expenditures

Household expenditure surveys are carried out throughout the world and have recently been used to test for son preference. The test is remarkably clever. Many of the goods that households consume can be identified as "adult" goods. They are items consumed only by adults, such as cigarettes and cosmetics. Sometimes expenditure surveys also record purchases of adult clothing by men and women. Data on these expenditures can then be analyzed to ask whether the presence of additional children, and whether girls or boys in particular, affect the share of expenditures on these adult goods. Holding the household budget constant (by including in the regression a variable for total household expenditures), an additional boy might affect expenditures on adult goods more than an additional girl would, if parents spend more heavily on boys than on girls. Such evidence would be consistent with son preference.

This line of thinking was originally developed by Rothbarth (1943) to enable comparisons of income for households with different demographic structures. The thrust of Rothbard's analysis was that a household earning $5,000 with two adults and three children ought to be considered poorer than a household earning the same income but with only two adults and no children. But how much poorer? To make a comparison, one needed an estimate of how many children were equivalent to an adult. The equivalence scale proposed by Rothbard was to see how much an additional child "cost," in the sense of how much an additional child shifted spending away from adult goods toward other expenditures. If an additional child caused expenditures on adult goods to fall by $100, then that could be a measure of how much a child reduced the income available to adults. The "real" income of the household with three children would be $4,700. Rothbard's intuition was that having a child was like having a reduction in income when it came to adult goods. However, that may not be the case. If having a child changes *preferences* away from adult goods, then the intuition is invalid. For example, one could easily imagine that having a child reduces alcohol and tobacco consumption regardless of family earnings, so there is no reduction in income. Testing whether consumption of adult goods really is independent of the demographic structure of the household is then a prior requirement to calculating the equivalence scale.

If one imagines that children can be measured as a continuous number (rather than integers), a statistic known as the outlay equivalent ratio may be calculated. This is the ratio of the change in expenditures on adult goods to changes in children, over the change in expenditures on adult goods over changes in income, normalized by expressing the ratio in relation to per capita expenditure (Deaton 1997, 229–235):

$$\pi_{jk} = \frac{\dfrac{\partial p_j q_j / \partial c_k}{\partial p_j q_j / \partial y}}{\dfrac{y}{c}}$$

Here, π_{jk} is the outlay equivalent ratio, p_j is the price of a given adult good, q_j is the quantity purchased of the adult good, c_k is the number of persons in a particular demographic category (i.e., children aged zero to five), c is the total number of household members, and y is total household expenditures. The numerator in the ratio is the increase in expenditures on adult goods associated with a one unit change in children in a particular category. The denominator is the increase in expenditures on adult goods associated with a one-unit change in household income. Suppose an additional child lowers expenditures on an adult good by $25, while an additional dollar in income raises expenditures by $0.90. The ratio is normalized by dividing by the mean per capita expenditure for the sample. Suppose this were $500. The outlay equivalent ratio would then be –.055. An additional child lowers expenditures on adult goods by the same amount as a 5.5 percent reduction in household income.

A fair number of papers have now used the expenditure data collected in household surveys to calculate outlay-equivalence ratios. Deaton (1989) finds no evidence of favoritism toward boys using the 1985 Living Standards Survey from Côte d'Ivoire. Haddad and Reardon (1993) find little evidence of pro-boy behavior in Burkina Faso, while Kebede (2000) finds some evidence that Ethiopian households have some pro-girl bias in infancy that switches to pro-boy bias in childhood. Appleton, Chess, and Hoddinott (1999) analyze data from the Integrated Household Survey of Uganda, collected in 1992–1993. The survey covered approximately 10,000 households and was designed to be representative of most of the country. Major consumption expenditures were recorded using a 30-day recall. Table 8.7 reports the calculated outlay equivalent ratios. The first column gives the shares in the household budgets for adult goods. The mean for the sample of households is about 7 percent of expenditures going toward adult goods. Men's goods represent a much larger share than women's goods. It is, after all, a man's world. The outlay equivalent ratios suggest that it is a boy's world, too. Moving down the pair of columns for children aged zero to five, one notes that the ratios are larger for boys than for girls in every case except one (meals out). Sometimes the differences in ratios are very large indeed (tobacco, men's clothing, women's footwear). Cosmetics has a positive ratio; apparently the presence of more children in the household leads to an increase in expenditures on cosmetics rather than a decrease. One might imagine cosmetics as a typical gift to a woman, from her husband, following childbirth. The ratio for cosmetics is negative for older children. For older children more generally, the ratios are still larger for boys than for girls in the majority of cases, and when they are not larger they are very similar. Of all the pairs of ratios, there are none where girls are very much larger than boys, while one-third of the pairs have the boy

Table 8.7 Mean Budget Shares per Household and Outlay Equivalence Ratios for Adult Goods, Uganda

	Budget shares (%)	Boys 0–5	Girls 0–5	Boys 6–14	Girls 6–14
Alcohol	2.74	−0.82	−0.62	0.19	0.00
Tobacco	0.90	−2.17	−0.62	−2.13	−1.41
Meals out	0.98	−0.41	−0.42	−0.76	−0.93
Entertainment	0.28	−0.36	0.01	−0.59	−0.37
Men's clothing (incl. footwear)	0.74	−0.55	−0.38	−0.56	−0.62
All potential men's goods	5.64	−0.17	−0.09	−0.54	−0.47
Women's clothing (excl. footwear)	0.91	−0.21	−0.07	−0.58	−0.50
Women's footwear	0.06	−0.23	−0.12	−0.56	−0.47
Cosmetics	0.29	0.06	0.02	−0.48	−0.47
All potential women's goods	1.26	−0.17	−0.09	−0.54	−0.47
All potential adult goods	6.90	−0.45	−0.30	−0.55	−0.58

Source: Reproduced from Appleton, Chessa and Hoddinott (1999, 8, 11), Tables 1 and 4.

ratio almost twice as large in magnitude. Boys cause larger shifts in expenditures away from adult goods.

Female Circumcision

For young girls, no health issue may be more important than circumcision, or female genital mutilation (FGM) as it is increasingly called (Rahman and Toubia 2000). The practice varies in severity, from relatively harmless nicks in western and southern Africa, to complete infibulation in Sudan and Somalia, involving removal of the labia majora, labia minora, and clitoris and sewing together of the vagina, leaving only a small opening for urine to pass through. The World Health Organization has four categories for the practice: Type 4 is the mildest form, involving any pricking, piercing, incising or stretching of the clitoris or other vaginal tissue; Type 1 is known as clitoridectomy and may involve complete removal of the clitoris; Type 2 involves removal of the clitoris as well as excision of the labia minora; Type 3, known as infibulation, has the vagina stitched together after removal of tissue.

There is no doubt that there are serious health complications from circumcision, particularly when carried out in rural areas without access to sterile procedures and antibiotics. There, the procedure itself, sometimes using unsterile razors or knives, and unsterile thread and needles for infibulation, can easily lead to life-threatening infections. Infibulation requires a surgical procedure to "open" the vagina for childbirth, and then is usually followed by a "reclosing" of the vagina, with concomitant complications.

Sexual intercourse may be very painful. Certainly it will be less pleasurable for the woman, on average.

Because the practice is often officially banned (though rarely enforced), limited scientific survey research on the health complications caused by the practice has been carried out. More recently, however, studies from a number of countries have become available. Jones, Diop, Askew, and Kabore (1999), for example, report on detailed interviews with women who presented themselves to health clinics in Burkina Faso and Mali. Just under 95 percent of women in both countries had some form of circumcision or FGM. (These percentages are not representative, since women who had been circumcised were more likely to be coming to the clinic, both because they are older and because, as the authors find, circumcision causes health complications.) In Burkina Faso most women fell into category Type 1, while in Mali almost two-thirds were in Type 2. Consequently, also half of the health complications in Mali involved hemorrhage, while in Burkina Faso keloid cysts and stenosis were more common complications. Women who had undergone circumcision (most commonly around age ten) were more likely to have obstetric complications and genital infections.

Not all of the evidence confirms health complications, it should be noted. Larsen and Yan (2000) find no evidence that circumcision affected fertility outcomes in three countries with moderate incidence of circumcision.

There is no mystery about how the practice is sustained, and particularly why it might be women, rather than men, who act as adamant supporters of the practice. Enforcing circumcision of young girls can be a Nash equilibrium. Each woman in a social group has a best strategy regarding circumcision: (1) Regardless of personal belief or experience, act as if circumcision is absolutely required for transition to womanhood; (2) Sanction any woman who does not act likewise; (3) Sanction any women who do not sanction women who disobey the norm, in word or in deed. If all women share these strategies, they become the norm, then each individual woman will clearly adopt the strategy in her own interest. The logic of the norm is self-fulfilling once a threshold of "believers" is reached.

Moreover, girls can be taught by their parents that being uncircumcised is equivalent to being unclean. They may be taught that an adult woman is a circumcised woman and that an uncircumcised woman remains a child. The possibility that the norm becomes internalized and becomes part of the identity of both younger and older women is not to be discounted, as the following two literary extracts suggest (see also Dirie [1999, 37–46]). The first is from Ngugi wa Thiong'o's novel, *The River Between:* "I want to be a real woman. I want to be a real girl, a real woman, knowing all the ways of the hills and ridges. Circumcision did not prevent [our parents] from being Christians. I too have embraced the white man's faith. However, I know it is beautiful, oh so beautiful to be initiated into womanhood. You learn the ways of the tribe. Yes, the white man's God does not quite satisfy me. I want. I need something more. . . . Surely, there is no tribe that does not circumcise. Or how does a girl grow into a woman?" (1965, 16, as cited in Gordon [1997, 26]). The second is from Charity Waciuma's novel, *Daughter of Mumbi:*

> About this time, we lost many of our good friends when they went through the circumcision ceremony. Because we Christian girls had not "been to the river" we were unclean. We were not decent respectable people and mothers would not have the shame of letting their daughters be seen in our company. It was believed that a girl who was un-circumcised would cause the death of a circumcised husband. Moreover, an un-circumcised woman would be barren. When the other boys and girls—and their parents—came to realise that we really never would be circumcised it was something of a scandal. We became a laughing-stock, the butt of their jokes. (as reproduced in Waciuma [1994, 84])

Fear of opprobrium and identity roles learned and reinforced throughout childhood can lead people to follow social customs regardless of the harm they may cause.

* * *

The studies discussed in this chapter suggest that there is little evidence of strong son preference in Africa, at least the kind of son preference that results in sizable differential mortality of girls and boys, or differential fertility behavior as the sex of children is revealed at birth and parents make updated fertility decisions, or health treatment. There is, however, some evidence of moderate but statistically significant differentials in excess mortality, especially when using an appropriate reference group with high overall mortality, and some evidence from expenditure data indicating preferences for boys. Moreover, the practice of female circumcision, which clearly affects the health of girls adversely, means that the problems of the girl child have to be taken seriously in African countries much as in Asian countries.

9

Investments in Education

> The needs and sensibilities of the women in my family were not considered a priority, or even legitimate. That was why I was in Standard Three in the year Nhamo [my brother] died, instead of in Standard Five, as I should have been by that age.
>
> —*Tsitsi Dangarembga,* Nervous Conditions

Although the typical African family does not intentionally neglect the health and nutrition of a daughter to any large degree, it does neglect her education. This was especially true for the past. Table 9.1 shows that literacy rates are lower for women. More tragically, the gaps are wider, percentagewise, in the countries with the lowest literacy rates. For Burkina Faso and Niger, women's literacy rates are far below those of men. The lone exception, again, is Botswana, where women's literacy rates are higher than men's. Literacy rates are rapidly improving for young women but remain below 50 percent for a good number of countries. The table excludes a number of war-torn countries for which statistics were not available, such as Congo (DRC), Somalia, Sierra Leone, and Angola. For these, schooling attainment has probably worsened considerably, for both men and women.

African countries are thus close to the more discriminatory societies of South Asia in terms of schooling for girls. Figure 9.1 shows the very low initial ratios of literacy rates in the two regions when compared with East Asia and Latin America. There has been considerable catch-up, partly as a result of changing incentives for schooling girls, changing norms, and deliberate education policy.

Disturbingly, data on enrollment rates presented in Figure 9.2 suggest that the gender catch-up in Africa may have stalled, while that of South Asia continues. There is considerable evidence that the demand for schooling has declined, as the quality and returns to schooling decline with the poor overall economic growth described in Chapter 2 (Bennell 2002). But supply-side factors are also implicated in the lamentable state of education

Table 9.1 Literacy Rates in African Countries, 1999

	Overall Adult Literacy Rate	Adult Female Literacy Rate	Females Aged 15–24 Literacy Rate
Benin	39.0	23.6	36.9
Botswana	76.4	78.9	91.9
Burkina Faso	23.0	13.3	22.2
Burundi	46.9	39.0	59.9
Cameroon	74.8	68.6	93.1
Cape Verde	73.6	65.1	85.4
Cen. Afr. Republic	45.4	33.3	56.9
Chad	41.0	32.3	57.7
Comoros	59.2	52.1	61.1
Congo, Rep.	79.5	73.0	96.3
Côte d'Ivoire	45.7	37.2	58.1
Djibouti	63.4	52.8	78.1
Ethiopia	37.4	31.8	51.8
Gambia	35.7	28.5	47.6
Ghana	70.3	61.5	87.3
Guinea-Bissau	37.7	18.3	32.5
Kenya	81.5	74.8	93.7
Lesotho	82.9	93.3	98.4
Liberia	53.2	36.9	54.1
Madagascar	65.7	58.8	75.6
Malawi	59.2	45.3	59.9
Mali	39.8	32.7	58.1
Mauritania	41.6	31.4	40.4
Mauritius	84.2	80.8	94.3
Mozambique	43.2	27.9	44.8
Niger	15.3	7.9	13.2
Nigeria	62.6	54.2	82.5
Rwanda	65.8	59.1	80.5
Senegal	36.4	26.7	40.7
South Africa	84.9	84.2	91.0
Sudan	56.9	44.9	70.0
Swaziland	78.9	77.9	90.8
Tanzania	74.7	65.7	87.8
Togo	56.3	39.6	57.6
Uganda	66.1	55.5	71.3
Zambia	77.2	70.2	84.6
Zimbabwe	88.0	83.8	95.5

Source: World Bank Development Indicators (2002).

in most countries. Both parents and states are responsible for the manifest neglect of girls' education.

Low literacy rates are worrisome even in the absence of gender disparities. The remotest villager apprehends that schooling enables the realization of one's capabilities. Literacy is essential in the modern world. Education and literacy probably have large spillover effects. Many researchers think that education is a cost-effective way to encourage economic growth. Educated people are more productive people, and educated people innovate. Everyone else benefits from the productivity and innovation of the educated.

**Figure 9.1 Literacy Rate Ratio, Female-to-Male
(Percentage of Females and Males Aged 15–24)**

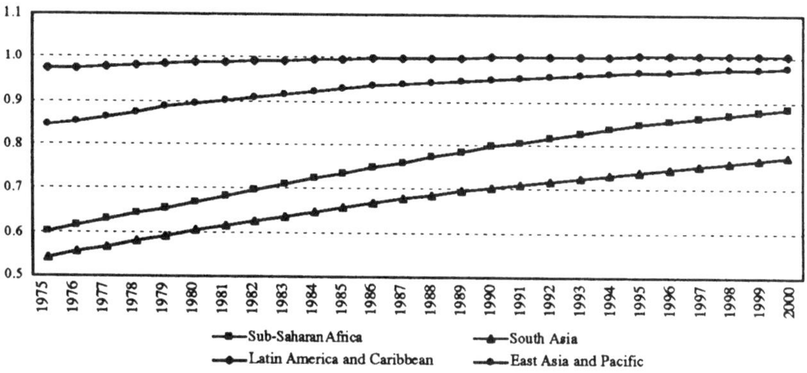

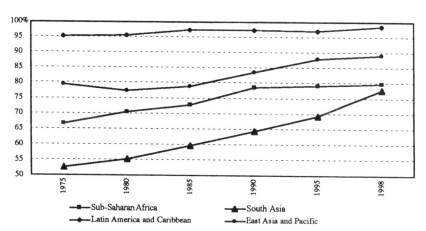

Source: World Bank Development Indicators (2002). Low- and middle-income countries only.

Figure 9.2 Ratio of Girls to Boys in Primary and Secondary Education

Source: World Bank Development Indicators (2002). Low- and middle-income countries only.

Investments in education yield high social returns, and investments in girls even more so (Schultz 2002). Rather than building dams, the World Bank and other donors should target their money toward girls' education. So, at least, goes an influential strand of development thinking.

Why Are Girls Neglected When It Comes to Education?

In most societies, parents decide how much education a child receives. Girls in Africa may be undereducated because parents think there is a low return to educating girls. Female graduates may not get jobs. They may earn lower wages than males. Parents may also prefer to educate boys for personal reasons. An educated girl may not respect her parents. She may refuse to marry a spouse chosen by parents. Parents may think it unseemly for a girl to be in a classroom with boys

The literature on the economic basis for schooling decisions is vast (Alderman and King 1998; King and Hill 1993). Models of education decisions, however, are not very informative. Investments in the education of children are investments in the future, and the future is not like a dog that comes when you whistle. The future is uncertain. Actions taken today with effects for tomorrow depend on expectations about the future. These expectations are hard to observe, let alone measure. This fact stymies comprehensive investigation of the determinants of schooling decisions that parents make for their children. The decisions depend on the expectations parents have, which are not observed by the researcher.

For example, the returns that parents expect from investments in their children will depend on the extent to which grown children transfer resources back to their parents when their parents are older and children are earning incomes. This expectation depends, in turn, on the norms that will enforce such transfers. Filial piety may induce children to care for their parents, but fear of shame and ostracism may be necessary in the breach. Not all societies care for the elderly; Turnbull's (1972) famous study of the Ik people of Uganda is a case in point. As their economic situation deteriorated, younger generations of the Ik abandoned their elders to starvation.

Parents also care about the welfare of their children. Their altruism may lead them to invest heavily in children who have especially bad prospects when they reach adulthood. The rewards of altruism, much like expectations, are not observable.

For these and other reasons, generating a single model of education decisions with testable implications is hard. The chapter therefore proceeds by briefly sketching three models of education decisionmaking before turning to some of the empirical findings. Each model emphasizes a different aspect of the education decision and will be more or less appropriate for different levels of analysis. The first is more appropriate for a population that has variation in parents' wealth, income, and education levels. The second is more appropriate for societies with different ethnic groups that have different norms regarding the relations between parents and children. The third is more appropriate when societies have lots of variation across localities, especially where smaller, tight-knit subcultures are prominent, as in some urban and peri-urban areas.

Investments When Returns to Schooling Differ by Gender of Child

Consider a model of the tradeoff between educating a son and educating a daughter. Suppose the utility function is such that only the present consumption of the parents and future earnings of the children matter for the parents. Parents act in concert and have two children, a boy and a girl. The parents choose education levels to maximize a function of present consumption and future earnings of the two children. The parents only care about the total income of the children; perhaps they suppose that the siblings will share their income. The parental utility function is $U(c_1, y_g + y_b)$, where c_1 is the consumption level for the parents in period one and y_g and y_b are the earnings of the girl and boy, respectively. Earnings or wages are higher if the child is more educated, as depicted in Figure 9.3. The marginal or extra return to schooling is always higher for the boy than for a girl if they have equal levels of schooling; for equal education levels, $y_b'(x_b) > y_g'(x_g)$, where x_i is the level of education of person i. Girls with lower levels of schooling may of course have higher marginal returns than well-educated boys. The marginal return to schooling might be higher for a girl who goes from no schooling to completion of primary school, compared with a boy who goes from seventh grade to twelfth grade. But for the same education levels, the marginal returns are lower for girls.

Suppose education is free, but if a child goes to school he or she cannot work to earn money for consumption in the present (imagine the parents are sick and cannot work). Someone has to work if the family is to eat. For ease of analysis, there is no consideration of leisure time, so that time spent in school is subtracted from time to work, so that after school a child earns $w(T - x)$ where T is the total number of years available for work at child wage w. In reality, the cost of schooling also includes out-of-pocket fees and expenses, such as transport and textbooks.

Intuitively, the parents will allocate more to the boy, since by assumption the return to educating the boy is always higher than the return to educating the girl if they have equal levels. At the margin, the parents will favor the boy. But let us set up the problem as a maximization problem and

Figure 9.3 Hypothetical Relation Between Years of Schooling and Earnings

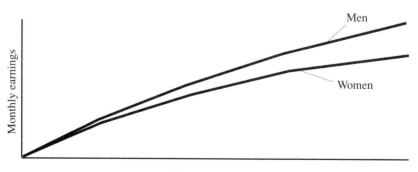

thus analyze the maximization conditions. The problem is to choose x_g and x_b to maximize the function:

$$U (c_1, y) \text{ subject to}$$
$$c_1 = w(T - x_g) + w(T - x_b)$$
$$\text{and } y = y_g(x_b) + y_g(x_g)$$

The more education, x_i, a child receives, the higher his or her future income will be, but the lower the current consumption of the parents. The condition for maximizing utility is that the marginal returns from investing in the education of the boy should equal the marginal returns from investing in the girl, and these in turn should equal the marginal returns (in terms of satisfaction, or utility) to parental consumption. This may not sound like much, but the basic apparatus may now be used to analyze what will happen if something changes. For example, changing social institutions that reward girl education with higher income will lead to greater investment in girl education. The model predicts that investment in girls will be responsive to changes in the economic environment. These predictions can be tested: when the returns to schooling increase for girls, do parents invest more in their education? This is nothing more than the income and price elasticity of schooling for girls. These are important parameters for designing education policies. If the elasticities are very low, then nonprice incentives and policies might have to be offered to raise girls' schooling.

Investments When Returns to Parents Differ by Gender of Child

Suppose instead that the returns to education are identical, but that parents care about how much of the child's future earnings will be transferred to them. As seen in the previous chapter, transfers to parents depend to some degree on whether marriages are virilocal, uxorilocal, ambilocal, or neolocal. Parents might also receive transfers from the bride or groom of their child, or the family of the bride or groom, as reward for parental investments in the form of marriage payments. (As defined previously, bridewealth refers to payments made from the groom's side to the bride's side; dowry is the reverse.)

Consider the effects of norms on transfers, marriage payments, and virilocality on daughter investment in a simple two-period model (Rammohan and Robertson 2001). In the first period, parents work and decide how much to invest in their daughter. In the second period, the daughter gets married and parents retire and live on the returns from the investments they may have made in their daughter, in the form of marriage payments and transfers, and the returns from other investments (e.g., in other children, financial savings, productive assets, and insurance). Assume again that parents have a joint utility function, and they choose levels of investment in their daughter I_d and in other investments I_o to maximize the following expression:

$$U(c_1) + U(\theta_m(I_d, n_m) + \theta_t(I_d, n_v, n_t) + \theta_o(I_o))\ s.t.\ y_1 = c_1 + I_o + I_d,$$

where c_1 is consumption in period one, n_m measures the strength of norms about payments at marriage, n_v represents the virilocality norm, and n_t represents the norm to give transfers when parents are elderly and retired. The function $\theta_m()$ determines to what extent investments in daughters are compensated in the marriage market by receipt of bridewealth. The function $\theta_t()$ represents the expectation of transfers from the daughter in old age and depends on the level of investment in the daughter, norms about how far away the daughter will live after marriage, and norms about whether the daughter is expected to contribute to the care of her parents in their old age. The function $\theta_o()$ is the expected return on other investments, in particular investments in sons. The level of current income or assets, y_1, is the constraint. Parents are typically credit-constrained in terms of making investments in children or in insurance for future compensation in old age. Otherwise all children able to "pay back" their educations would complete the entire course of schooling. Because of credit constraints, different families with different wealth levels will confront different implicit prices for credit, as some families are rationed.

Maximization leads to equations for the level of investment in daughters and other investments, $I_d(y_1, n_m, n_v, n_t)$ and $I_o(y_1, n_m, n_v, n_t)$, that show how these levels depend on the strength of norms and the parental assets or income. Levels of investment also depend on the $\theta_i()$ functions that describe the expected returns to investments in daughters as opposed to other investments. Both norms about payments and transfers and the responsiveness of these to levels of investment will affect parental decisions. Investments in daughters increase, relative to other investments, if parents receive higher bridewealth for more educated daughters in the marriage market, if daughters are more likely to send transfers to parents or care for them in old age, and, of course, if daughters live closer to parents.

Investments When Returns Depend on What Peers Do

Ethnic norms about marriage payments and fealty to parents can be taken as "historical," or "cultural." They are part of the structure that people take as given. Likewise, investment decisions may also be influenced by more local, neighborhood norms. Akerlof suggested that these norms matter when "the impact of my choices on my interactions with other members of my social network may be the primary determinant of my decision, with the ordinary determinants of choice (the direct additions and subtractions from utility due to the choice) of only secondary importance" (1997, 1006).

In developing countries, one can think of a number of reasons why parents would be influenced by social norms, or shared local expectations, in their schooling decisions. Prospects in the local marriage market (and hence, implicitly, old-age insurance for the parents) may depend on status, which may in turn be defined by educational attainment. If people in a locality do not like marriages where women are more educated than their husbands, then everyone is afraid of overeducating daughters. The risk is too high that the daughter could end up a spinster. Children are also influenced by local norms, and schoolyard norms that discourage girls' education may suppress a child's desire for more schooling.

A graph illustrates the main idea behind models of neighborhood or peer effects. Figure 9.4 measures the costs and benefits of schooling on the vertical axis and the proportion of peers enrolled on the horizontal axis. As more peers are enrolled, the costs of schooling decline; the individual child is less likely to be ostracized. But the benefits also decline. More children enrolled means more crowding in the classroom, for example. The graph may be interpreted as a kind of dynamic story. If the enrollment rates are lower than the cutoff point *A,* then the benefits of schooling fall below the costs, and parents will not send their children to school. The equilibrium rate of schooling for girls is zero. If enrollment rates are above *A,* then the benefits of schooling exceed the costs, and all girls are enrolled. Different neighborhoods have different enrollment rates for historical reasons, and these feed back into current enrollment decisions.

Empirical Findings

Regression analysis of the determinants of enrollment has some measure of schooling as the dependent variable. This might represent current enrollment, schooling attainment in years, or completion of primary or secondary school. The explanatory variables include the age and gender of child; household variables such as the parents' education levels, wealth, or income; and the price and quality of schooling.

The typical empirical analysis neglects gender issues, focusing on more general issues. One such question concerns the price elasticity of schooling. The sensitivity of enrollment and attainment to the costs of schooling is an important parameter in the politically charged debates over whether schooling should be free or fee-based (Behrman 1993). There is great interest in finding out whether moderate fees dissuade parents from educating their children. A related question is whether parents are credit-constrained in sending their children to school. If capital markets worked well, then all children would attend school if the rewards to schooling exceeded the opportunity costs. But if poor parents could not borrow, then poor children

Figure 9.4 Hypothetical Costs and Benefits of Schooling That Depend on Social Norm

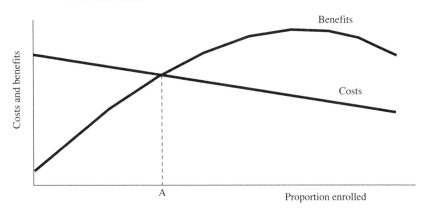

would not enroll and rich children would, perpetuating the divide between poor and rich. Many studies find that the wealth and income of parents matters a great deal in determining the education levels of their children (Filmer and Pritchett 1999; Glewwe 1999, 119). This is very strong evidence that parents are constrained in their ability to borrow against the future earnings of their children. Children who go to school are able to more than compensate their parents for the lost income and direct costs of schooling. Yet parents do not make the investments. The reason must be that they cannot borrow in anticipation of the expected higher earnings of their children. They need the income of their children now. Unfortunately, few studies test whether the wealth effect–cum-credit constraint typically matters more for boys than for girls.

Despite the focus on other issues, some gender-related results can be gleaned from the literature. The coefficient estimated for how being a girl or boy affects enrollment and attainment is interesting. The birth of sons or daughters is random, and there is little daughter neglect in African societies leading to premature abortion or death. This means that the estimated coefficient on the dummy variable for whether the child is a boy or girl measures how much less parents send their daughters to school, controlling for indicators of parental status and school costs. (If rich parents had fewer daughters, as the Trivers and Willard [1973] hypothesis predicts, then the indicator of household wealth would be correlated with the gender variable, and interpreting the coefficients on the two variables would be problematic because of the resulting multicollinearity.)

For many recent analyses using African data, this coefficient on the gender dummy variable is insignificant, reflecting the converging enrollment rates for younger girls seen in Table 9.1 and Figures 9.1 and 9.2.

Glewwe and Jacoby (1995), for instance, use a sample of 1,757 children from the Ghana Living Standards Survey of 1988–1989 to test the importance of early childhood malnutrition for schooling. They include a dummy variable for gender of the child. That variable ends up not being significant; neither is it significant in a regression estimating dropout age. There would seem to be no overall gender differences in schooling for this sample of Ghanaian children. A statistical analysis from South Africa also finds no gender difference in enrollment for girls in black families, and a small favoring of girls in white families (Maitra and Rammohan 1999). There are exceptions; as mentioned, Chernichovsky (1985, 327) found that in Botswana girls were more likely to be enrolled and also more likely to remain in school longer.

The real interest in empirical analyses of schooling is whether the coefficients of various explanatory variables differ by the gender of the child (Deolalikar 1993). There are few studies that include these interaction terms.

Al-Samarrai and Peasgood (1998, 404) analyze a sample of almost 3,000 Tanzanian households and find that the family head (almost always male) having completed primary school increases the chance of a boy being enrolled by 11 percent, and only increases girls' enrollment by 5 percent. The effects are almost exactly reversed for the spouse having finished primary school. Girls' enrollment rises by 11 percent, boys by only 4 percent. This result would be remarkable if it were robust, because the policy implications are so immediate. Girls do not go to school because their mothers did not go to school. If the cycle is broken, with the current generation of girls given encouragement to remain in school, there will not need to be a proactive policy favoring girls in future generations. Unfortunately, other studies find just the opposite result. Tansel (1997), using data sets comparable in size to those in the Tanzanian study, finds that in both Ghana and Côte d'Ivoire the fathers' education has a greater effect for daughters than the mothers' does.

If any parental characteristic affects enrollment of children, parental death probably is one. The HIV virus that causes AIDS currently infects more than one-third of adults in southern Africa. The children of adults who die are sometimes left orphaned and almost surely suffering from catastrophic changes in livelihoods. There is little formal insurance to mitigate the lost income of a deceased parent, and because the pandemic is so widespread, local safety nets offer little assistance. Recent research, consequently, has tried to measure the effects of deaths of parents on the schooling of children (Urassaa et al. 1997). Gordon (2002), for example, uses the Kwazulu Natal Income Dynamics Survey from 1993 and 1998. She finds that children who had a parent die were less likely to have progressed the same number of grades as children who did not have deaths in the family. As seen in Figure 9.5, however, the gender differentials were small and

Figure 9.5 Ratio of Female to Male School Achievement for Children with and Without Parental Death

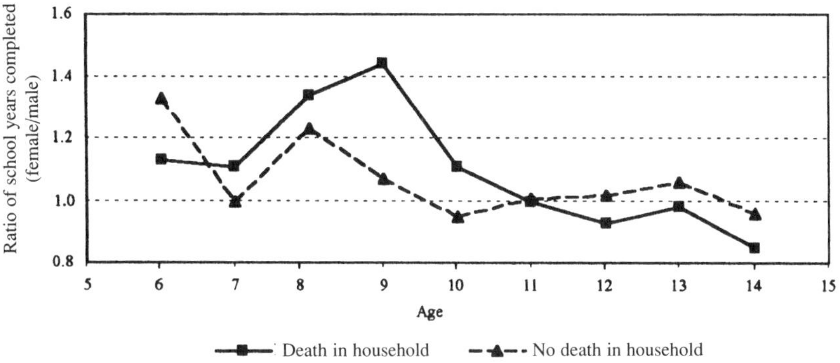

Source: Calculations by Deanna Gordon, using Kwazulu Natal panel data.

went in girls' favor. During primary school years, girls who experienced an adult death in their households completed more schooling than boys, compared with households without parental deaths.

There are few studies of how parents' ability to "capture" the higher earnings of their educated children affects schooling decisions or how local, gendered norms affect schooling outcomes. (For an example from Indonesia, see Levine and Kevane [2003].) That neighborhood-level variables affect schooling decisions and outcomes, and that these affect boys differently from girls, has been discussed extensively in studies of education in industrialized countries. These variables are not always interpreted as proxies for social norms; sometimes they are called "social learning" variables, and sometimes "peer-group" effects. Whatever these variables are called, they seem to be as important as individual or household-level variables for studies conducted in the United States, and they seem to vary by gender (Ellen, Mijanovich, and Dillman 2001; Elliott 1999; Ensminger, Lamkin, and Jacobson 1996; Entwisle, Alexander, and Olson 1994; Marpsat 1999).

There are several statistical problems in trying to estimate the effects of social norms on schooling decisions. Focusing on the role of social norms means considering what other people—the reference group—are doing. This gives rise to the "reflection problem": that group and individual behavior are spuriously correlated because of omitted variables (Manski 1993). Recent work has suggested methods of partitioning data among social groups that live in the same geographic area but have different local cultures or norms (such as co-resident religious groups) that overcome the reflection problem. Munshi and Myaux (1998) in particular find that in Bangladesh the aggregate behavior of a woman's religious group is an important determinant of contraception use, while the behavior of co-resident women belonging to other religions does not affect contraception choice. Their finding, using a panel and controlling for village effects, that a change in contraceptive use for a person depends on the change in that person's own religious group's aggregate behavior, but does not depend on the change in the other group's behavior, would seem to weigh decisively against the reflection problem. It seems highly unlikely that across villages there were two correlated, but omitted, variables that changed in ways that affected contraceptive behavior for one group but not the other. As of yet, no work on education determinants in developing countries has incorporated their insights.

As a last point, mention should be made of a very important problem in estimating the determinants of enrollment. Presumably, the single most important variable is the parents' estimate of the economic returns to schooling or "human capital." If girls are rewarded less in the labor market for their extra schooling, then parents will school them less. These parental estimates are not observable and instead must be determined by the analyst. Mincer (1974) is widely credited as the first serious and sustained empirical work estimating the effects of schooling on wage rates, and "Mincer equations" have now been estimated for most countries of the world, using data from surveys of workers in urban labor markets. The equations typically look as follows:

$$wages = \beta_0 + \beta_1 E + \beta_{,2} E^2 + \beta_3 S + \beta_4 X + \beta_5 O + \varepsilon$$

where E is years of experience, S is years of schooling, X are individual characteristics, O is a set of dummy variables for occupational and gender categories, and ε is a random error term. When wages are measured in natural logarithms, this makes the coefficient on schooling interpretable as the rate of return from an extra unit of schooling. Schooling is typically measured in years. With estimates of the coefficients in hand, one can then calculate an estimate of the net returns for schooling (see Glewwe [1999, 5–8]) for a clear and concise discussion; also Knight, Sabot and Hovey [1992]). The analyst calculates the earnings profile from age twelve, say, to retirement, for a person with no schooling and for a person who has completed primary schooling. The person with no schooling earns a wage early on, while the person who goes to school earns nothing until graduation. The present discounted value of the earnings profiles can then be used to calculate an implied, constant annual rate of return. The difference between the returns is the extra return from schooling.

These estimated returns are more like realized historical returns, rather than the expected returns on which contemporary decisions are based. Any estimate of the returns for education depends on expectations about the future. If everyone decided to get a secondary school diploma, the returns might turn out to be quite low. Most likely, many would be unemployed. If everyone dropped out of secondary school, then the few who remained would earn high returns. The future is not always like the past. Moll (1996) shows that for South Africa the returns for schooling turned out to be considerably lower than what many had probably thought, as the economy turned sour in the 1980s and 1990s.

Glick and Sahn's (1997) study of returns for schooling in Guinea merits attention. They control for the selection problem of differing entry into the informal sector, private sector, and public sector. Wage profiles differ in each of these sectors. Women in the informal and public sectors earned less than men, only half as much in the self-employed sector and 20 percent less in the public sector. Women in the private sector earned more, but that was because private sector female wage workers were more educated than their male counterparts. Once account is taken of the differing experiences and educations of men and women, the gender wage gaps were all against women, and were substantial for some sectors.

Table 9.2 reproduces the results from a recent study of the returns for schooling. Nielsen and Westergård-Nielsen (2001) use a household survey of 26,084 adults interviewed in 1993 in Zambia. Incomes are very low for the people in the sample, with the majority of people earning considerably less than a dollar per day at the market exchange rate. Men and women work in both formal and informal sectors, so the authors first estimate an equation that predicts which sector the person will work in. Once that selection is controlled for, the authors can then estimate the effect that extra years of schooling has on wages and income. The returns for schooling are very low in urban areas, on the order of 2 percent per year, and this only for men. For rural areas the returns are on the order of 8 percent and are roughly equal for men and women. As expected, completion of primary school, included as a dummy variable, boosts earnings in urban areas but not in rural areas.

Education and Macroeconomic Growth

If the samples of adults in the workforce reveal increases in wages and incomes of those with more schooling, then such growth should be mirrored in the aggregate data. As schooling rates increase in a country, its GDP per capita should rise. The country might see an increase in its longer-term rate of the GDP growth if better-educated people innovate more. Moreover, there are nonprivate, social returns to schooling that might enhance growth prospects (McMahon 1999; Schultz 2002). Health, fertility, contraception, and schooling of children are improved, especially with women's schooling (Ainsworth, Beegle, and Nyamete 1996). For example, Subbarao and Raney find that "the elasticities of fertility and infant mortality

Table 9.2 Annual Returns to Schooling, Zambia

	OLS			Full Model	
	All (1)	Formal (2)	Informal (3)	Formal (4)	Informal (5)
Urban areas:					
Females:					
School	0.000	0.002	0.001	0.001	0.017
School > 7	−0.098[a]	0.015[a]	0.099[a]	0.093[a]	0.328[a]
Males:					
School	0.023[a]	0.023[a]	0.021[a]	0.011	0.023[a]
School > 7	0.055[a]	0.054[a]	0.058[a]	0.015	0.021

	All (1)	Self-Employed (2)	Employed (3)	Self-Employed (4)	Employed (5)
Rural areas:					
Females:					
School	0.093[a]	0.070[a]	0.115[a]	0.062[a]	0.122[a]
School > 7	0.008	0.041	0.058	0.072	−0.063
Males:					
School	0.073[a]	0.068[a]	0.082[a]	0.074[a]	0.097[a]
School > 7	−0.003	−0.025	0.056	0.071[a]	0.202[a]

Source: Reprinted with permission from Nielsen and Westergård-Nielsen (2001), Table 5, p. 376, "Returns to Schooling in Less Developed Countries: New Evidence from Zambia" in *Economic Development and Cultural Change,* published by the University of Chicago Press, copyright 2001 by the University of Chicago.
Notes: a. Indicates significance at a 5 percent level.

with respect to female education substantially exceed those with respect to family planning and health programs" (1995, 404–405). It is surprising, then, to find that the macro evidence is far from clear.

As seen in Chapter 2, the primary method for assessing the importance of various sources of growth is the cross-country growth regression. Growth of GDP per capita is the dependent variable, and country characteristics are the independent variables. When measures of schooling are included as explanatory variables, they sometimes have low and insignificant coefficients. Sometimes the coefficients are negative. Subsequent studies have addressed some of the numerous econometric problems particular to estimating the effects of schooling on growth, and do find larger, positive coefficients (Krueger and Lindahl 2001; Pritchett 2001). There are some general points that should be made about interpreting the coefficients of education levels in growth regressions. Large and significant coefficients may not be what they seem. Bils and Klenow (2000) note three reasons for why the coefficients might be biased. First, high enrollment rates may serve as a proxy for changes in labor force numbers relative to dependents. The more workers there are relative to dependents, the more production can be invested rather than consumed. More investment equals more rapid growth. Second, high enrollments may be due to other factors that also generate economic growth. Schooling and growth are correlated, yes, but there is no causal connection. Peace and security, for instance, may lead to more schooling and more economic growth. Finally, the causality may actually be reversed. People who live in countries with expected rapid GDP growth may spend an increasing fraction of their incomes on schooling. The schooling responds to the growth, rather than causing it. Bils and Klenow try to quantify each of the three effects and conclude that the direct effect of schooling on growth is probably less than one-third of the estimated effect. It is, however, still positive.

Parents are not the only decisionmakers in the schooling problem. The providers of education may themselves have gender biases. The education policies that governments implement are mostly about the quality of education provided, rather than access. Glewwe (1999) has argued convincingly that the estimates of returns for schooling described above are not helpful in understanding the benefits from improving quality. For that, measures of schooling outcomes, such as test scores, are required. Test scores and other indicators of quality may generate new insights into how education policy is gendered. The developed countries have seen extensive debates over how boys and girls learn in the classroom and what the long-term effects are of different pedagogies. Glewwe (1999, 136–141) finds evidence that test scores are lower for girls in Ghanaian middle schools, but his small sample size prevents him from attempting to determine the specific aspects of school quality that might generate this result.

Finally, it should be recalled that in Africa the majority of the colonial regimes were distinctly pro-boy when it came to education. French and British schools were originally only for boys. The sons of chiefs were sent to colonial schools and to Paris; daughters were left at home. In Sudan, for example, Babiker Badri established the first small school for girls in 1907, after considerable conflict with the colonial power. Sir James Currie, at the time director of the Educational Department of the British administration of the Sudan, is quoted as having taken the position: "I would myself prefer that the government should not undertake the task [girls' education] for some time. But . . . I cannot see that any possible harm can accrue from starting something here" (Afhad University 2003). Badri's school survived for many years as a lonely outpost of progressive education.

These pro-boy policies changed well before independence, but a structure had been set. Since all the early educated persons were boys, they formed all the top layers of the education hierarchy. This disproportion was then replicated, as older men in the education hierarchy promoted their male protégés, leaving educated women behind as teachers in primary schools. Education ministries have not made girls' schooling a top priority, preferring instead to be gender-neutral. But neutrality has implicitly favored boys.

10

Development Projects for Women

No, I don't like this "women improvement" not because they are trying to improve. . . . But my wives go there and then they drink corn beer, and then they come home and then they don't answer properly. Women should be peaceful and respectful in the house . . . now you are a good person to tell them how to improve and, above all, how to be quiet.
— *Faay Kuykishwang, elderly Cameroonian farmer, 1958*

Why did the Whites make us have our women wear clothes? I had twenty wives. When they were naked, all I had to do was grunt here in my abaa and twenty women would shush in their twenty kitchens. When they got cloth to wear, I could call all day, and they would continue to chatter as if I didn't exist.
— *Cameroonian chief Enama Elundu Menge*

The grim circumstances outlined in previous chapters demand outside intervention; otherwise they will continue as before. The conditions are grim for women because, as such, they make conditions less grim for men. Men are disinterested in altering the male-favoring structures that gender economic activity.

Into this situation step development projects and programs that rely primarily on outside funding (i.e., those that are not the outcome of a domestic political bargain, the subject of the next chapter). Development projects involve well-defined activities funded from a pre-allocated budget and usually have a specified deadline. There are many success stories, but also many failures. Numerous development projects fail to plan adequately for what happens after their completion. The project may have very high maintenance costs and no budget to cover them. The project may not have any incentives for managers to continue effectively after the project end. The project may not generate any revenue, either directly or socially, and thus may be perceived by local counterparts to the donors as a cost rather than a benefit.

Gender projects may involve building meeting halls; designing programs for adult literacy; purchasing cooperative mills to alleviate the work burden of pounding and grinding grain by hand; establishing cooperative gardens, farms, fisheries, and orchards; improving livestock and poultry rearing; giving vouchers to students to attend school; and raising consciousness about legal rights and processes. The typical gender project specifies that the beneficiaries of the project should be women and that women in the community participate and coordinate the planning and implementation of the project.

These programs go under the rubric women in development (WID) and have a short but controversial history (Kabeer 1994, 11–39). One of the easiest things in the world to do is to pay people to appear to heed your advice. Many gender projects are like that. Wealthy countries organize projects. The projects involve distributing valuable technologies, commodities, skills, resources, and opportunities. A condition or purpose of the project is that women must attend monthly meetings, or that a woman must be on the organizing committee, or that women must get some fraction of the benefits. The project recipients are grateful for the help and candidly understand the project intentions. They listen patiently. The men grudgingly accept. The women who are to benefit feel a little empowered. Perhaps now things really will change. Most likely, they will not.

The history of project interventions contains many lessons, and the history of those intended to change gendered structures many more. This chapter focuses on the experiences of microcredit programs, which have expanded exponentially in Africa. Microcredit programs have been studied extensively in other countries and offer some important lessons for proper impact evaluation and project improvement.

Microcredit for Women

Microcredit projects targeted toward women are tremendously important in the current landscape of development projects (Morduch 1999). This is more true of Asia and Latin America, but African countries are rapidly catching up. Microcredit projects are being funded across the continent, and existing projects are expanding rapidly. The situation has evolved to a point where analysts are concerned about competition among microcredit institutions for the same clients, leading to overlending and defaults.

The microcredit movement emerged during the 1980s, mainly because of the remarkable achievements of the Grameen Bank in Bangladesh. Grameen had managed to grow rapidly for a decade, lending mostly to poor women, with repayment rates above 95 percent. Since the bank charged high interest rates, the high rate of repayment meant that the bank was closer to the path of financial sustainability than any previous institution. The secrets to its successful strategy were widely disseminated. First, the bank recognized that poor people did not have collateral, so substituted joint liability for collateral. In effect, groups of borrowers cosigned each other's loans. If one person in the group did not repay, the others would be liable for their debt and might suffer penalties from the lending institution. Second, the bank conditioned loans on agreement to a weekly repayment schedule. Rather than leaving the borrower to her or his own devices for six months or a year, all borrowers were required to sit down together every week. Third, the bank combined the weekly repayment meetings with what can only be called "empowerment messages." Borrowers were to agree to "sixteen decisions." Among them: to grow vegetables all year; to forgo dowry; to plan for smaller families; and to use pit latrines. The weekly meetings were also a time when borrowers would parade and publicly proclaim their commitment to the sixteen decisions. Finally, on the staff side, loan agents were motivated by "high-powered" incentives, where their promotion within the Grameen system and their generous retirement pensions were linked to performance.

The combination of joint liability; weekly meetings; shared, public commitments; and high-powered staff incentives generated the institution's remarkable performance. Clearly, the four elements generated synergies that one alone may not have accomplished. Weekly meetings enabled joint liability to work, because the cosigners would be required to meet together regularly and compare notes. The public performance of the sixteen decisions probably inculcated a shared sense that defaulting on loans was more than just a financial problem; it was a moral and personal failure. Staff success was directly tied to group success.

Joint liability has attracted much interest among academics because there are a number of ways that it could work to generate high repayments (Ghatak and Guinnane 1999; Conning 1999). Three advantages of joint lending must be highlighted: social pressure, mutual insurance, and screening through self-selection. The small groups of borrowers who are jointly liable may better exercise pressure against a recalcitrant borrower. A loan officer coming from a distant town might have few effective threats against a villager, but other villagers can hurt a fellow borrower who is not repaying. They may ostracize her; they might confiscate her personal belongings. They can embarrass her through gossip. All of these small punishments may induce a defaulter to repay. The stick of sanctions can be supplemented by a carrot of mutual insurance. In a small group, should misfortune strike one borrower, the others might agree to repay for the defaulter. The default may have been due to sickness or crop loss, not to any fault of the borrower. Finally, the self-selection of borrowers into groups means that the joint liability system has borrowers screen themselves. No borrower would like to be in a group with a known credit risk. Individuals in a group-lending situation are thus more likely to repay than if they were individual borrowers.

This does not mean that joint liability is a panacea and easily replicated around the world (MkNelly and Kevane 2002; Woolcock 1999). Numerous details must be ironed out for successful implementation. What should happen to a loan were the borrower to die? Should the cosigners really be liable? How should groups be reconstituted as borrowers drop out, as their circumstances change through marriage or migration or other events?

When lending large amounts to mostly illiterate and powerless poor people, Grameen agents are vulnerable to abuse their positions. Elaborate and effective accounting controls, combined with spot visits, must be enforced from the beginning. The culture of the institution must be one of flexibility, forgiveness, and compassion for borrowers but ruthless determination to deal with embezzlement and fraud among bank staff.

A Microcredit Project in Burkina Faso

Microcredit programs have been so successful they have spawned a large and growing literature reporting on program experiences and methods for evaluation (Cheston and Reed 1999; Hulme 2000; Kevane 1996; Navajas et al. 2000; Pal 1995). The earlier discussions on households and on social norms of labor control suggested that programs targeted toward women could have two effects. One effect would be to alter the bargaining positions of men and women within households. Giving women access to credit would enable them to live more independently of their husbands. If bargaining in the household broke down, so that women had to retreat to their "separate sphere" of childcare and household management without much assistance from their spouse, then access to outside credit would tremendously strengthen their bargaining positions. A second effect would be to empower women in the extrahousehold domain. If social norms that favored men were upheld as Nash equilibria, with people following the norms simply because others followed them, then credit programs for women might induce enough women to violate the norm, have practice belie the norm, and induce a snowball effect. Even when men actively collude to enforce a norm, giving women alternatives enables them to more effectively secure their own interests and undermine the norm.

Evaluators are, in the first instance, interested in the effects of credit programs in alleviating poverty for women and children whatever the mechanism: whether directly, through the credit effect on the household as a whole, or indirectly, as an increase in household bargaining power or as a change in community-wide gender relations. The effects may be captured by examining measures of income, health, consumption, or time allocation, as well as fuzzier measures of happiness and self-esteem. These effects may be thought of as the accomplishments of a household, or as a set of outcomes and behaviors chosen by the household given the resources available to it and its members.

An evaluator observes these choices and wants to know whether they were caused in part by the introduction of the credit program. Many evaluations are qualitative, questioning participants about their experiences and asking them to assess the program. The remainder of this section discusses the results of one such evaluation, conducted by the author. The program was called Credit and Savings with Education and was intended to facilitate rural women's access to credit and health and nutrition education in Burkina Faso. The project is implemented by the Union des Caisses Populaires du Burkina Faso (UCPBF), an umbrella organization for several hundred local savings and credit cooperatives. Freedom from Hunger, the international nongovernmental organization that developed the program, hoped the project would have three effects: (1) raise the incomes women earned directly through their own market activities; (2) improve the knowledge of rural women, isolated to some degree from radio programming and other popular media, concerning modern health and nutrition practices; and (3) reinforce and deepen the bonds of collective solidarity among women, enabling them to participate more directly in village and regional institutions that affect their lives. The ultimate goal was to improve food security and nutritional status.

Mechanics of the Credit and Saving with Education Program

Credit and Savings with Education applies the principle, discussed above, that credit could be delivered at low cost to rural women by organizing distribution and repayment through self-selected groups that monitored their own performance. The loan program works as follows: Loans are issued to the group as a whole, in cycles of four to six months, from a local credit cooperative (Caisse Populaire), a member of the UCPBF. Each group is supervised by a project agent (*animatrice*). At the end of a cycle every woman tells the animatrice how big a loan she would like for the next cycle. Maximum loan sizes start at 25,000 CFA for the first four cycles, then increase to 150,000 CFA. At an exchange rate of 600 CFA per dollar, then, loan sizes ranged from $40 to $250. The animatrice holds a meeting at the beginning of each cycle, and loans are disbursed. The officers of the association and two witnesses (usually men) sign for the loan, while each woman thumbprints for her individual loan. During the cycle, repayment meetings are held every week or every month, depending on the age of the association. Interest payments are 10 percent of the loan total. Many associations also add a 10 percent interest charge placed into an association fund. Repayments of interest and principal are not left for the end of the loan cycle; they commence immediately.

At the weekly repayment meetings the animatrice will also collect savings from every member. Initially savings of 10 percent of the loan were mandatory, but the rule has now been relaxed and savings are voluntary. The animatrice places the savings into the association account at the Caisse Populaire and distributes them at the end of every cycle. They earn no interest. Most women choose to withdraw their savings rather than roll them over for another loan cycle.

Occasional participation and membership fees are collected at the beginning of each cycle. Many associations fine members for absences from meeting or for arriving late (these fines vary from 25 to 50 CFA). These fines and fees, together with the 10 percent surcharge, are placed into the association account at the Caisse Populaire. Association officers reimburse travel and meal expenses connected with association business from the fund. But the bulk of the fund remains to be used either for special association projects (contributing to school construction or building a community center) or for making internal loans. The group itself had the authority to set the terms of repayment for any such internal or emergency loans.

For the first five cycles, weekly repayment sessions are linked to education sessions during which the animatrice presents a health or nutrition topic, offering a few key recommendations for practice and trying to engage in group discussions and encourage questions and problem-solving. Topics have included desirable breastfeeding, weaning, and food preparation practices; treatment of diarrhea; use of local clinics; the connection between health and spoiled or dirty food; family planning basics; and the importance of vaccinations. The lessons presented and discussed are developed with the participation of health experts from the Burkina Faso Ministry of Health.

Communities and Activities

For the evaluation, three credit associations were selected randomly from the group of nine that had gone through at least six credit cycles (i.e., were at least two years old) and that had a relatively high (greater than 50 percent) proportion of borrowers to savers. The associations were located in the villages of Tingandogo, Nagreongo, and Ipendo. Each village was visited for approximately one week. During that time an attempt was made to interview all current members of the association, as well as community leaders, teachers, nurses, and other key persons in the community. Sometimes interviews were organized as group discussions, especially when several women in the same compound were members. Women who had never joined the program or who had left the program were interviewed when they were encountered. Program coverage was extensive, and there seemed to be no barriers to joining; women who were currently not members were either sick, had been traveling, or had recently married into the village.

Women in all three villages carried out a variety of income-generating activities. Most common was brewing *dolo* (sorghum beer). Some women specialized in germinating and selling the sorghum used for the beer. Another common activity was preparing *soumbala,* a flavoring and addition to stew made from the pods of the *néré* tree. On market days many women would set up a small fire and deep fry fritters made from flour. Other women sold deep-fried peanut paste or peppery doughballs (often eaten with milk). The normal profits earned on market days (every three days), ranged from 700 to 1,000 CFA, but they were highly variable.

Differences among the villages shaped the market opportunities for women, and these are important for understanding the effects of the loan component of the project. Tingandogo women were borrowing considerably larger amounts than women in Nagreongo or Ipendo. Tingandogo also exhibited greater increases in membership, low drop-out, and larger loan sizes. (At the beginning of the program, membership in Tingandogo was at 36; it then increased to 42 members in the fourth cycle, and 60 by the sixth cycle). Many women consistently borrowed the maximum available. Ipendo, by contrast, saw high drop-out rates and small loan sizes. Nagreongo had limited change in membership and only saw larger loan sizes in the sixth cycle.

What features of the villages explain these broad patterns? Tingandogo was located only 12 kilometers south of Ouagadougou, on the main Burkina-Ghana axis. Traffic on the unpaved, dusty road was heavy. Thirsty, hungry travelers made frequent stops for meals and dolo. The entire area was densely settled. Many residents had family living in Ouagadougou. An irrigated plain near the village provided off-season employment. There could be no doubt the village was the more prosperous of the three.

Ipendo straddled a paved "highway" where cars and busses whizzed by without stopping; the village was very dispersed, separated into six quarters stretching over several miles. A large school and market area defined the village center. The actual market, however, was very small; women spoke of it as being saturated by small-scale vendors eking out tiny profits. One woman laughed when asked whether she might take a larger loan; she had been thinking of taking a smaller loan. "The market is completely full," she said. Another woman said there was not a lot of profit in expanding her activity, and she was nervous that if she took a larger loan she might not be able to repay. Asked why they did not make more soumbala, one group replied that the nearby village of Goudin was not known as "the village of soumbala" for nothing. Women there already produced more than local markets could handle; there was already too much that remained unsold.

Fifty kilometers to the east of Ouagadougou, on the paved road to Niger, the women of Nagreongo named their association Zoeyande, which translates roughly as, "having fear of shame." This accurately symbolized the cautious approach women had adopted when deciding how to use their loans in the light of an extraordinary market opportunity presented to the village. Ordinarily Nagreongo was a sleepy village. The local market was even smaller than that of Ipendo. The regional center of Ziniaré seemed far away. The land was unproductive. The fields of most families were far from the village, and people spent the rainy season in their fields, sometimes 15 kilometers from the village. Only a small irrigation project nearby offered dry season work. Because the women were Muslim they did not make dolo.

But in 1995 Nagreongo became a household word in Burkina Faso. About two years earlier, roughly the same time the program was beginning, a local woodcutter named Seydou Bikenga started making a name as a healer. Toward the beginning of 1995 his reputation exploded. The "miracle worker of Nagreongo" was enabling deaf-mutes to hear and speak, making paralytics walk, curing AIDS, boosting the fertility of childless women, and performing a thousand other small cures and miracles. Buses from all over Burkina started transporting the sick and hopeless to his encampment about seven kilometers from Nagreongo village. Wealthy patrons donated buildings to shelter the seriously ill; a Frenchman gave the healer a new Renault. The other traditional healers of the area, led by Seydou Bikenga, were holding meetings with local government officials and health workers. Local newspapers featured stories about Nagreongo—sometimes negative, implying that the village had become a center for contraband health products and merchants avoiding normal market taxes. Radio France International featured him on a regular broadcast. From Dakar to Bamako to Cotonou, people were coming to Nagreongo.

These massive flows of people created an instant demand for a large market; every day thousands of people needed to eat or buy condiments to prepare their meals. But women from Nagreongo were slow to respond, in general. While some young men worked so hard in the market they had not returned to the village in months, most women continued with their agricultural activities. The market was left to women from other villages, to market women from Ouagadougou, and to strangers.

Economic Impact of Loans

Women were quick to sing the praises of the program. "Before, I used to sell millet after harvest to get some money to start my commerce, but now I can keep the millet stored to feed the children," said one woman in Nagreongo. Others reported they had more money to pay school fees, buy meat or fish to improve sauces, or purchase new clothes for themselves and their children. Women from Ipendo recounted the story of how they feared that if they took loans they would be hauled off to Sabou jail for nonrepayment, but now they realized that they could use the money and easily repay.

Two facts lend weight to these positive assessments by participants. First, the scale of women's income-generating activity had increased for virtually all participants. On average borrowers had increased the scale of their activity by 80 percent. Roughly one-third of the respondents had more than doubled the scale of their activity. Second, many women were making significant investments in increasing or improving their productive capacity. In Tingandogo especially, women were making significant investments in *marmite* (heavy aluminum cooking pots) and *canari* (clay cooking pots). They were in the process of creating long-term ties with clients and merchants. They were establishing regular sites in Ouagadougou markets. They were improving their hangars (thatch shelters) and dolo cabarets in their local market.

Ouedraogo Lucie, the Tingandogo midwife and wife of the village administrator, was perhaps the premier, if somewhat exceptional, example of how the loan program was fundamentally altering local production. She had used her latest loan of 150,000 CFA to buy three large marmite—#55—at 50,000 CFA each. A six-year old child can fit comfortably inside a #55 marmite, just to give an idea of how big it is. Most village women think the largest possible marmite is #20 or #25; in Nagreongo women were only using #10 pots. Lucie's marmite were embedded in a clay oven, but she intended to replace it with cement her next loan cycle. She had already bought a sack of cement at the beginning of the loan program to build her hangar in the market. Innovating was not new to her; she had switched from making rice and selling on the side of the road about seven years ago, finding that dolo was less work. Lately she had started selling liquor. On a good day in the market she came home with 2,500–3,000 net of expenses; on a bad day she might have to give much of her dolo away and barely recover the costs of the germinated millet and firewood.

Women making soumbala in Tingandogo were well positioned to take advantage of the program. Nikiema Mariam was typical. She had increased her production from three plates to eight, in the rainy season, and in the dry season could sometimes make four to five *tiin* (a large container, equivalent to eight plates). She was buying a sack of néré (used in soumbala) at a time, up to 25,500 CFA. She tried to sell to other women vendors in Ouagadougou, rather than walk around the markets herself. She had been regularly buying canari, two to three a year at 1,000 each, and this year also replaced all of her filters, and bought several large metal basins for 2,500–3,000 each. She bought an improved metal stove and also had some men build a cement hearth. Tapsoba Mariam had similarly increased to producing three tiin of soumbala from slightly under one tiin. She went every day to the Dassassgho market in Ouagadougou to sell, and claimed to make between 500–1,000 per tiin.

An example of how women seized upon the extraordinary market opportunity in Nagreongo was the mother and daughter team of Tapsoba Mamounata and Diallo Rasmata. They ran "restaurants," selling rice and sauce. Rasmata had worked for months in the market of the *guerisseur,* making a 50-kilo sack of rice every two days. During the last month, however, the number of people coming to be healed had decreased, and more and more women were coming to sell as the agricultural season drew to a close, so she had moved back to the Nagreongo market. She now prepared three plates of rice every market day. Her mother prepared two plates every day, and both made sauces from cabbage, soumbala, boullion cubes, pepper, tomato paste, peanut butter, and occasionally meat. Both claimed to be able to sell, easily, their whole production and take home net of expenses roughly 2,500 per day. They had been making significant investments. Mamounata had hired men to build a hangar by the Ouaga road, paying about 4,000 for the material and labor. Her daughter Mamounata had bought serving plates, a large metal basin to hold the rice, benches, tables, and other material, spending close to 20,000. Mamounata seemed exactly the kind of woman a credit program should be encouraging; she had started making fried dough and cookies but switched to the restaurant when she saw she could make more money. The irony of this mother-daughter success story is that it was Rasmata who could or would not repay her loan, the cause of much consternation in the Zoeyande association.

There was a fairly strong correlation (.44) between working capital and profits per day involved in an activity. The increase in scale had a direct effect on returns per day's work because most women operated at excess capacity; they were usually constrained by their working capital, not their fixed capital. The typical village woman making dolo, soumbala, or germinated millet would have enough marmite and canari to expand production; what she would not have is enough cash on hand to pay for the néré or sorghum. Furthermore, for most of these activities expanding the scale would not increase labor time significantly: Stirring a half filled pot uses the same amount of time as stirring a full pot. Tending a fire for a small pot takes the same time as tending the fire under a large pot. While time spent in marketing extra production would necessarily increase, no women indicated they had less time available for child care or leisure.

The positive effects described above characterized most, but not all, program participants. Child care was, of course, a constraint on women's activities. Nikiema Blandine from Tingandogo, for instance, had always sold germinated millet. Since starting the program she had increased her sales from two tiin per week to four. She continued to buy the millet in the village market and sell to the village dolo makers, and she did not know if she could get better prices in Ouagadougou. The margin per tiin was only 250 CFA; she said this margin remained throughout high and low prices. The only tools she needed were canari, which she had previously purchased and had not needed to replace. She said she might start borrowing more, but with four small children she did not have the time to market the germinated millet.

Within villages there were numerous women who had changed little. Many women of Zoeyande in Nagreongo seemed to be pursuing the same activities they always undertook, not having changed their behavior because of the guerisseur, nor even having changed much with the loan program. They continued, by contrast with women in Ipendo and Tingandogo, to not specialize, instead spreading their time and capital across several activities carried out on a very small scale. They said they were too busy with agricultural work to do market activity. They said they needed bicycles to go to the market of the guerisseur. They said there was a problem of obtaining enough water to do soumbala on a larger scale. They said they were too old, or didn't have enough money.

Congo Mariam, for example, sold peppers and salt in the market, purchased rice to clean, and also stocked sorghum and millet. Her much younger co-wife Wangrawa Ami also processed foodstuffs for the market. Neither had ever gone to sell in the guerisseur market. Tapsoba Zoenabo borrowed 100,000 CFA and carried out several small activities: She bought a sack of sweet potatoes for 6,000, and boiled some for each market day. She bought two sacks of karité nuts (for about 6,000) to make butter later in the dry season. She had bought about 5,000 worth of millet to store. She made fritters in the marketplace twice a week, earning roughly 500 each time after expenses. Finally, she said that during the previous loan cycles she used to make soumbala, but stopped when the raw ingredients became too expensive. A second Tapsoba Zoenabo also divided her time and 10,000 loan between two activities, making fried groundnut paste and soumbala. She bought five plates of peanuts at a time, spending about 2,750, and claimed to have very little profit.

The cautious response illustrates the importance of risk. The possibility that the guerisseur market would be temporary, and its coinciding with the beginning of the rainy season, cautioned against making significant investments in securing a market position. In the beginning many preferred to plant; who could have known that the popularity would continue? Once planting was completed, the perceived costs of abandoning the fields for the market were much higher. The risk associated with home production is also still perceived to be high because of illnesses. Women are very concerned that if they, or someone in their household, falls ill they will be unable to continue their production and will not be able to repay the loan. They know stories like that of Kaboré Marie, who had an infected leg through two loan cycles and could not make or sell dolo; she had to sell her pigs and stocks of peanuts and left the program. The greater the loan taken and used in production, the greater the risk.

Caution and an unwillingness to invest substantial amounts in production are intimately linked to problems relating to the perceived size of markets.

The women of Tingandogo have a large urban market 12 kilometers away, they have steady road traffic willing to stop and make final purchases before arriving in Ouagadougou, and they have their own village market serving a relatively well-off district; their capacity to sell is virtually unlimited as long as their prices are competitive. The markets of Ipendo and Nagreongo, by contrast, are small. In Ipendo sorghum, millet, néré, and other products were purchased using small bowls to measure quantities of 50 to 100 CFA, rather than the larger measures. It was not unusual to find women speaking of buying 100 bowls of grain. Clearly the market was not used to bulk purchases or sales, such as would be permitted by loans of 100,000 CFA. Regional markets like Sabou and Ziniaré were saturated. Asked why not go to Sabou regional market, one woman replied with a sad tale: she had sent her son that very week to sell karité butter and he came back having sold only 50 CFA worth at the end of the day. There was little road traffic, though both were on main roads.

A vicious circle of high transport costs keeps markets less dense, while transport costs are high precisely because markets are not dense and there is too little traffic. Bicycles were commonly used in Tingandogo to ride to Ouagadougou, but in Ipendo their absence meant that women in general did not know how to ride, and found it frivolous to consider investing in a bicycle.

This problem of many villages having very small markets, and of many women in those villages being reluctant to take the risk of substantially increasing their scale, is very important when considering the possibilities for "deepening," for having the same number of borrowers returning higher interest payments that would eventually cover the costs of credit delivery and supervision. There is a need for careful financial calculations of the costs of servicing villages that are more isolated from large markets. These costs may then be compared with the costs of servicing larger villages, which would allow better planning for sustainable expansion.

Even before addressing these issues of "coordinated" interventions, the credit program, like many others, had another mystery. Only a handful of women used much more than 10,000 CFA for variable expenses (like Tapsoba Zoenabo above), but many were taking loans of 50,000 or 100,000 CFA. This pattern of taking large loans but only using a small portion of the loan as working capital continues even today, according to sources in the villages. Why? What were they doing with the remainder?

There are four possibilities. One is that because repayments commence immediately, women need to take large loans to preserve a smaller amount of working capital. For example, a 10,000 CFA loan, where the borrower will repay 12,000 over six months, enables the woman to work with an average of 8,000 the second month, and only 6,000 the third, and so on (assuming she has no other source of working capital). A 50,000 CFA loan would similarly translate into a working capital of 40,000 for the second month, 30,000 for the third, and so on. This is not quite the whole story, since women are also earning profits on the loans and can use those profits to maintain their working capital. If the woman could set aside 200 per market day, then on a 10,000 CFA loan she would be able to maintain her working capital intact and have the full amount at the end of the loan period. The program requirement of requiring continuous payment of principal over the loan period cannot explain the large size of loans relative to variable capital used.

A second possibility is that husbands were appropriating the extra funds for use on their own activities. The occasional woman did admit that she had given part of her loan to her husband or to a son. Sawadogo Zarata in Nagreongo was one. After questioning her about her making fritters, which used about 2,000 of her 100,000 CFA loan, she began saying that she stocked millet and groundnuts and karité, but then could only recall 3,000 or 4,000 in purchases. Finally she said that she had given the loan to her husband and son, both of whom sold clothing and shoes in all the local markets, including the guerisseur market. Ilboudo Habibou of Nagreongo also had a great deal of difficulty accounting for her 100,000 loan; after a lengthy discussion she said she had given the funds to her husband.

In general, men claimed to have no involvement whatsoever with the loan program. This claim may be reasonable given cultural norms about maintaining separate budgets. Suppose it were the case that husbands appropriated loans because they had profitable activities. One might ask, then, why women weren't using their loans for the same kinds of activities? Perhaps the reason was that women liked to keep their income separate, out of the control of the husband. But then why would they place themselves in such a disadvantageous position as letting their husband determine whether or not they could repay?

A third possibility for explaining the large size of loans is that both men and women have tremendous pressures to hold ready cash or "liquid" commodities like grain. Emergencies and market opportunities are ever-present possibilities, and short-term credit is unavailable. Households may view the 20 percent interest charge as a low price to pay for having a stock of cash on hand. They may be worried about a return to the high inflation that followed the devaluation of the CFA at the end of 1993, when prices increased at rates approaching 60 percent per year. Were inflation again to shoot up from its low rates, a family would want to be able to immediately acquire commodities that would be rising in value.

Finally, the fourth and related possibility is that women were realizing that it could be profitable to speculate on seasonal variations in the prices of grain, peanuts, dried beans, or other agricultural products. Recall the two Zoenabos from Nagreongo. One took a very small loan of 10,000, one a large loan of 100,000. When asked what she might do with 100,000, the second Zoenabo offered that she might buy a sack or two of produce to use a raw material slowly over time. Basically, she, and many other women, were using their loans to ensure themselves of supplies at current prices. The largest sums invested in commodities were around 60,000–80,000 CFA; more common was to find a woman stocking 20,000 CFA worth of produce. This investment in stocks certainly explains part of the discrepancy between the large loan sizes and small size of working capital requirements.

Most likely, a combination of all four reasons explains the large discrepancy between sums borrowed and used on income-generating activities. This remains an important issue to be resolved through careful research.

Responding to the Challenges

The challenges confronting the credit program had to do with recovering costs and avoiding default. On the one hand, the program needs to encourage larger loans by overcoming fears of high risk and by dealing with the problem that many villages simply do not have extensive market opportunities. On the other hand, the program must discover the uses to which larger loans are being put. If borrowers are stocking agricultural produce (millet, sorghum, groundnuts, etc.), then steps should be taken to diversify or mitigate that general program risk. Certainly sessions on enterprise planning could incorporate discussions of the risk of stocking agricultural commodities. Women stock because they are concerned about price increases; none seemed to think that the prices of the products they stocked could fall. Prices did fall, of course, especially for sharply seasonal products. A woman could easily lose much of the value of her stocks by incorrectly holding a commodity going through a price downturn. Finally, if extra cash were being set aside, then the provisions and mechanisms for borrowing emergency loans need to be made more accessible and "trustworthy" (in the sense that a woman is very confident that funds will always be available).

Several other strategies might address these issues. One thinks of placing a lower cap on lending of 50,000 CFA, and requiring a guarantee for larger loans (as is done for men when they borrow from a Caisse Populaire). Many women own large marmite, bicycles, plastic barrels, jewelry, and so forth, and they could probably be convinced that access to 100,000 CFA loans was worth the small risk of losing assets. Another possibility is to restructure solidarity groups according to loan size, so that larger borrowers are responsible for each other, and to strengthen the responsibility of these smaller groups. The alternative of continuing with group responsibility is risking that two or three large defaults (of 150,000 or 200,000 CFA loans) will throw the entire association into indefinite senescence.

In that regard, the goal of the program is that women collectively exercise restraint and sanction recalcitrant repayers and prevent loans to known default risks. But perhaps the degree to which women are reluctant to control fellow villagers was underestimated. It seems likely that associations will have to experience several defaults before they take positive steps to limit the amounts riskier borrowers can take. This transition period will require more active intervention by the animatrice to guide the association, and steps should be taken to plan for this eventuality.

More enterprise education and training is needed. At present only a handful of women in the three villages reported changing from one activity to another. None mentioned innovations in the preparation process. Change made most women nervous; only rarely does one encounter a woman claiming to have changed from making one product to another because there was more profit. An exception was a woman from Tingandogo who went to a friend in Ouagadougou, toward the end of the dry season and requested that she teach her how to make *coura-coura,* the fried groundnut paste. Then with her 50,000 CFA loan she bought a sack of peanuts for 19,000, a frying dish for 1,000, and a grinding stone for 1,000. She started selling the oil and coura-coura, making two tiin for each market day and earning roughly 3,000. She says she wanted to do coura-coura because she had many children (five, including one breast-feeding), and the big, hot fires needed for dolo or soumbala would be dangerous for them. The point is that she had to go learn how to make coura-coura; one should perhaps not underestimate the specialization of women's knowledge. Organizing workshops and hands-on training is expensive, but perhaps women's group funds could partially contribute to the costs.

Quantitative Impact Assessments

Qualitative evaluations are a good start, but at some point quantitative evaluations are necessary to measure impacts. The main problem in estimating the impact of a program is that participation in the credit program is usually endogenous (Ravallion 1999). The borrowers decide whether to enter the program and what their level of commitment will be. Imagine that the credit program was in fact completely ineffective in changing any outcome of interest. People knew this but joined nevertheless because the program offered a chance to converse on a weekly basis with city folk. For entrepreneurial and wealthy villagers, the chance to interact with the program staff was an opportunity not to be missed. The evaluator looks at the participants in the credit program. They are healthy, wealthy, and have high self-esteem. The nonparticipants are poor and embarrassed. The evaluator concludes that the program is a big success. "Look how much healthier the borrowers are," she proclaims. Of course, the health and esteem outcomes are spurious, not caused by the program at all. They are an artifact of the evaluators' blindness to the problem of self-selection.

More formally, an evaluator might estimate the demand by the household for a set of outcomes, such as good health and nutritious food, conditioned on program participation (as measured by the cumulative quantity borrowed, for example. The level of participation in the credit program is given by:

$$C_{ijt} = \beta_{ijt} + \pi X_{jt} + \beta \varepsilon_{ijt}.$$

The level of the outcome conditional on participation is:

$$Y_{ijt} = \gamma X_{ijt} + \sigma Z_{jt} + \theta C_{ijt} + \mu_{ijt},$$

where the C_{ijt} included in the second regression is the predicted level of participation in the credit program rather than the actual participation. The subscripts refer to values of the variables for individual or household i, in village j, at time t. The symbols β, π, γ, θ, and θ stand for the vectors of coefficients to be estimated, corresponding to the vectors of explanatory variables X and Z. The X variables might include household demographics (such as the presence of small children), initial household wealth, and ethnic status, while the Z variables may be village-level variables such as proximity to paved roads and the presence of schools and health clinics. The interest in estimating the two equations is in the coefficient θ, which captures the effect of the program on the outcomes of interest. Do people who borrow more, or who participate in the program, have better nourished children?

Again, the problem in estimating these equations is that factors that determine participation may also be related to program outcomes, but in a spurious way (errors across equations may be correlated). To give an example of spurious correlation of program participation with good outcomes, if placement of credit program were deliberate rather than random, then if placement were among the most poor, a comparison of program area outcomes effect with nonprogram area outcomes (the "control group") would be expected to underestimate the program effect. The program deliberately selected to locate in an area where success would be hardest. People who participated would not have good outcomes, but this would be the result of the selection.

One standard way to resolve this selection problem is to find a variable correlated with program credit but not correlated with determinants of outcomes. There are not many such variables. Anything that might affect participation in the program is more than likely to be correlated with characteristics of the person or setting that partially determines the outcomes observed. Many evaluators have turned to a second method for evaluating the effects of the program. This method takes advantage of the slow but deliberate spread of credit programs through regions. The slow geographic expansion means that some villages are outside the "borders" of the credit program, and can be used as "control" villages. Most regions where programs are expanding have, at any moment in time, five groups of persons: eligible participants in program villages; eligible nonparticipants in program villages; ineligible nonparticipants in program villages; potentially eligible participants in control villages; and potentially ineligible nonparticipants in control villages. The evaluator can then look at the differences over time in behaviors and outcomes for these five groups and use the resulting differences in differences (over time and among the groups) to identify more confidently the real effects of the credit program.

A landmark study of the Grameen Bank by Pitt and Khandker (1998) was one of the first widely cited examples of this analysis. They found that age and sex of household head were very significant in determining program participation and borrowing levels. Household status was very important in determining access and participation. A woman living in a household with a younger male head typically borrowed smaller amounts. Women without spouses or even other men in the household participated less often. Credit did have large effects. Pitt and Khandker estimated that a 100 taka increase in credit for women led to an 18 taka increase in household expenditure, while for male borrowers the 100 taka increase in loan size would be predicted to increase expenditures by only 11 taka. The credit program also had a large effect in increasing women's non-land assets. Male labor supply typically declined, suggesting that the income effect of credit may have been leading to increased leisure time rather than higher incomes. Finally, there was evidence that the microcredit program improved the schooling of children.

There are few impact studies available for African microcredit programs. Coleman and Cadalen (1998) studied a program sponsored by Catholic Relief Services in Burkina Faso, which had intended to establish village banks that would eventually become self-sufficient lenders not requiring outside funding. The idea was that as villagers saw their incomes increase, they would increase their savings in the form of deposit accounts in the village bank, which the bank could then use to lend to other villagers. The program projected that by the end of the project the banks would be virtually self-sufficient.

Coleman and Cadalen's evaluation was not so optimistic. They surveyed nine villages, seven of which had been involved in a credit program for some time, while two of the villages had recently been included in the program area. Villagers in the two "control" villages had already self-selected into the program, so the authors had two dimensions to use to control the correlates of self-selection. First, some villages had not yet received the program. Second, people in the control villages had self-selected to obtain the credit but had not yet obtained the credit. If the authors had been able ask respondents about the outcomes of interest before the credit program and then after the credit program, they would have had a third control to correctly estimate the effect of the program. Unfortunately, their limited budget and intent of the survey (as a post-project evaluation) precluded the before-and-after questions.

Coleman and Cadalen go a bit overboard on the impact on outcomes, measuring over fifty outcomes. Of course, there will be some probability then that, just by chance, the impact of the program will be significant. In fact, the authors find that the program had almost no impact on the outcome variables. Only five of the coefficients capturing the impact are significant at the 95 percent level. This seems remarkably low for one of the poorest countries in the world, where the need for credit is presumably high. Table 10.1 presents a few of their findings. Note that the one outcome that is very large and significant is the impact on women's savings. Women saved 26,000 CFA more when they had the credit program available. There were no other large effects, except on men's labor time. Men seemed to reduce their work time in response to the program. Perhaps the empowering of women had an unintended backlash effect, as men decided to work less

Table 10.1 Effect of Credit Program on Household Outcomes, Burkina Faso

	Estimated Impact		
Dependent Variable (Measured in FCFA Unless Otherwise Noted)	For All Treatment Villages	For Village Banks Current in Repayment	For Village Banks Delinquent in Repayment
Women's business assets	20520.2	25658.59	14407.91
	(0.166)	(0.197)	(0.458)
Women's savings	26009.75[a]	33331.12[a]	14198.71
	(0.004)	(0.001)	(0.164)
Women's non-village-bank debt	–22701.65	–21390.37	–21819.59
	(0.067)	(0.12)	(0.126)
Men's business hours	–35.62[a]	–39.58[a]	–43.63[a]
	(0.002)	(0.009)	(0.006)
Girl's health index (1,2,3,4)	0.05	0.08	0.02
	(0.841)	(0.758)	(0.956)
Boys' health index (1,2,3,4)	0.45	0.32	0.6
	(0.07)	(0.159)	(0.056)
N	362	239	209

Source: Reproduced from Coleman and Cadalen (1998, 41) Table C.
Notes: P-values are in parentheses. a. Indicates significance at .01.

hard for the well-being of the household. A more generous, but unlikely, interpretation is that men were spending somewhat more time at home while their wives profited from the credit opportunity.

Another interesting study by McIntosh (2002) evaluates a Ugandan microcredit program organized by FINCA, an international non-governmental organization. The program is directed exclusively towards women, and uses the group-lending organization of borrowers described above. At the time of the study, the program had some 25,000 clients. In early 2000, FINCA introduced two innovations into its credit program. The first gave borrowing groups more authority to control the terms of lending, in particular to change the length of the loan cycle and timing of repayments. Many groups wanted to switch from weekly to biweekly payment schedules. The second offered a health insurance package to the clients, but on condition that 60 percent of the clients in the borrowing group also enroll (to avoid having only very sick clients enrolling in the program). The health program was fairly expensive, at $15 per loan cycle. AIDS has exacerbated the already high morbidity and mortality rates in Uganda, though, so people might value health insurance and be willing to spend a considerable fraction of their incomes to obtain it.

McIntosh wanted to study the impacts of these innovations on borrowing and repayment behavior. The problem with running a simple regression to see whether participation in the new programs affected behavior is that participation is very clearly and deliberately endogenous. The strategy McIntosh adopted was to create artificial control groups by exploiting the geographical variability in the way the innovations were introduced. Table 10.2 shows the control groups. There were three geographic regions. In the first, groups were offered the possibility of changing the repayment schedules. In the second, groups were offered the health insurance program. In the third, neither innovation was offered. Within each geographic area, groups had to vote on whether to accept the innovations. McIntosh organized mock elections in the areas not receiving a particular innovation, in order to construct a sample of "choosers" even when the program was not actually offered. The hypothesis is whether the "treatment" of the innovation caused an improvement in the outcomes, and the nonchoosing population of groups can be used as control group to see how any geographic-specific effects (an outbreak of Ebola in the northern regions, for instance) may have affected group performance.

The outcomes studied are measures of group performance; the interest here was in how the innovations improved group performance, not on the impact of the innovations on client well-being. Some results are reproduced in Table 10.3. The columns report results for two different regression techniques. The outcome measures are new clients (the percentage of new clients to a group); dropout (the percentage of clients that dropped out of their group); savings (the average level of savings in the village bank); loans (the average loan size for the village bank); and grades (a measure of repayment performance and attendance at meetings). The coefficients reported indicate the effect of the program on group performance. For the innovation in repayment scheduling, McIntosh finds that dropout rates were significantly reduced, with no other impacts. Since reducing meetings to every other week, and also reducing dropouts, unambiguously lowers the

Table 10.2 Experimental Design for Impact Evaluation, Uganda

Program Implemented in Region	Choosers	Non-Choosers
Biweekly repayment program	Offered and accepted	Offered and unaccepted
Insurance program	Offered and accepted	Offered and unaccepted
Control	Unoffered and accepted	Unoffered and unaccepted

Source: McIntosh (2002, 9).

Table 10.3 Effects on Group Outcome of Participation in Program Innovation, Uganda

Innovation: Biweekly Repayment	Method 1	Method 2
New Clients	−2.7306	−2.8325
	(−0.8183)	(−0.8426)
Dropout	−6.9059[a]	−7.7971[a]
	(−1.9874)	(−2.2215)
Savings	1202.7	1188.3
	(0.4993)	(0.4847)
Loans	22.8	33
	(0.0194)	(0.0029)
Grades	0.1915	0.1904
	(1.6285)	(1.6094)
N	348	348
Innovation: Health Insurance		
New Clients	5.3226[b]	5.6981[b]
	(1.9261)	(2.0352)
Dropout	3.1809	3.2743
	(0.8152)	(0.8362)
Savings	−3176.2[a]	−3177.9[a]
	(−2.9703)	(−2.9748)
Loans	45.7	28.1
	(0.0337)	(0.0203)
Grades	−0.1106	−0.1105
	(−0.8754)	(−0.8711)
N	316	316

Source: Reproduced from McIntosh (2002, 21).
Notes: T-statistics are in parenthesis. a. Indicates significance at .05; b. indicates significance at .10.

program costs to FINCA, McIntosh concludes this was indeed a successful innovation. The health insurance program had more ambiguous effects. The number of new clients increased more rapidly in the treatment areas. New clients joined the program to take advantage of the insurance. Moreover, the savings rate of clients declined. Perhaps clients previously maintained cash savings in order to meet unforeseen medical expenses. With insurance, they no longer had to maintain their savings. The impact of the changes from the program point of view could be negative, especially if the sustainability of the insurance and savings programs are important goals. Given the rapid influx of new members more likely to be sick and take advantage of the insurance, the prospects for sustainability seemed less rosy.

Microcredit and microinsurance programs offer possibilities to target women, as the poorest of the poor, in ways that increase their incomes, strengthen their bargaining power within the home, and undermine discriminatory social norms. This possibility, however, is contingent on careful and flexible implementation. Flexibility, in turn, demands proper techniques of evaluation. The literature on the evaluation of women's microcredit projects is evolving rapidly, and new efforts are being made to construct, or even incorporate into program design, the monitoring of control groups. This enables a researcher to answer the question: What would have happened without the credit program?

11

New Directions

The possibility of the formation of gender blocs dividing all production units right in the middle should not be underestimated; in protest movements or rituals of reversal . . . such blocs manifest a strikingly physical reality.

—Mahir Saul

The mouth of a woman is her quiver.

—Mossi proverb

Gender structures sometimes change as a result of deliberate actions that people take in their capacities as citizens. The previous chapter discussed how outside donors use their financial wherewithal to transform gender structures. At the end of the day, these induced changes can only be a catalyst for reform that comes from within. Citizens, particularly women, have to assert their rights to equal treatment and often have to demand that governments fulfill their obligations to remedy past inequities.

One of the enduring tragedies of African polities is that so few of their political leaders accord the full status of citizenship to all persons within the territorial boundaries they administer. Too often, leaders have followed the colonial lead and treated whole categories of persons as subjects rather than as citizens. These leaders justify their exclusion with reference to the colonial era. They sometimes justify their exclusion with reference to the current practice of European countries, some of which continue to have restrictive nationality laws that effectively maintain hierarchies of citizenship. Women, like some ethnic groups, are also often treated as lower-class citizens.

As people struggle for their freedoms and rights they clash with entrenched interests. Movements to effectively enfranchise and empower women as citizens carry a double burden. Women as newly enfranchised citizens are likely to oppose dictatorial regimes, and women as empowered actors are likely to threaten their husbands and fathers. The same double burden was seen in the colonial era.

There are a wide variety of historical and contemporary cases illustrating how blocs of women emerged as important political actors, restructuring norms and laws that affected their lives (Dike 1995; Dorward 1983). Sometimes these movements have responded to specifically gendered structures perceived to be especially unfair to women, and sometimes they have protested against policies that were not specifically gendered.

Studying gender politics offers a new and rich field of analysis, yet very few statistical analyses are currently available. Anecdotes and case studies constitute the main empirical evidence by which theories are evaluated. There are classic issues of positive political economy that can be addressed in new ways with a focus on gender issues. Female voters, like other voting blocs, need to be mobilized to have high degrees of participation in elections, when their individual votes have only marginal effects. What are the mechanisms through which political entrepreneurs create gendered political movements? African polities are often described as "patrimonial," meaning that holders of power survive not through widely recognized and accepted legitimacy in the office but rather through distribution of resources from the office to select constituencies. The officeholder is the patron of his or her constituencies rather than a fiduciary for the public interest. Why then do women seem to rarely participate in this patronage politics, either as patrons or clients? Where is the "matronage" system of African politics? Finally, violence remains a widespread option as a means of acquiring political power. Again, though, women seem to rarely participate in violent social movements. Young men have dominated that domain of action.

Urgent Politics: The AIDS Crisis and Botswana

According to UNAIDS, the United Nations agency charged with coordinating the global response to HIV/AIDS, about 2.2 million men, women, and children died from AIDS in sub-Saharan Africa in 1999. More than 25 million people, more than 8 percent of the population, are currently living with HIV. There is great variability across the continent, with southern and central Africa being much harder hit than other areas. Women are more affected by HIV in Africa than in other parts of the world, with infection and death rates comparable or higher to those of men (Marcus 1993).

Sexual activity is not usually thought of as economic behavior, but the grave threat of transmission of diseases such as AIDS, and consequent economic costs for individuals and societies, has placed sexual practices at center stage in some debates about economic development in Africa. Biology makes for obvious common sexual practices: penises will be inserted into vaginas around the world. But the passive voice of that statement is already a clue to the enormous variety of sexual activity that may take place among humans. Does the *man* insert his penis into the woman's vagina, or does the *woman* insert his penis into her vagina? What sexual activities precede and follow insertion and withdrawal? How much sexual activity is produced by same-sex subcultures? How are the terms of trade negotiated between prostitutes and clients? As these questions suggest, sexuality is gendered, complex, and very much about political economy. There are several excellent treatments of this topic (Baylies and Bujra 2000; Kuate Defo 1998; Le Coeur and Khlat 2000; Renne 2001; Tuck 1994).

One of the ironies of the AIDS pandemic is that the highest rate of infection is in Botswana. As has been seen in practically every chapter in the book, Botswana stands out as a leading country in sub-Saharan Africa (Maipose and Matsheka 2000). Political leadership and institutions have been responsible and stable, a rarity on the continent. Both major political parties have had quotas of 30 percent female representation on their party lists standing for election, and 17 percent of parliamentarians are women, considerably higher than the continental average. A woman sat as a Supreme Court justice. It had the highest growth rate in GDP per capita on the continent. Most births take place in well-equipped clinics. Mortality rates are low. Girls typically have more schooling than boys. The female literacy rate has been higher than that of men. Botswana is one of the most urbanized countries on the continent. Women aged 15–24 are least likely to be married, compared with other countries. Polygyny has largely disappeared. A woman's age when giving her first birth has been well above the continental average.

Yet the adult HIV infection rate in Botswana is estimated to be 38.8 percent, higher than in any other African country, as can be seen in Figure 11.1. Life expectancy at birth is down to 44 years, from the high 60s. There are 69,000 orphans in a population of about 770,000 adults aged 15–49. That is about one orphan for every ten adults.

How did Botswana, so successful and progressive on gender relations compared with the rest of the continent, end up with such a high rate of infection and tremendous loss of life? And why with an infectious disease like AIDS, for which, as experts have long been warning, the subordinate status of women, unable to exercise control over their own sexuality, was a major factor in the spread of the epidemic?

The answer to this question, which is only now being asked, seems to come from a nightmarish alliance of two factors. The first is the structure of the Botswanan economy. The second has to do with the demographic implications of increasing gender equality and especially of self-ownership. About the first, not much can be done. There can be little doubt that the structure of the Botswanan economy contributed to the rapid spread of HIV in the country (Drimie 2002). Botswanan men work in mines, for long months of the year, and live in barrack-style dormitories. Sex workers are easily available on the outskirts of these mining towns. Cities in Botswana are also heavily male. Botswanan men also migrate to South Africa to pursue work. Finally, young men still go off on long cattle treks in the interior of the country. (The conditions are ripe for spread of sexually transmitted diseases and HIV.)

Figure 11.1 Percentage of Adult Population Infected with HIV/AIDS

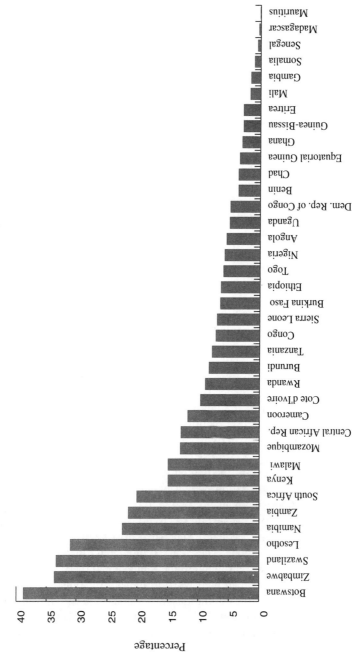

Source: U.N. AIDS website, http://www.unaids.org/en/resources/epidemiology.asp
Note: Adult population is defined as ages 15 to 49.

The second factor suggests more careful attention to new directions of political and legal change taking place on the continent, change that will be necessary to manage the growing pressures that arise as traditional structures of male control over the lives of women break down. Comaroff and Roberts (1977) noted some time ago a rapid evolution of marriage and cohabitation norms from the prewar period described by Schapera (1938), when extramarital births were rare and marriage was early. They argued that a tradition of polygyny continued to shape the attitudes of men toward marriage and that sequential relations with a succession of young women had replaced the simultaneous plural marriages of the past. Children resulting from these temporary unions joined the kinship group of their fathers if a marriage was perceived to have existed; if none existed, children remained in the agnatic unit of their mother, but the woman was entitled to compensation and child support.

Older women, left behind to manage a rural service economy and care for children, and financially supported by their absent husbands, have little incentive to restrict the sexual activity of their daughters, who increasingly become sexually active at early ages. The higher incomes that come with relative prosperity also generate leisure time, and a culture more oriented toward "young males." But because of the economic structure, young men are mostly unable to follow through on mutual desires for monogamous relationships, and so both men and women enter into multiple, serial, and sometimes simultaneous sexual relationships. Suggs (2002) offers a nuanced analysis of the masculinization of bars and alcohol consumption. A culture of machismo is emerging from the breakdown of the earlier culture of patriarchy and polygamy. Disturbing trends toward a greater incidence of sexual violence among relative strangers—rape—exacerbates the problem. These circumstances are ideal for the transmission of HIV.

The problem, in short, is that growing gender equality has produced a new set of social structures across the continent (May 2003). These structures may have their downside, and unfortunately HIV has come at the wrong time. Advocating a return to earlier gender structures is irresponsible, given that HIV has now compounded the changes that led in the first place to new, more equal structures. Botswanan society is left, then, with the task of creating new social institutions and policies to manage both the AIDS crisis and the behavioral patterns that make preventive action so difficult. New political directions must be found.

The Convention for the Elimination of Discrimination Against Women

One source of new direction comes from the Convention for the Elimination of Discrimination Against Women (CEDAW). The United Nations

General Assembly adopted CEDAW in December 1979, and the convention entered into force in September 1981, after it had been ratified by 20 states. As of early 2003, 172 states had ratified CEDAW.

CEDAW is an international treaty intended to guarantee rights for women and sets standards for women's rights in the political, cultural, economic, social, and family sectors. The convention delineates many forms of gender discrimination, from the obvious to the subtle, and calls for specific actions to remedy discrimination. CEDAW defines discrimination as: "[any] distinction, exclusion or restriction made on the basis of sex which has the effect or purpose of impairing or nullifying the recognition, enjoyment or exercise by women, irrespective of marital status, on the basis of equality between men and women, of human rights or fundamental freedoms in the political, economic, social, cultural, civil, or any other field." Articles 2–16 describe specific ways in which discrimination can and should be avoided in public, governmental, and family life. CEDAW establishes women's rights to reproduce, vote, hold public office, establish credit, enter into contracts, and be employed. Furthermore, CEDAW establishes women's rights to healthcare and education. CEDAW guarantees women's rights to retain nationality and the nationality of their children. Article 16 concerns rights in marriage, and establishes that women should have the "same rights [as men] entering into marriage . . . during marriage and at its dissolution." CEDAW calls for equality in the legal system and legislation as a basis for the end of discrimination. The convention also calls on states to take proactive measures outside of the domain of law to ensure redress for past discriminatory practices. Articles 17–22 of CEDAW provide for a limited enforcement mechanism. They established the UN Committee on the Elimination of Discrimination Against Women. The committee's task is to monitor the progress made on "legislative, judicial, administrative and other measures adopted to give effect to the provisions of the conventions." State performance is to be judged by the committee based on progress reports submitted the first year after ratification and then every four years. The UN-CEDAW committee is comprised of 23 experts on women's human rights and meets annually to discuss the state reports of that year and to make nonbinding recommendations on how CEDAW could be further implemented in particular states.

Article 29 of CEDAW is an optional suggestion that disputes that might arise concerning the convention be settled through arbitration by the International Court of Justice. However, this is nonbinding because reservations against it may be made at anytime. A new optional protocol developed by the committee in 1999 gives individual women the right to complain to the UN-CEDAW committee about abuses of their CEDAW rights.

As this brief summary of the major articles of the convention makes clear, CEDAW is part of a new generation of human rights treaties, in which, as Clark expressed it, "the obligations incumbent upon a state party are not reciprocal obligations owed to the other states parties but unilateral obligations owed to citizens of that state party" (1991, 287).

African states were early ratifiers of CEDAW. Figure 11.2 shows that states with predominant Muslim populations have been the slowest to adopt the convention and have the most nonadopters of CEDAW. These states see CEDAW as incompatible with their domestic law. Patterns of ratification for different groups of countries are even more skewed if the numerous reservations to the convention made by some ratifiers are taken into account (Clark 1991; Cook 1990; Jenefsky 1991). Article 28 of the convention states that reservations may be made at the time of ratification or accession. However, reservations that are "incompatible with the object and purpose of the convention" are prohibited. Of the 172 countries that have ratified the convention, 55 have done so with reservations to one or more of the articles, and the more serious reservations have mostly been from Muslim countries. The only African state among them was Niger. A cursory examination of the reservations of many of these states suggests that they are incompatible with the object and purpose of the convention. For example, Kuwait reserved the right to continue to exclude women from voting. Other ratifiers of the convention have objected to the reservations of these predominantly Muslim states.

There is some evidence that CEDAW has led states to take serious steps to implement provisions of the conventions. One of the more well-known

Figure 11.2 Ratification of CEDAW Treaty by Developing Countries

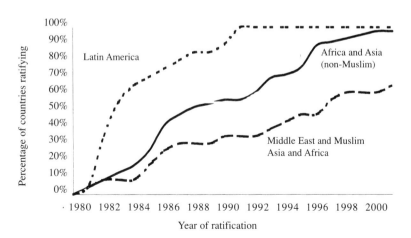

Source: CEDAW website

instances comes from Botswana, where a human rights attorney named Unity Dow challenged the Botswana nationality law. This law gave full citizenship status to children of a man married to a foreign woman, while denying citizenship status to children of a woman married to a foreign man. As in many other countries, children were deemed to take the nationality of their fathers, irrespective of the nationality of the mother or even location of their birth. The court opinions favoring Ms. Dow against the government cited CEDAW and the government's obligations to bring its domestic law into conformity with the international convention that it had signed and ratified. Ms. Dow went on to become a member of the High Court of Botswana.

Another well-known case had the Tanzanian High Court invalidating in 1990 customary law that prevented women from inheriting clan land from their fathers. The case is summarized on the International Labour Organization website (2002):

> Holaria Pastory brought a court challenge to the Haya customary law that prevented her from selling clan land. She had inherited land from her father, through his will, but when she tried to sell it her nephew applied to have the sale voided. Tanzania's Declaration of Customary Law clearly prohibited her sale of the land in section 20 of its rules of inheritance. Pastory argued that this constraint on women's property rights violated the Constitution. The court was faced with the difficulty of interpreting a constitutional guarantee of freedom from discrimination that did not make any specific reference to women. The court relied on the fact that the Tanzanian Government had ratified the Convention on the Elimination of All Forms of Discrimination Against Women (CEDAW), as well as other international treaties and covenants, to find that women were constitutionally protected from discrimination. The court stated that "the principles enunciated in the above named documents are a standard below which any civilised nation will be ashamed to fall." The High Court decided that the rules of inheritance in the Declaration of Customary Law were unconstitutional and contravened the international conventions which Tanzania had ratified. Thus, the rights and restrictions around the sale of clan land are the same for women and men.

One last example illustrates the scope of CEDAW to effect change. A gender activist, Sara Longwe, sued the Lusaka InterContinental Hotel. The hotel had a policy that unaccompanied women were not allowed onto its premises. The motive was to discourage prostitution. Ms. Longwe, however, saw the policy as being discriminatory: an unaccompanied woman was presumed guilty and denied entry into a "public space." Unfortunately, the Longwe case seems not to have been precedent-setting, for a new Lusaka High Court judge dismissed a similar case brought by Elizabeth Mwanza in 1997. She, too, was evicted from a hotel for being unaccompanied by a man. Sara Longwe argued in an open letter published in local newspapers that the judge had contravened CEDAW and given carte blanche to gender discrimination.

CEDAW has tremendous potential to serve as a template for structuring change in discriminatory laws. Women's associations across Africa are being trained and sensitized to the important political rights open to them under CEDAW. The coming years will see increasing efforts to ensure local judicial enforcement.

Women in National Politics

When judiciaries, operating in accordance with CEDAW, cannot bring about new political and legal institutions, elections might. A wave of democratization is sweeping much of the African continent. Whether these democracies turn out to be mere facades for autocratic rule is still unclear. But women are able to play an important role on the continent. One area of research is to determine whether women are likely to use their political voices to effect change. Unfortunately, little is known about gender patterns of voting in African elections. There is an active debate in the political science literature over how women in Western countries moved, over the post–World War II period, from being less likely to participate in politics and more conservative to being more likely to participate and more liberal.

One of the more interesting, and more hopeful, studies available is Wantchekon (2002). The author, a native of Benin, was able to use his connections there to convince presidential candidates Mathieu Kerekou and Nicephore Soglo to participate in an unusual experiment. Each candidate worked closely with a team of researchers to craft two campaign messages. One message emphasized how the candidate would bring jobs and pork barrel projects to the village. The other message emphasized the politician's role in ensuring national unity and national progress. So one set of messages was all about clientelism and patronage, while the other set of messages was all about honesty, integrity, and national interest above partisan interest. The experimenters then located villages at random, and campaigners went to those villages and delivered campaign messages, over the election cycle, that were either clientelistic or nationalistic. Wantchekon and his team then used exit polls to interview people about their voting behavior.

Table 11.1 presents the results of a regression analysis from the study explaining people's voting behavior. Each column reports the coefficients from a regression explaining whether a person voted for a particular candidate or not. If yes, the dependent variable is coded as one, if no, then the dependent variable is zero. So a positive coefficient means the variable led people to be more likely to vote for the particular candidate. The messages that the experimenters crafted were scored on an ascending scale, so that a

Table 11.1 Probit Analysis of Nationwide Vote for Kerekou and Soglo, Benin

	Kerekou	Soglo
Constant	−1.204[a]	−2.823[a]
	(0.33)	(0.51)
Sex	−0.426	0.58
	(0.27)	(0.40)
Age	−0.001	0.008
	(0.00)	(0.01)
Past	1.576[a]	1.591[a]
	(0.14)	(0.22)
Treatment	0.436[b]	1.062[a]
	(0.17)	(0.25)
Message	0.299[b]	0.779[b]
	(0.12)	(0.24)
Bariba	0.264	−1.001[b]
	(0.17)	(0.34)
Adja	−0.424[b]	−0.388
	(0.20)	(0.33)
Fon	−0.835[a]	0.825[b]
	(0.23)	(0.33)
Sex*Message	0.16	−0.692[b]
	(0.14)	(0.25)
N	1017	1017

Source: Reprinted with permission from Wantchekon (2002, 46), Table VI. Copyright by Leonard Wantchekon.

Notes: Bariba, Adja, and Fon are ethnic dummy variables. Past is a dummy variable indicating whether the respondent voted for the candidate in the previous 1996 election.

a. Indicates significance of 0.01. b. Indicates significance of 0.05.

more patronage-oriented message scored higher. People in general responded favorably to these narrow, self-interested messages. The coefficient on the variable "message" is positive and significant. But women behaved differently, in the case of voting for the national opposition candidate Soglo (Kerekou was the former dictator). If Soglo's message were more clientelistic, women were less likely to vote for him. The coefficient on the interaction term "Sex*Message" is negative and significant. If these results are generalizable, then the empowerment of women has hopeful implications for the future of democracy in sub-Saharan Africa.

Many elected regimes are already demonstrating the seriousness with which they consider women's votes, and more challenges may be inevitable following ratification of CEDAW. There has been a wave of reform of laws of inheritance, also known as laws of intestate succession.

Nevertheless, contradictions between customary and statutory laws regarding women's inheritance can be seen in many countries. In Zambia, statutory laws have been partial to women, but they are typically ignored in favor of customary laws that work against women's interests. When it comes to the inheritance of property, the patrilineal and matrilineal societies of Zambia privilege male agnatic ties over conjugal ties. Widows therefore are not eligible to inherit property and face an onslaught of "property grabbing" by their husbands' relatives. Munalula and Mwenda (1995) report that recent statutory laws provide legal protection to widows, either by allowing their husbands to make wills declaring the nature of his wives' inheritance, or through the Intestate Succession Act of 1989, which permits widows a 20 percent share of their husbands' property.

Fortmann and Nabane (1992) outline a similarly contentious legal environment that demonstrates the importance of pro-female advocacy in Zimbabwe. Many male Zimbabweans argue that in traditional tenure widows have "no right to inherit and are therefore without even the theoretical protection provided to divorcees by the Matrimonial Causes Act" (p. 5). The Zimbabwe Supreme Court upheld a version of customary law that did not recognize the right of a widow to be appointed as heir to her deceased husband's intestate estate. But other legal actors have taken a different view: "Community courts have with increasingly frequency appointed widows as the heir to their deceased husband's estate when he dies intestate" (p. 5). New national laws passed in the 1990s guaranteed that a daughter may inherit land, thus preventing the deceased husband's family from taking the land in cases where a widow had no sons. Another law allowed a grace period of one year before a husband's customary heirs could acquire his property, which gave a widow an opening to negotiate a settlement with her husband's relatives. In 1999, the Zimbabwe Supreme Court reversed the rights that women had gained to inherit property. They rejected a claim made by a daughter to the estate of her dead father, after her brother had evicted her. The judges opined that "the nature of African society relegates women to a lesser status, especially in the family. A woman should not be considered an adult but only a junior male" (Cloud 1999, 4). Much work remains to be done.

Appendix:
Tools for Analysis

This appendix contains brief introductions to three tools of analysis that are used implicitly and explicitly throughout the book: supply-and-demand analysis; game theory, the Nash equilibrium in particular; and regression analysis.

Supply-and-Demand Analysis

The supply-and-demand model for understanding markets is a basic tool of the social sciences. This model is useful for thinking about situations where large numbers of people are transacting some commodity or service. The model is very common in economics, where it is a staple of introductory courses. It is also used implicitly in many other disciplines. The phenomenon of globalization, much discussed today, is partly about the increasing spread of market transactions. Goods and services that were formerly allocated via nonmarket mechanisms are increasingly being allocated via market mechanisms. So understanding how markets function is an essential beginning for any discussion of structure in society.

Market structures thrive where people have individual property rights and are free to transfer those rights to people in return for a consideration. The usual supply-and-demand analysis asks how many exchanges or transactions are made in a given time period and at what terms. The most important term of the transaction is the price at which a piece of property, an asset, a good, or a service is exchanged. The model of supply and demand supposes that the price fluctuates until all the willing buyers, at that price, are buying from willing sellers, at that price. If the price were any other price, some willing buyers or sellers would not find anyone to transact with. That other price would not be an *equilibrium* price.

The concept of equilibrium in a social situation is an important element of supply-and-demand analysis. People interact in markets to pursue their interests, however broadly or narrowly defined. What is the outcome of their interactions? Just by using the phrase, "the outcome," we are already halfway to the concept of equilibrium. In real life, people interact continuously and simultaneously. The planet does not sleep at the same time, and neither do markets. Every moment there is an outcome of the interaction of people in markets. Which outcome is *the* outcome? The equilibrium approach to the outcomes is to suppose something like this: *the* outcome is a kind of average outcome of all the outcomes over a reasonably short time period, and is the outcome that people, again on average, actually think will be the outcome. I know the price of Japanese yen fluctuates by the second on foreign exchange markets. But when I travel to Japan, I have in my head an idea about how many yen I should get for a dollar. For me, the outcome of the foreign exchange market is the price. The market is in equilibrium when my reasonable expectations accord with the actual outcomes. The market is not in equilibrium when there is a large discrepancy between my reasonable expectations and what is happening. An equilibrium is a situation in which what people think is going to happen (according to the models they have in their heads about the way social interactions work) does happen. The models are validated. Suppose what happens is not what people had thought. Then, equilibrium reasoning goes, people might change their actions, expectations, and models. The state of disappointment ought not to persist, since people would change their behavior.

The reality of the world must be a continual process of learning and change, with some people satisfied and others disappointed. No social scientist believes that anything is really "in equilibrium" all of the time. But people do expect to go to work each morning, or to study, or to find coffee in the coffee shop, and that is what happens in many instances.

The idea of equilibrium in the supply-and-demand model can be illustrated with a graph, as in Figure A.1. The horizontal axis measures the quantity of the good or service being transacted, while the vertical axis measures the price. Suppose the good being transacted were home-brewed beer, a typical women's product in many countries. At different prices there would be different quantities supplied and demanded. The quantities may vary smoothly with the prices, in which case the behavior of people in the market can be represented by supply-and-demand curves (or lines). The demand curve represents how much beer consumers wish to purchase, at any given price. At high prices, potential beer consumers reduce their purchases, consuming less alcohol in general and substituting away from beer toward other, cheaper libations. At low prices, they want to buy large amounts of beer. The supply curve represents how much beer suppliers are willing to sell, at any given price. At high prices, beer brewers are willing to work long hours and supply lots of beer to the market. At low prices, beer brewers may find their time more valuable in other activities, and so many withdraw from the market. As drawn, there is only one price where the quantity supplied is equal to the quantity demanded. That is the equilibrium price of beer, p^*.

Figure A.1 Supply and Demand in Beer Market

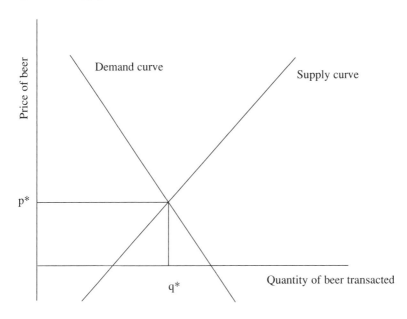

The idea that social states are in equilibrium enables us to apply one of the most powerful tools in the social sciences. This is the method of seeing how an equilibrium changes when the initial situation is altered in some way. Typically, analysis is restricted to simple changes, where the initial situation is altered along only one dimension. The idea is to see how an *exogenous* variable (the one changing) affects the other, *endogenous*, variable (the one changed). An exogenous variable is determined outside the model and is said to be *independent*. Endogenous variables are determined, according to the model, by exogenous variables. They are the *dependent* variables. This method is known in economics as the method of comparative statics and as the method of applying *ceteris paribus,* or "holding other factors constant."

In terms of our beer example, if exogenous weather desiccated sorghum seedlings so that there was little production, then women would have to pay a very high price for sorghum to germinate and brew into beer. Women would be willing to supply the same amount of beer only if the price of beer were higher. Alternatively, if the price of beer stayed the same, many women would withdraw from the beer market, leaving only the most efficient women still producing. The supply curve *shifts to the left,* as in Figure A.2. The new equilibrium price for beer would be *p**,* a higher price. Part of the increase in costs to the beer brewers is passed on to the beer customers. The price of beer is the endogenous variable, and its rise is explained by the change in exogenous weather. How much the price rises

Figure A.2 Supply and Demand in Beer Market After Weather Shock

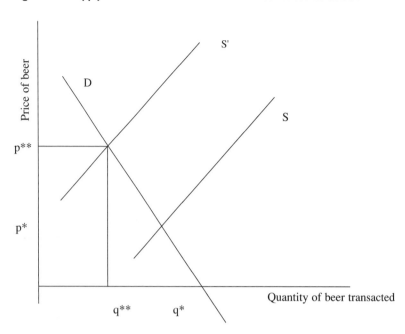

depends on the shift in the supply curve and the slopes of the supply-and-demand curves.

Supply-and-demand analysis is powerful because it focuses attention on how exogenous changes will affect producers and consumers in a market. For some goods and services, market participants will include virtually everyone in society. This is the case with labor markets and capital markets. The wage, the price of labor, is of obvious importance. The extent to which exogenous changes affect wage rates will depend, according to the model, on the slopes of supply-and-demand curves. The slopes themselves might change in response to exogenous changes. Some economists think that the globalization phenomenon of the 1990s involved the demand curve for labor in any particular country getting flatter (more *elastic*). Any exogenous policy change that mandated new employment conditions, such as tighter occupational safety regulations, would then reduce employment without improving wage rates. The costs of the mandates are borne by the laborers rather than by the employers.

In the real world many variables change at the same time, and one rarely has an opportunity to observe instances of ceteris paribus. In the analysis of government policy one might assume that only one variable, the policy, will change. However, even here a problem arises, because changes in government policy might be caused by other forces. They are themselves endogenous. For example, suppose an African government changes divorce laws to make divorce easier for women. After the implementation of the new laws, fewer women get married in the "marriage market." Did the divorce law somehow cause the decrease in marriage rates, or did legislators change the laws in recognition or anticipation of a social phenomenon that was already leading to a decline in marriage? Causality is difficult to determine when a purported causal factor may itself have been caused by another factor through a related process.

The Concept of a Nash Equilibrium

Many economic settings are characterized by anonymous and atomistic interaction, as in the supply-and-demand model, where individual actions have a negligible effect on the economic environment. Other settings are strategic settings, where the action one takes is influenced by and in turn influences the actions of others. Everyone is familiar intuitively with these types of settings. As in chess, one finds oneself thinking, "If I do this, then she will do that, but if she thinks I will do that, she might do something else altogether, and besides, what do I think she will think that I will think . . ." The theory of how to analyze these settings is game theory, and strategic thinking is the essence of game-theoretic situations.

Nash (1951) developed an influential equilibrium concept for analyzing these types of settings. He proposed that when each person's strategy was his best strategy, given his expectations of everyone else's strategy, and when each person's expectation of the other's best strategy was indeed that person's best strategy, then no one would want to change his strategy, and so the set of strategies having this property would be the equilibrium of the game. No other strategies would be the outcome because by definition those other strategies would not be best responses to others' best strategies.

An example should help clarify the concept. Figure A.3 describes the payoffs to men and women in a situation of conflict. Perhaps the men and women are deciding on a rule over how labor is allocated or crops divided. Men and women have to decide whether to fight angrily at the meeting or to come in a cooperative mood. When they fight, they waste energy on loud, angry meetings, which keeps them from working. People get all worked up, hoping that their anger might intimidate the other side. Of course, if the other side is conciliatory and ready to cooperate, they might give in more speedily when faced with an angry crowd. The payoffs from the interactions of men and women are as indicated in the table. The numbers represent the total value to men and women from the various outcomes. If women choose to fight and men to cooperate, then the women get

Figure A.3 Fight or Cooperate? Prisoner's Dilemma

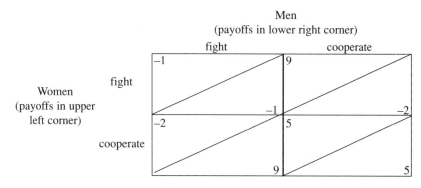

9 and the men get –2. If the situation is reversed, with women cooperating and men fighting, then the women get –2 and the men get 9.

What is the Nash equilibrium? Consider men and women in turn. If the men think the women are going to cooperate, then the men should fight and get 9. If the men think the women are going to fight, the men should fight, too, and get –1 instead of –2. So the men should fight no matter what they think the women will do. The same logic applies to the women, and so the Nash equilibrium has both of them fighting. Of course, they are then both made worse off; joint cooperation is the better outcome. Both women and men cooperating maximizes total surplus. They do not waste their time and energy being angry. However, neither side can credibly commit to cooperate. Perhaps there is no mechanism in local society that can enforce a promise not to fight. If one side cooperates, the other will grab all of the benefits from cooperation.

Suppose the game is repeated over time. Every year the same game is played from here to eternity. What should men do? Fight, or cooperate? Now the game is more interesting, and there is the possibility of a self-enforcing good equilibrium, where both cooperate. Why? Because a Nash equilibrium could be sustained by each having a strategy of cooperating as long as the other side also cooperates, and fighting for the rest of time if the other side fights. If the other side has this strategy, then it may be in the interest of the first to also abide by the strategy. Not necessarily, though. Each side will weigh the benefits of "cheating" against the costs of living for the remainder of the time in the fight-fight equilibrium.

Consider another version of the game, in Figure A.4, with slightly different numbers. Now there are two possible equilibria. If the men think the women are going to concede, they should fight, and if the women think the men are going to fight, they will indeed concede. The reverse also holds. There is no way to know which equilibrium will hold in practice. When this game is repeated over time, the optimal strategies for the parties may be somewhat different. One way to think about this is to suppose that what people have are strategies about when to concede. That is, about when to stop fighting and begin cooperating. In this strategy, they fight up to a certain point in time, at which point, even if the other party has not conceded, they cooperate. Suppose men had reputations of being always and everywhere willing to fight. Women should then cooperate immediately. Suppose women had reputations of being always and everywhere willing to fight. Men, then, should cooperate immediately. Now suppose women in society were not sure what the men were like: they thought there was a 90 percent chance that men were the kind who would cooperate and only a 10 percent chance that they would fight. Now, the correct strategy for women might be to fight for a specific number of periods, say three, and then either concede or continue fighting. After three periods, say, where the men fought every period instead of cooperating, the chances that the men really were the fighting "type" increase. It no longer pays to keep fighting them and sustaining losses. Of course, the men have similar problems with assessing the real nature of women's character and deciding how many periods to fight.

This kind of repeated game and equilibrium is very interesting because it illustrates how it is possible to model a difficult real-world problem in which people fight for a finite period of time and then cooperate, without there having been any change in the underlying game. This accords well with the intuition about "wars of attrition." Some wars and conflicts suddenly end on terms remarkably similar to terms that were proposed many periods earlier (Alesina and Drazen 1991; Bulow and Klemperer 1999; Haccou and Glaizot 2002). Why were so many resources and opportunities wasted? Presumably, something like the war of attrition was going on.

A Model of Collusion

This section develops a simple model that shows how collusive behavior by men may be sustained as a Nash equilibrium. The model draws on the theory of cartels, such as the Organization of Petroleum Exporting Countries

Figure A.4 Fight or Concede? War of Attrition

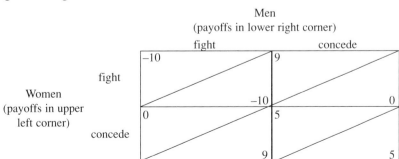

(OPEC). This theory raises the question as to how a cartel survives when each cartel member has an interest in cheating. Models of cartels suggest that a cartel may survive when the short-term benefit from cheating on the cartel may be less than the longer-term benefits from abiding by the cartel rules. In the model developed here, the long-term benefit of obtaining the labor of the wife at a lowered wage outweighs the short-term advantage of hiring more labor at the low wage. The model draws on a fairly large literature on how village labor markets work and how discriminatory collusion can be sustained (Akerlof 1980; Bardhan 1979; Osmani 1990). The intuition captured by the model is expressed by Bassett, writing about cotton cultivation in Côte d'Ivoire:

> One man told a story that spoke to the origins of these gender struggles taking place at the cotton market. He said that one day during the 1993/1994 market period, he was at the market selling his wife's cotton. When his turn came to weigh and load her cotton, a number of men spoke up and said that their wives were not growing cotton so they were not going to help him lift his wife's bales onto the scale and load them into the truck. They departed from the marketplace. This left the remaining men in the socially awkward position of being viewed by other men as "working for their wives." My informant expressed his discomfort at being publicly humiliated for not behaving in ways that conformed to ideals of male dominance and power. . . . Like other men in the village, he too feared that if his wives gained some economic autonomy they would not longer respect him and refuse to work in household fields. After this incident, the men who had been assisting their wives decided that they would no longer support their efforts to grow cotton. (2002, 365)

Consider a local village economy composed of M pairs of men and women, and suppose that husbands and wives have access to production functions that are quadratic in the labor applied:

$$F(l) = K^i l - l^2$$

where K^i, $i = (m,f)$ for the husband (male) and wife (female), represents the different endowments of productive resources, or capital, or "access to activities." So more labor raises production according to how big K is, but then the squared term gets bigger and the laborers are getting in each other's way and production no longer increases. As the Wolof proverb has it, "Ten digging, ten filling—lots of dust, no hole." Husbands are assumed to have more capital, $K^m > K^f$, and the endowments are assumed to be non-tradeable (only men can "own" land, only women can make sorghum beer).

If the M husbands and the M wives in the local economy are free to trade labor (but not capital) in a competitive market, the market equilibrium will have the more productive husbands hiring the wives. The husband's demand for labor is found as the solution to the following maximization problem:

$$max \ F(T + l^d) - wl^d$$
$$l^d,$$

which yields a demand for labor, $l^d(w)$, that depends on the wage, the husband's capital, and the time, T, available to the husband to work on his fields (this time is assumed to be fixed):

$$l^d(w) = 1/2(K^m - 2T - w).$$

Similarly, the wife chooses how much labor to supply to the labor market at the prevailing wage:

$$max \ F(T - l^s) + wl^s$$
$$l^s,$$

which yields a supply of labor, $l^s(w)$, that also depends on the wage:

$$l^s(w) = 1/2(2T + w - K^f).$$

In a competitive equilibrium the wage adjusts so that the total supply of labor Ml^s equals the total demand for labor Ml^d, and so the competitive wage will be:

$$w^c = 1/2(K^m + K^f - 4T).$$

What happens when the husbands have a norm that they do not hire each other's wives? In this case, if a husband abides by the norm and if his wife indeed cannot find employment outside the home, he is in a position to obtain her labor at a much lower wage. He is a "monopsonist." Specifically, the husband takes his wife's supply of labor function as given and chooses a wage that maximizes his return (of course, he cannot hire any other labor, since he is abiding by the norm):

$$max \ K^m(T + l^s(w)) - (T + l^s(w))^2 - wl^s(w)$$
$$w.$$

This yields an optimal wage to offer the wife:

$$w^m = 1/3(K^m + 2K^f - 6T),$$

While $w^m < w^c$, the husband cannot hire as much labor at this lower wage, so we need to check that his profits are higher, that he prefers this monopsonistic position to the competitive situation. We compare then the profits in the two situations:

$$
\begin{aligned}
\pi^c &= K^m(T + l^d(w^c)) - (T + l^d(w^c))^2 - w^c l^d(w^c) \\
&= K^m(T + 1/2(K^m - 2T - 1/2(K^m + K^f - 4T)) - (T + 1/2(K^m - 2T - \\
&\quad 1/2(K^m + K^f - 4T))^2 - w^c(1/2(K^m - 2T - 1/2(K^m + K^f - 4T)) \\
&= K^m(T + K^m/4 - K^f/4) - (T + K^m/4 - K^f/4)^2 - w^c(K^m/4 - K^f/4).
\end{aligned}
$$

And if we let $X = K^m - K^f$, we have,

$$
\pi^c = K^m(T + X/4) - (T + X/4)^2 - w^c(X/4).
$$

Similarly,

$$
\begin{aligned}
\pi^m &= K^m(T + l^s(w^m)) - (T + l^s(w^m))^2 - w^m l^s(w^m) \\
&= K^m(T + X/6) - (T + X/6)^2 - w^m(X/6).
\end{aligned}
$$

After manipulation we find:

$$
\pi^m - \pi^c = (3/144)X^2 > 0.
$$

The more productive the husband's capital, the greater the benefit from colluding. (He may be able to make even more money by exploiting his wife if he makes a "take it or leave it" offer that specifies the amount of time she has to work for him, rather than letting her decide based on the offered wage rate.)

While the husband benefits from being the only buyer of his wife's labor, he may be tempted to cheat on the norm by offering to hire other women at a wage just a bit higher than the low wage *their* husbands offer them. He can then hire a lot of labor at a low wage and earn a large return on his production. Of course, this has to be weighed against the foregone profits in future periods, when the other husbands "retaliate" against his cheating by offering their wives the competitive wage. To see whether these short-term benefits are greater than abiding by the norm, the profits from hiring as many laborers as he pleases must be calculated. We assume that he can hire them at exactly the same monopsony wage. (He would have to offer a slightly higher wage, but since the women know that if they *do* work for an employer not their husband then the collusive equilibrium will be broken, they will be happy to work for another man at the same wage their husband paid them.) To find the value of that benefit we first note that the "cheating" husband hires N women to solve the problem:

$$max \; K^m(T + Nl^s(w^m)) - (T + Nl^s(w^m))^2 - wNl^s(w^m)$$
$$N.$$

The value of N that solves this problem is given by:

$$N^* = (K^m - w^m - 2T)/(2l^s).$$

Substituting this into the expression for total profits we find:

$$\pi^{m,cheating} = K^m(T + N^*l^s(w^m)) - (T + N^*l^s(w^m))^2 - w^mN^*l^s(w^m)$$
$$= K^m(T + X/3) - (T+X/3)^2 - w^m(X/3).$$

It should be noted that:

$$\pi^{m,cheating} - \pi^m = (1/36)X^2.$$

Now the husband discounts the profits from an infinite number of future periods by a discount factor σ. This discount factor is a fraction. If it were 0.9, that would mean that a dollar received in the next period was worth $0.90 received today. The higher the discount factor, the more a person is willing to be patient and receive income in the future rather than in the present. A husband will prefer to abide by the norm if:

$$\pi^m + \sigma\pi^m + \sigma^2\pi^m + \; ..... \; > \pi^{m,cheating} + \sigma\pi^c + \sigma^2\pi^c + \; ....$$

or,

$$1/(1 - \sigma)\pi^m > \pi^{m,cheating} + \sigma/(1 - \sigma)\pi^c.$$

This may be rewritten as:

$$\sigma/(1 - \sigma) > (\pi^{m,cheating} - \pi^m)/(\pi^m - \pi^c) = 4/3.$$

or,

$$\sigma > 4/7,$$

which seems reasonable, even for an agrarian economy where the future is regarded with unease. The bottom line is that men could sustain collusive norms that prevent their wives from realizing the full value of their labor in the marketplace.

Collusion need not be the only explanation for occupational segregation. One fascinating theoretical paper by Francois (1996) argues that occupational segregation by gender could occur as a Nash equilibrium. The gendered outcomes in industrial economies emerge as a pattern of uncoordinated behavior generated by shared expectations rather than as the result of collusion. In the model, production takes place under two different processes. One process requires motivation because worker effort and care cannot be monitored; the other process is easily monitored. The work force of the first process is motivated when the wage is at a premium; then workers will work hard for fear of being fired and having to return to the low wages paid to workers on the other process. Francois notes that the premium to workers in the first process could be partially composed of extra bargaining power within the household. When one member has a premium-earning job and the other does not, the first member is in a better bargaining position. The consequences of this, if recognized by employers, follow immediately. If employers know that other employers only hire men for premium-paying jobs, then they also will only hire men. If they hired a woman, chances would be high that her husband would also have a premium-earning job, and so her premium would be "nullified"—her husband would be able to match her bargaining position. The equilibrium is arbitrary in the sense that another equilibrium with all employers hiring women rather than men also exists.

These illustrations of strategic situations suggest some of the richness and importance of this area of study for the economics of gender. One can think of objections to the Nash equilibrium approach, however, especially when thinking of applying it to the real world. Perhaps people do not know much about the other people playing and so have no ability to know what their best strategy is. Perhaps people do not have the mental capacity to actually compute best strategies. Perhaps people have an inherent dislike for strategizing in this way. Perhaps strategies in this period depend on strategies that are expected in future periods and so extend down through infinity and may not be calculable. Also, there is no guarantee to the analyst that every strategic situation has a Nash equilibrium. Moreover, many plausible situations will have more than one Nash equilibrium.

Data Indicating Discrimination?

Suppose that a researcher has measured the hourly wage rates earned by men and women working in urban Lusaka. On computing the average wage rates for the entire sample, the researcher notices that the rates for women are only half the rates for men. She immediately reports this finding to the local newspaper, which promptly runs the screaming headline: "Discrimination Against Women in Lusaka Labor Markets!" The article recounts several anecdotes of women working in the same company receiving lower wages than men and then suggests the statistical evidence confirms the presence of discrimination. Does it?

Regression analysis is one of the social sciences' most important tools for answering this and other basic questions. The problem with the researcher's interpretation should be readily apparent. She may have jumped the gun in her eagerness to confirm her gut feeling that employers discriminated against women. She neglected to consider that the reason for the disparity in wages might be due to disparities in qualifications and experience rather than discrimination. Consider, for example, the simple possibility that discrimination did exist in the past but has disappeared in recent years. Older workers, with more experience and seniority, are all men, and younger workers are evenly divided between men and women, earning comparable wages. The researcher's sample, however, contains a mix of older and younger women, so that men, on average, appear to earn higher wages. Only the older men do, in fact.

Regression Analysis as Cross-tabulation

"Regression analysis" is the term used to encompass a variety of statistical techniques used to analyze and explain variation in some outcomes. Basically, the techniques are more sophisticated ways to construct cross-tabulations. A "crosstab" is a table where the average of some outcome variable is computed separately for different groups. The groups are typically assumed to be exogenous. So, for instance, a crosstab might show the average growth rates of GDP per capita for African countries and non-African countries, further categorized by whether the states are legitimate or not (determined by some measure of the continuity of precolonial rule). The crosstab might show that legitimate African countries had rates of economic growth just as high as legitimate states elsewhere and that illegitimate states everywhere had lower rates of growth. This might be strong evidence that legitimacy of the state mattered for economic growth. In the wage rate case, the relevant crosstab would have average wage rates computed for younger men and women and older men and women. The table would have four cells, with the cell for older women perhaps empty because there are no observations. The crosstab might make clear that the wages of older men were higher than the wages of younger workers, and that the wages of young men and women were roughly even. The crosstab might show no evidence of discrimination.

A crosstab *controls for* a factor (age or experience in the labor force) that might explain some outcome (the wage rate). A regression, generally speaking, is a technique for controlling for certain factors when explaining the correlation between another factor and some outcome. In testing the proposition that men earn more than women, the age or experience of men in the sample of workers needs to be controlled for. The essence of the regression method is to posit a linear relationship between the explanatory variables and the outcome variable and then calculate the "partial" correlations between each variable of interest and the outcome variable. These partial correlations are known as the regression coefficients, and they tell us how much a change in one variable, holding constant the other variables, changes the outcome variable (the ceteris paribus assumption of much economic reasoning).

The workhorse method for calculating these coefficients is known as the method of ordinary least squares (OLS). The OLS method is to choose values for the regression coefficients that minimize the sum of squared deviations between the actual outcome variable and the outcome predicted by the chosen regression coefficients. Suppose the relationship between some explanatory variables X_1, X_2, X_3 and X_4, and a dependent variable Y were assumed to be linear. Every observation constitutes a set of Xs and a Y for each country or worker, to continue the examples above. Every observation, moreover, is assumed to be observed or recorded with some small error. Imagine an "error term," ε_i, that captures the deviation of the observation from what would have been predicted. This error term is assumed to be random. For every observation, then, the following relationship holds:

$$Y_i = \beta_0 + \beta_1 X_{1i} + \beta_2 X_{2i} + \beta_3 X_{3i} + \beta_4 X_{4i} + \varepsilon_i.$$

The OLS method involves selecting values for the coefficients (β_0 to β_4) that minimize the following expression:

$$\Sigma(Y_i - \beta_0 - \beta_1 X_{1i} - \beta_2 X_{2i} - \beta_3 X_{3i} - \beta_4 X_{4i})^2,$$

the sum of the squared deviations.

Suppose there were just one explanatory variable. Figure A.5 illustrates the scatter of points that are observed in the data. Each point represents an observation, such as country or worker, and the levels of X and Y associated with that observation. These might be wage rate and age of a worker, or the legitimacy of the state and the growth rate of GDP for that state. The figure gives a possible candidate line that fits those points. Is this line the best fit? One criterion for determining the best fit is the least squares criterion. The line should minimize the sum of squared deviations of the actual value of Y from that predicted by the regression line. That deviation is also known as the residual, so the method of least squares minimizes the sum of squared residuals.

Fortunately for the student, any computer can now estimate a regression line using either statistical software or spreadsheet software such as Excel or Quattro Pro. The data is entered in columns, with one column for each variable. Each row is an observation (e.g., a worker or country). The

Figure A.5 Data and Example of Fitted Line and Residual Error

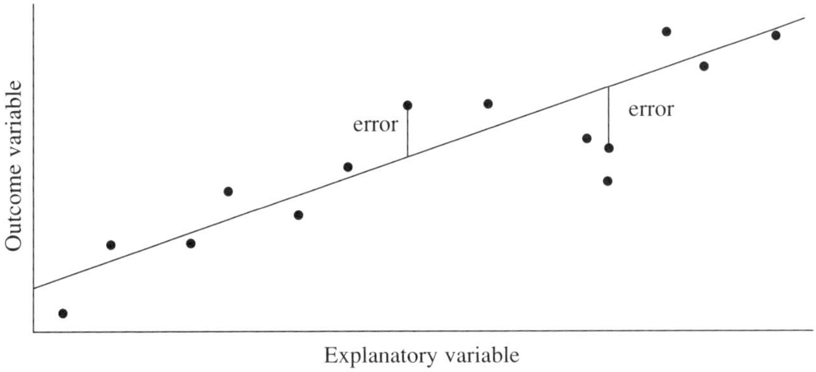

software produces the estimated values of the coefficients for each X that minimizes the sum of squared residuals. Informally, this is called "running" a regression, as in "I just ran a million regressions!" The first coefficient, β_0, is sometimes called the *constant term* or *intercept term,* and is not usually of interest. The other coefficients are the partial correlations, and are usually called the *slope coefficients,* or sometimes the *estimated coefficients.* The coefficients are interpretable as partial derivatives, indicating how much one variable changes when another variable changes. These partial derivatives have a special symbol, ∂, that is found every so often in this book. The expression $\partial W/\partial X$ stands for "how much W changes when X changes by one unit." This is the estimated coefficient in a regression with W as the dependent variable and X as an independent variable.

Regression output also includes a *t-statistic* (or z-statistic) reported for each estimated coefficient, which can be used as an indicator of statistical confidence in the estimate of the coefficient. The general rule of thumb is that for an estimate to be worth talking about, the t-statistic should be greater than 1.96 in absolute value. The reason we need a t-statistic is simple. The regression method will of necessity produce an estimate of every coefficient. But some of these estimates will basically be arbitrary, since there might be very little variation in the explanatory variable. For example, if we wanted to explain the frequency of indigestion in a population and included the number of eggs eaten per day, the regression software will generate an estimate of the coefficient. But this coefficient is likely to be meaningless. We are pretty sure that nobody in our sample eats enough eggs to get indigestion (at least compared with other sources of stomach indigestion). There is just not much variation in egg eating (presumably because people refrain from eating too many eggs!). The t-statistic will not be greater than 1.96 in absolute value, and we can ignore the estimated coefficient.

The t-statistic for a coefficient will also depend on the overall explanatory power of the regression, and this is conventionally measured by the R^2 statistic. This statistic indicates the fraction of the overall variation in the outcome variable that is explained by the variables included in the regression. The R^2 statistic varies from a low of zero to a high of one. The better the regression overall, the more confidence one can have that the estimated coefficient on a particular variable is indeed worth considering. There is no rule of thumb about how high the R^2 statistic should be. In time series data, where the observations are for different years or months, it is very common to have R^2 statistics above .90. For cross-sectional data, such as samples of households, the R^2 statistic may be as low as .05 and the regression still considered informative.

Two special kinds of variables may be included in regression analyses and are often the most important variables of concern to social scientists. One kind of variable is known as a *dummy variable*. This is a variable that takes on values of zero or one, according to some criterion. Zero could stand for men and one for women. Zero could stand for urban and one for rural. Combinations of dummy variables could represent more complex categories. A first dummy variable could take on value one for urban men and zero otherwise. A second could take value one for urban women and zero otherwise. A third dummy variable could take on value one for rural men and zero otherwise.

There is no need to include a fourth dummy variable for rural women in the regression. Indeed, including such a fourth variable would make it impossible to compute the regression coefficients. The four dummy variables together perfectly explain the variation in wage rates. The deviations of observed outcomes from the predicted outcomes will add up to exactly zero if the coefficients on the dummy variables are simply the mean values of the outcome for those categories and the coefficients for other variables are zero. So the rule is to omit one of the dummy variables when these are grouping the data into different categories.

The regression coefficient estimated for a dummy variable may be interpreted as the difference between the expected value of an observation in that category and the expected value of an observation from the excluded or omitted category, when other effects from other variables are controlled for. Returning to the example of wage rates and possible discrimination, it should now be clear that the coefficient of interest in a regression equation explaining variation in wage rates is the coefficient on a gender dummy variable.

The other special kind of variable is a composite variable created by multiplying one variable by a dummy variable. This is known as an *interacted variable*, and the coefficient measures how the partial correlation between the outcome and the continuous explanatory variable differs from one category to another. The categories are captured by the dummy variable. So, for instance, a regression equation may be:

$$Y_i = \beta_0 + \beta_1 X_{1i} + \beta_2 X_{2i} + \beta_3 D_i + \beta_4 D_i X_{2i} + \varepsilon_i.$$

Now, β_2 measures the effect of X_2 on Y for observations that fall into the zero category of the dummy variable, while $\beta_2 + \beta_4$ measures the effect of X_2 on Y for observations that fall into the other category of the dummy variable. In explaining differing wage rates, interaction terms could help control for possibly differing returns to age and experience for men and for women.

The usefulness of the regression analysis approach can be further illustrated with a more concrete example of the comparison between the wages earned by men and those earned by women. Two equations might be estimated, one for each gender:

$$w_m = \beta_{m0} + \beta_{m1} E_m + \beta_{m2} E_m^2 + \beta_{m3} S_m + \beta_{m4} X_m + \beta_{m5} O_m + \varepsilon_m$$
$$w_f = \beta_{f0} + \beta_{f1} E_f + \beta_{f2} E_f^2 + \beta_{f3} S_f + \beta_{f4} X_f + \beta_{f5} O_f + \varepsilon_f,$$

where w_m and w_f are the wages of individual mean and women, E is years of experience, S is years of schooling, X are individual characteristics, O is a set of dummy variables for occupational categories, and ε is a random error term, for males and females. The difference between the average wages of men and the average wages of women can now be decomposed into the following:

$$\hat{w}_m - \hat{w}_f = (\beta_{m0} - \beta_{f0}) + (\beta_{m3} - \beta_{f3})\, \hat{S}_f + (\hat{S}_m - \hat{S}_f)\beta_{m3},$$

where $\hat{w}_m$ and $\hat{w}_f$ are the mean level of wages and $\hat{S}_m$ and $\hat{S}_f$ are the average levels of schooling for men and women, respectively. The decomposition was first proposed by Oaxaca (1973), and it suggests that the difference in average wages is due to three factors. First is the difference in the intercept coefficients, which might be a measure of basic discrimination in the market for labor. Second is the difference in returns to schooling, as captured by the estimates from the regression of the slope coefficients. This also might be due to discrimination. Third is the difference in average levels of schooling, which is not due to discrimination in the marketplace (though it might be caused by discrimination in education opportunities). The Oaxaca decomposition can be used to estimate what part of the wage differential is due to differences in schooling attainment and other measures of ability or experience, and what part is unexplained by the included factors and hence is attributable to discrimination. Of course, the analyst can never include all variables that are relevant in explaining wages—many are unobserved to all save the employer—so the measurement of discrimination is never precise. The decomposition enables the analyst to better guess at the upper bound of discriminatory effects in the labor market.

Table A.1 shows how much of the gender wage gap is explained by differing levels of schooling and experience for men and women in various African countries. The typical gender wage gap has women earning wages 75 percent of those of men. About half of the 25 percent gap is explained by lower education levels of women, and half remains unexplained. It is tempting to suppose that the unexplained half is due to discrimination against women in labor markets. Women with the same levels of education and experience earn lower wages. But there are many problems with estimating wage equations. Finding that not all of the variation in wages is explained may be due to some of these problems (see below).

To recapitulate briefly on why statistical analysis is important, suppose that a researcher has measured the incomes of men and women in households in a large number of villages in Zambia, and then also recorded the nutritional status of the boys and girls living in the household. The researcher categorizes the households into three groups: rich, middle, and poor, according to the total household income per person in the households.

Table A.1   Relative Earnings of Women and Men Adjusted for Differences in Human Capital

Country and Year of Data	Relative Pay	Unexplained Pay (%)	Source	Wage Source/ Sample
Côte d'Ivoire 1985	76	*	Tzannatos 1998	hourly wage
Côte d'Ivoire 1988	81	*	Tzannatos 1999	hourly wage
Ethiopia 1990	78	119	Appleton, Hoddinott, and Krishnan 1999	urban workers
Guinea 1990	45	58	Glick and Sahn 1997	hourly wage
Kenya 1986	63	60	Agesa 1999	urban workers
Tanzania 1971	75	17	Knight and Sabot 1991	manufacturing monthly wage
Tanzania 1980	86	4	Psacharopoulos and Tzannatos 1992	urban workers, manufacturing, monthly wage
Uganda 1992	72	74	Appleton, Hoddinott, and Krishnan 1999	urban workers
Zambia 1993	74	65	Nielsen 2000	national survey

Source: Reproduced from World Bank (2001, 301–306), Appendix 3.

Note: Unexplained pay above 100% means that working women are more qualified (say, in terms of education) than men. Without gender bias, women's wages would not only have been larger than their current wages but greater than men's wages.

Then the researcher computes the average levels of nutritional status for each income group. It turns out that the nutritional status of children is actually lower in the richer groups. How could this finding be explained? It may be that we are calculating our averages without controlling for some other variable. For instance, it may be that in wealthier households most of the income is earned by men. Women, say, very rarely earn high incomes. When men earn most of the income in a household, they then get a disproportionate share of the power to make decisions in the household. Men do not care to spend income on children, so the richer family actually spends less on the nutrition of children. OLS regression analysis is needed to control for both the level of overall household income and for the share of that income controlled by the man and the share controlled by the woman.

Problems with Estimating Wage Equations

There are two big problems with estimating the wage equations and interpreting the estimated coefficients as partial correlations, as unbiased estimates of the effect on wages of varying the levels of the explanatory variables. These problems are known as the *sample selection* problem and as the *omitted variable* problem. The two problems are related, but at this level are best treated separately.

Take the omitted variable problem first. The omitted variable in the wage equation case is ability. People with high wages may have unobserved talents or abilities. These abilities are the real reason for their high productivity and consequent high wages. Even if education does not improve productivity (and hence wages), it is positively correlated with ability, which does affect wages. Without an independent measure of ability, the equation will clearly not capture the independent effect of more schooling on wages (Card 2001; Griliches 1977).

The sample selection problem is a bit more complicated. Suppose men and women decide whether to be in the labor market according to some tradeoff that they make between the value of the time working, as measured by the wage they are likely to earn, and the value to themselves of staying at home and tending the children. For social reasons, women are saddled with much of the childcare burden. Thus, many women who have lots of children work at home and not in the market. In the market, wages are determined solely by educational level. If one estimated a wage equation on the sample of observed wage earners—which often does not include women with lots of children—then one might think education does not affect wages that much. This is because if one assumes that the more children a woman has the more likely she might have less education (if only because having children takes up so much time, and women bear the brunt of that time allocation problem), then lots of women with low education are being excluded from the sample. Those with low education who are in the sample are two groups: one with few children and getting low wages; the other with many children, low education, and more likely to be in the labor market because for some unobserved reason they earn high wages. That is why they chose to be in the labor market in the first place, despite having lots of children. The selected sample overly represents women whose education is low but who have high wages for other reasons. So the effect of education on wages is muted because the sample has been self-selected in a way that mutes the correlation between education and wages.

There are ways to correct for both the unobserved ability bias and sample selection problem. The adept at statistical analysis are referred to the extensive literature (Ashenfelter and Zimmerman 1997; Behrman and Deolalikar 1995; Behrman and Rosenzweig 1999; Miller, Mulvey, and Martin 1997; Rosenzweig 1995).

References

Acemoglu, D. 2002. *Why not a political Coase theorem? Social conflict, commitment and politics.* Working paper, Cambridge, MA: National Bureau of Economic Research.

Acemoglu, D., S. Johnson, and J. A. Robinson. 2001. The colonial origins of comparative development: An empirical investigation. *American Economic Review* 91:1369–1401.

Acemoglu, D., and J. A. Robinson. 2000a. Democratization or repression? *European Economic Review* 44:683–693.

———. 2000b. Political losers as a barrier to economic development. *American Economic Review: Papers and Proceedings* 90:126–144.

Adam, L. 1947. Virilocal and uxorilocal. *American Anthropologist* 49:678.

Adams, B. N., and E. Mburugu. 1994. Kikuyu bride-wealth and polygyny today. *Journal of Comparative Family Studies* 25:159–166.

Afhad University. 2003. History of the Ahfad University for women. Omdurman: Afhad University.

Agesa, Richard U. 1999. "The urban gender wage gap in an African country: findings from Kenya." *Canadian Journal of Development Studies/Revue Canadienne D'études Du Developpement* 20, no. 1:59–76.

Agüero, J. M. 2002. *Are intra-household allocations efficient? Evidence from Brazilian data.* Working paper, University of Wisconsin-Madison.

Ainsworth, M., K. Beegle, and A. Nyamete. 1996. The impact of women's schooling on fertility and contraceptive use: A study of fourteen sub-Saharan African countries. *World Bank Economic Review* 10:85–122.

Akerlof, G. 1980. A theory of social custom, of which unemployment may be one consequence. *Quarterly Journal of Economics* 94:749–775.

———. 1997. Social distance and social decisions. *Econometrica* 65:1005–1027.

Akerlof, G. A., J. L. Yellen, and M. L. Katz. 1996. An analysis of out-of-wedlock childbearing in the United States. *Quarterly Journal of Economics* 111:277–317.

Alderman, H., and E. King. 1998. Gender difference in parental investment in education. *Structural Change and Economic Dynamics* 9:453–468.

Alesina, A., and A. Drazen. 1991. Why are stabilizations delayed? *American Economic Review* 81:1170–1188.

Allen, D. W. 1992. Marriage and divorce—comment. *American Economic Review* 82:679–685.

Almroth, S., and T. Greiner. 1979. *The economic value of breastfeeding.* Rome: Food and Agriculture Organization of the United Nations.

Al Samarrai, S., and T. Peasgood. 1998. Educational attainments and household characteristics in Tanzania. *Economics of Education Review* 17:395–417.

213

Amadiume, I. 1987. *Male daughters, female husbands: Gender and sex in an African society.* London: Zed.

Ancey, G. 1983. *Monnaie et structures d'exploitations en Pays Mossi, Haute-Volta.* Paris: Editions de l'office de la recherche scientifique et technique d'outre-mer.

Anderson, B. S., and J. P. Zinsser. 2000. *A history of their own: Women in Europe from prehistory to the present.* New York: Oxford University Press.

Anderson, G. M., and R. D. Tollison. 1998. Celestial marriage and earthly rents: Interests and the prohibition of polygamy. *Journal of Economic Behavior & Organization* 37:169–181.

Anderson, S. 2000. *Why the marriage squeeze cannot cause dowry inflation.* Working paper, Tilburg: Center for Economic Research, Tilburg University.

———. 2001. *Why dowry payments declined with modernization in Europe but are rising in India.* Working paper, Tilburg: Center for Economic Research, Tilburg University.

Andre, C., and J. P. Platteau. 1998. Land relations under unbearable stress: Rwanda caught in the malthusian trap. *Journal of Economic Behavior & Organization* 34:1–47.

Appleton, S., I. Chessa, and J. Hoddinott. 1999. *Are women the fairer sex? Looking for gender differences in gender bias in Uganda.* Working paper, Oxford: Center for the Study of African Economies.

Aryee, A. F. 1997. The African family and changing nuptiality patterns. In *Family, population and development in Africa,* edited by A. Adepoju, 78–96. London: Zed Books.

Asare, B. 1995. Women in commercial agriculture: The cocoa economy of southern Ghana. In *Women and sustainable development in Africa,* edited by V. James, 101–112. Westport, CT: Praeger.

Ashenfelter, O., and D. J. Zimmerman. 1997. Estimates of the returns to schooling from sibling data: Fathers, sons, and brothers. *Review of Economics and Statistics* 79:1–9.

Austin, G. 1993. Human pawning in Asante, 1800–1950: Markets and coercion, gender and cocoa. In *Pawnship in Africa: Perspectives on debt bondage,* edited by T. Falola and P. E. Lovejoy, 119–159. Boulder, CO: Westview.

Bacon, R. W. 1988. *A first course in econometric theory.* Oxford: Oxford University Press.

Balaban, E., and R. V. Short. 1994. *The differences between the sexes.* Cambridge: Cambridge University Press.

Bardhan, K., and S. Klasen. 1998. Women in emerging Asia: Welfare, employment, and human development. *Asian Development Review* 16:72–125.

Bardhan, P. K. 1979. Wages and unemployment in a poor agrarian economy: A theoretical and empirical analysis. *Journal of Political Economy* 87:479–500.

Barnes, T. 1992. The fight for control of African women's mobility in colonial Zimbabwe, 1900–1939. *Signs* 17:586–608.

Barnett, T. 1977. *The Gezira scheme: An illusion of development.* London: F. Cass.

Bassett, T. J. 2002. Women's cotton and the spaces of gender politics in northern Côte d'Ivoire. *Gender, Place, and Culture* 9:351–70.

Bassett, T. J., and D. Crummey. 1993. *Land in African agrarian systems.* Madison: University of Wisconsin Press.

Bayart, J.-F. 1985. *L'état au Cameroun.* Paris: Presses de la Fondation Nationale des Sciences Politiques.

Baylies, C. L., and J. M. Bujra. 2000. *AIDS, sexuality, and gender in Africa: Collective strategies and struggles in Tanzania and Zambia.* London: Routledge.

Becker, G. 1981. *A treatise on the family.* Cambridge, MA: Harvard University Press.

Behrman, J. 1993. Analyzing human resource effects: Education. In *Understanding the social effects of policy reform,* edited by L. Demery, M. A. Ferroni, and C. Grootaert, 114–136. Washington, DC: World Bank.

Behrman, J. R., and A. B. Deolalikar. 1995. Are there differential returns to schooling by gender? The case of Indonesian labour markets. *Oxford Bulletin of Economics and Statistics* 57:97–117.

Behrman, J. R., and M. R. Rosenzweig. 1999. "Ability" biases in schooling returns and twins: A test and new estimates. *Economics of Education Review* 18:159–167.

Bennell, P. 2002. Hitting the target: Doubling primary school enrollments in sub-Saharan Africa by 2015. *World Development* 30:1179–1194.

Bernal, V. 1988. Losing ground—women and agriculture on Sudan's irrigated schemes: Lessons from a Blue Nile village. In *Agriculture, women and land: The African experience,* edited by J. Davison, 131–156. Boulder, CO: Westview.

Bernard, S. J. 1966. *Les bisa du cercle de Garango.* Paris: CNRS-CVRS.

Berry, S. 1988. Property rights and rural resource management: The case of tree crops in West Africa. *Cahiers des Sciences Humaines* 24:3–16.

———. 1993. *No condition is permanent: The social dynamics of agrarian change in sub-Saharan Africa.* Madison: University of Wisconsin Press.

———. 2000. *Chiefs know their boundaries: Essays on property, power, and the past in Asante, 1896–1996.* Social history of Africa. Portsmouth, NH: Heinemann; Oxford: J. Currey; Cape Town: D. Philip.

Besteman, C. 1995. Polygyny, women's land tenure, and the "mother-son partnership" in southern Somalia. *Journal of Anthropological Research* 51:193–213.

Bils, M., and P. J. Klenow. 2000. Does schooling cause growth? *American Economic Review* 90:1160–1183.

Bledsoe, C. 1990. No success without struggle—social mobility and hardship for foster children in Sierra Leone. *Man* 25:70–88.

Boni, N. 1962. *Crépuscule des temps anciens.* Paris: Présence Africaine.

Borgerhoff Mulder, M. 1987. On cultural and reproductive success: Kipsigis evidence. *American Anthropologist* 89:617–634.

———. 1988. Kipsigis bridewealth payments. In *Human reproductive behaviour,* edited by L. L. Betzig, M. B. Mulder, and P. W. Turke, 65–82. Cambridge: Cambridge University Press.

———. 1996. Responses to environmental novelty: Changes in men's marriage strategies in a rural Kenyan community. In *Evolution of social behaviour patterns in primates and man. Proceedings of the British Academy,* edited by W. G. Runciman, J. Maynard-Smith, and R. I. M. Dunbar, 203–222. Oxford: Oxford University Press.

Bowles, S., and H. Gintis. 2002. Behavioural science—Homo reciprocans. *Nature* 415:125–128.

Bowles, S., H. Gintis, and M. Osborne. 2001. Incentive-enhancing preferences: Personality, behavior, and earnings. *American Economic Review* 91:155–158.

Bradley, K., and D. Khor. 1993. Toward an integration of theory and research on the status of women. *Gender and Society* 7:347–379.

Brautigam, D. 1992. Land rights and agricultural development in West Africa: A case study of two Chinese projects. *Journal of Developing Areas* 27:21–32.

Brinig, M. F. 1990. Rings and promises. *Journal of Law, Economics, and Organization* 6:203–215.

Broekhuyse, J. T., and A. Allen. 1988. Farming systems research on the northern Mossi plateau. *Human Organization* 47:330–342.

Browning, M., F. Bourguignon, P. A. Chiappori, and V. Lechene. 1994. Income and outcomes: A structural model of intrahousehold allocation. *Journal of Political Economy* 102:1067–1096.

Browning, M., and P. A. Chiappori. 1998. Efficient intra-household allocations: A general characterization and empirical tests. *Econometrica* 66:1241–1278.

Bujra, J. 1977. Production, poverty, prostitution: "Sexual politics" in Atu. *Cahiers d'études Africaines* 17:13–39.

Bukh, J. 1979. *The village woman in Ghana.* Publications from the Centre for Development Research, Copenhagen, no. 1. Uppsala: Scandinavian Institute of African Studies.

Bulow, J., and P. Klemperer. 1999. The generalized war of attrition. *American Economic Review* 89:175–189.

Burr, M., and R. O. Collins. 1995. *Requiem for the Sudan: War, drought, and disaster relief on the Nile.* Boulder, CO: Westview.

Cadigan, R. J. 1998. Woman-to-woman marriage: Practices and benefits in sub-Saharan Africa. *Journal of Comparative Family Studies* 29:89–98.

Cain, M., S. R. Khanam, and S. Nahar. 1979. Class, patriarchy and women's work in Bangladesh. *Population and Development Review* 5:405–438.

Camerer, C. 1999. Behavioral economics: Reunifying psychology and economics. *Proceedings of the National Academy of Sciences* 96:10575–10577.

Campos, N. F., and J. B. Nugent. 2002. Who is afraid of political instability? *Journal of Development Economics* 67:157–172.

Caplan, A. 1975. *Choice and constraint in a Swahili community: Property, hierarchy, and cognatic descent on the East African coast.* London: International African Institute and Oxford University Press.

Capron, J. 1963. Univers religieux et cohésion interne dans les communautés villageoises Bwa traditionelles. *Études Voltaïques* 4:73–124.

———. 1973. *Communautés villageoises Bwa: Mali, Haute Volta.* Paris: Institut d'ethnologie.

———. 1981. *Des femmes et une société pour l'avenir.* Ministère de l'ensegnement supérieur et de la recherche scientifique, Centre national de la recherche scietifique et technologique.

Capron, J., and J. M. Kohler. 1978. De quelques characteristiques de la pratique matrimoniale Mossi contemporaine. In *Marriage, fertility, and parenthood in West Africa,* edited by C. Oppong, G. Abada, M. Bekombo-Priso, and J. Mogley, 187–223. Canberra: Australian National University.

Carbone, J. 2000. *From partners to parents: The second revolution in family law.* New York: Columbia University Press.

Card, D. 2001. Estimating the return to schooling: Progress on some persistent econometric problems. *Econometrica* 69:1127–1160.

Carney, J. 1988. Struggles over land and crops in an irrigated rice scheme: The Gambia. In *Agriculture, women, and land: The African experience,* edited by J. Davison, 59–78. Boulder, CO: Westview.

Carney, J., and M. Watts. 1990. Manufacturing dissent. *Africa* 60:207–241.

———. 1991. Disciplining women? Rice, mechanization, and the evolution of Mandinka gender relations in Senegambia. *Signs* 16:651–81.

Chanock, M. 1985. *Law, custom, and social order: The colonial experience in Malawi and Zambia.* Cambridge: Cambridge University Press.

Chattopadhyay, R., and E. Duflo. 2001. *Women as policy makers: Evidence from a India-wide randomized policy experiment.* NBER working paper, no. 8615. Cambridge, MA: National Bureau of Economic Research.

Cheater, A. 1982. Formal and informal rights to land in Zimbabwe's black freehold areas: A case-study from Msengezi. *Africa* 52:77–91.

———. 1990. The ideology of communal land tenure in Zimbabwe—mythogenesis enacted. *Africa* 60:188–206.

Chernichovsky, D. 1985. Socioeconomic and demographic aspects of school enrollment and attendance in rural Botswana. *Economic Development and Cultural Change* 33:319–332.

Cherry, R. 1998. Rational choice and the price of marriage. *Feminist Economics* 4:27–49.

Cheston, S., and L. Reed. 1999. Measuring transformation: Assessing and improving the impact of microcredit. *Journal of Microfinance* 1:20–43.

Cheung, S. N. S. 1972. Enforcement of property rights in children, and the marriage contract. *The Economic Journal* 82:641–657.

Chiappori, P.-A. 1997. "Collective" models of household behavior: The sharing rule approach. In *Intrahousehold resource allocation in developing countries: Models, methods, and policy,* edited by L. Haddad, J. Hoddinott, and H. Alderman, 39–52. Baltimore: Johns Hopkins University Press.

Chiu, Y. S., and B. R. Yang. 1999. The outside option, threat point, and Nash bargaining solution. *Economics Letters* 62:181–188.

Chodorow, N. 1978. *The reproduction of mothering: Psychoanalysis and the sociology of gender.* Berkeley: University of California Press.

Ciekawy, D. 1999. Women's "work" and the construction of witchcraft accusation in coastal Kenya. *Womens Studies International Forum* 22:225–235.

Cigno, A. 1991. *Economics of the family.* Oxford: Clarendon.

Claassen, C., and R. A. Joyce. 1997. *Women in prehistory: North America and Mesoamerica.* Philadelphia: University of Pennsylvania Press.

Clark, B. 1991. The Vienna convention reservations regime and the convention on discrimination against women. *American Journal of International Law* 85:281–321.

Cloud, Kate. 1999. *Gender and Agribusiness Project (GAP): Case Study, Cargill, Zimbabwe.* Working paper, Urbana: International Programs and Studies, University of Illinois.

Coale, A., and J. Banister. 1994. Five decades of missing females in China. *Demography* 31:459–479.

———. 1996. Five decades of missing females in China: Incidents of sex-selective abortion and female infanticide as reported in Chinese censuses and fertility surveys. *Proceedings of the American Philosophical Society* 140:421–450.

Coase, R. H. 1988. *The firm, the market, and the law.* Chicago: University of Chicago Press.

Coetzee, J. M. 1999. *Disgrace.* New York: Viking.

Cohen, L. 1987. Marriage, divorce, and quasi rents; or, "I gave him the best years of my life." *Journal of Legal Studies* 16:267–303.

Cole, H. L., G. J. Mailath, and A. Postlewaite. 1992. Social norms, savings behavior, and growth. *Journal of Political Economy* 100:1092–1125.

Coleman, B., and M. Cadalen. 1998. *Community banks for the women of Tanghin-Dassouri department.* Working paper, Ouagadougou, Burkina Faso: Catholic Relief Services.

Collier, P., and J. W. Gunning. 1999. Explaining African economic performance. *Journal of Economic Literature* 37:64–111.

Collier, P., and A. Hoeffler. 1998. On economic causes of civil war. *Oxford Economic Papers—New Series* 50:563–573.

———. 2000. *On the incidence of civil war in Africa.* Working paper, World Bank.

Collins, R. O. 1983. *Shadows in the grass: Britain in the southern Sudan, 1918–1956.* New Haven, CT: Yale University Press.

Colson, E. 1958. *Marriage and the family among the plateau Tonga of northern Rhodesia.* Manchester, UK: Manchester University Press, for the Rhodes-Livingstone Institute of Northern Rhodesia.

Comaroff, J., and S. Roberts. 1977. Marriage and extra-marital sexuality: The dialectics of legal change among the Kgatla. *Journal of African Law* 21:97–123.

Commission on Population and Development. 2000. *World population monitoring, 2000: Population, gender and development.* New York: United Nations.

Conning, J. 1999. Outreach, sustainability, and leverage in monitored and peer-monitored lending, *Journal of Development Economics* 60:229–248.

Cook, R. 1990. Reservations to the convention on the elimination of all forms of discrimination against women. *Virginia Journal of International Law* 30:643–716.

Cornwall, A. 2001. Wayward women and useless men: Contest and change in gender relations in Ado-Odo, S.W. Nigeria. In *"Wicked" women and the reconfiguration of gender in Africa,* edited by D. Hodgson and S. McCurdy, 67–83. Portsmouth, NH: Heinemann; Oxford: J. Currey; Cape Town: D. Philip.

Cronk, L. 1991. Wealth, status, and reproductive success among the Mukogodo of Kenya. *American Anthropologist* 93:345–360.

Dacher, M., and S. Lallemand. 1992. *Prix des épouses, valeur des soeurs; suivi de les représentations de la maladie: Deux études sur la société Goin, Burkina Faso.* Paris: L'Harmattan.

Dangarembga, T. 1989. *Nervous conditions.* Seattle: Seal.

Dauphin, A., B. Fortin, and G. Lacroix. 2002. *A test of collective rationality within bigamous households in Burkina Faso.* Working paper, Québec: Université Laval.

Davison, J. 1988. *Agriculture, women, and land: The African experience.* Boulder, CO: Westview.

———. 1995. Must women work together? Development agency assumptions versus changing relations of production in southern Malawi households. In *Women wielding the hoe: Lessons from rural Africa for feminist theory and development practice,* edited by D. Bryceson, 181–199. Oxford: Berg.

Deaton, A. 1989. Looking for boy-girl discrimination in household expenditure data. *World Bank Economic Review* 3:1–15.

———. 1997. *The analysis of household surveys: A microeconometric approach to development policy.* Baltimore: Johns Hopkins University Press, for the World Bank.

Dei, G. 1994. The women of a Ghanian village: A study of social change. *African Studies Review* 37:121–146.

Deolalikar, A. B. 1993. Gender differences in the returns to schooling and in school enrollment rates in Indonesia. *Journal of Human Resources* 28:899–932.

Dercon, S., and P. Krishnan. 2000. In sickness and in health: Risk sharing within households in rural Ethiopia. *Journal of Political Economy* 108:688–727.

Dey, J. 1981. Gambian women: Unequal partners in rice development projects? *Journal of Development Studies* 17:109–122.

Dickerman, C. W., and G. Barnes. 1989. *Security of tenure and land registration in Africa: Literature review and synthesis.* Working paper, Madison: University of Wisconsin Land Tenure Center.

Dike, P. C. 1995. *The women's revolt of 1929: Proceedings of a national symposium to mark the 60th anniversary of the women's uprising in south-eastern Nigeria.* Lagos: Nelag and Co.

Dirie, W. 1999. *Desert flower: The extraordinary journey of a desert nomad.* New York: William Morrow.

Dnes, A. W. 1998. The division of marital assets following divorce. *Journal of Law and Society* 25:336–364.

———. 1999. Applications of economic analysis to marital law: Concerning a proposal to reform the discretionary approach to the division of marital assets in England and Wales. *International Review of Law and Economics* 19:533–552.

Dollar, D., and R. Gatti. 1999. *Gender inequality, income, and growth: Are good times good for women?* Policy research report on gender and development working paper series, no. 1. Washington, DC: World Bank Development Research Group/Poverty Reduction and Economic Management Network.

Donald, M., and L. Hurcombe. 2000. *Representations of gender from prehistory to the present.* New York: St. Martin's.

Dorward, D. C. 1983. *The Igbo "women's war" of 1929: Documents relating to the Aba riots in eastern Nigeria.* East Ardsley, U.K.: Microform Ltd.

Doss, C. 1997. *The effects of women's bargaining power on household health and education outcomes: Evidence from Ghana.* Working paper, Williams College.

———. 2001. Is Risk Fully Pooled Within the Household? Evidence from Ghana. *Economic Development and Cultural Change* 50:101–30.

Downs, R. E., and S. P. Reyna. 1988. *Land and society in contemporary Africa.* Hanover, NH: University Press of New England, for the University of New Hampshire.

Drewett, R., D. Wolke, M. Asefa, M. Kaba, and F. Tessema. 2001. Malnutrition and mental development: Is there a sensitive period? A nested case-control study. *Journal of Child Psychology and Psychiatry and Allied Disciplines* 42:181–188.

Drimie, S. 2002. *The impact of HIV/AIDS on rural households and land issues in southern and eastern Africa.* Working paper, Pretoria: Human Sciences Research Council.

Drylands Programme. 1999. *Land tenure and resource access in West Africa: Issues and opportunities for the next twenty-five years.* London: International Institute for Environment and Development, Drylands Programme.

Dube, L. 1997. *Women and kinship: Comparative perspectives on gender in south and south-east Asia.* Tokyo: United Nations University Press.

Dyson, T., and M. Moore. 1983. On kinship structure, female autonomy, and demographic behavior in India. *Population and Development Review* 9:35–60.

Easterly, W. 2001. *The elusive quest for growth: Economists' adventures and misadventures in the tropics.* Cambridge, MA: MIT Press.

———. 2003. *Can foreign aid buy growth?* Working paper, New York University.

Eckel, C. C., and P. J. Grossman. 1998. Are women less selfish than men? Evidence from dictator experiments. *Economic Journal* 108:726–735.

Edlund, L. 2000. The marriage squeeze interpretation of dowry inflation: A comment. *Journal of Political Economy* 108:1327–1333.

Edlund, L., and R. Pande. 2001. *Why have women become left-wing? The political gender gap and the decline in marriage.* Working paper, Columbia University.

Ehrenberg, M. R. 1989. *Women in prehistory.* London: British Museum.

Elbadawi, I., and N. Sambanis. 2000. Why are there so many civil wars in Africa? Understanding and preventing violent conflict. *Journal of African Economies* 9:244–269.

Ellen, I. G., T. Mijanovich, and K. N. Dillman. 2001. Neighborhood effects on health: Exploring the links and assessing the evidence. *Journal of Urban Affairs* 23:391–408.

Eller, C. 2000. *The myth of matriarchal prehistory: Why an invented past won't give women a future.* Boston: Beacon.

———. 2001. The myth of matriarchal prehistory—a response. *Religion* 31:265–270.

Elliott, J. R. 1999. Social isolation and labor market insulation: Network and neighborhood effects on less-educated urban workers. *Sociological Quarterly* 40: 199–216.

Englebert, P. 1996. *Burkina Faso: Unsteady statehood in West Africa.* Boulder, CO: Westview.

———. 2000a. Pre-colonial institutions, post-colonial states, and economic development in tropical Africa. *Political Research Quarterly* 53:7–36.

———. 2000b. Solving the mystery of the AFRICA dummy. *World Development* 28:1821–1835.

———. 2002. *State legitimacy and development in Africa.* Boulder, CO: Lynne Rienner.

Englebert, P., S. Tarango, and M. Carter. 2002. Dismemberment and suffocation: A contribution to the debate on African boundaries. *Comparative Political Studies* 35:1093–1118.

Ensminger, J., and J. Knight. 1997. Changing social norms—common property, bridewealth, and clan exogamy. *Current Anthropology* 38:1–24.

Ensminger, M. E., R. P. Lamkin, and N. Jacobson. 1996. School leaving: A longitudinal perspective including neighborhood effects. *Child Development* 67: 2400–2416.

Entwisle, D. R., K. L. Alexander, and L. S. Olson. 1994. The gender gap in math: Its possible origins in neighborhood effects. *American Sociological Review* 59:822–838.

Evenson, R. 1978. Time allocation in rural Philippine households. *American Journal of Agricultural Economics* 60:322–330.

Fafchamps, M. 1997. *Efficiency in intrahousehold resource allocation.* Working paper, Stanford University.

Field, A. J. 2001. *Altruistically inclined? The behavioral sciences, evolutionary theory, and the origins of reciprocity.* Ann Arbor: University of Michigan Press.

Filmer, D., and L. Pritchett. 1999. The effect of household wealth on educational attainment: Evidence from 35 countries. *Population and Development Review* 25:85–120.

Firmin-Sellers, K. 2000. Custom, capitalism, and the state: The origins of insecure land tenure in West Africa. *Journal of Institutional and Theoretical Economics* 156:513–530.

Fleuret, A. 1988. Some consequences of tenure and agrarian reform in Taita, Kenya. In *Land and society in contemporary Africa,* edited by R. E. Downs and S. P. Reyna. Hanover, NH: University Press of New England.

Folbre, N. 1986. Cleaning house: New perspectives on households and economic development. *Journal of Development Economics* 21:5–40.

Fortmann, L., C. Antinori, and N. Nabane. 1997. Fruits of their labors: Gender, poperty rights, and tree planting in two Zimbabwe villages. *Rural Sociology* 62:295–314.

Fortmann, L., and N. Nabane. 1992. *The fruits of their labours: Gender, property, and trees in Mhondoro district.* Harare: University of Zimbabwe Centre for Applied Social Sciences.

Fosu, A. K. 1992. Effect of export instability on economic growth in Africa. *Journal of Developing Areas* 26:323–332.

———. 1999. The external debt burden and economic growth in the 1980s: Evidence from sub-Saharan Africa. *Canadian Journal of Development Studies* 20:307–318.

———. 2001. Economic fluctuations and growth in sub-Saharan Africa: The importance of import instability. *Journal of Development Studies* 37:71–84.

———. 2002. Political instability and economic growth: Implications of coup events in sub-Saharan Africa. *American Journal of Economics and Sociology* 61:329–348.

Francois, P. 1996. *A theory of gender discrimination based on the household.* Kingston: Institute for Economic Research, Queen's University.

Frank, R. H. 1985. *Choosing the right pond: Human behavior and the quest for status.* Oxford: Oxford University Press.

Freidan, B. 1995. Beyond gender. *Newsweek,* September 4, 1995, 30–32.

Friedberg, L. 1998. Did unilateral divorce raise divorce rates? Evidence from panel data. *American Economic Review* 88:608–627.

Friedman, D. 1990. *Price theory: An intermediate text.* Cincinnati: Southwestern.

Gangadharan, L., and P. Maitra. 2002. *Testing for son preference in South Africa.* Melbourne: University of Melbourne.

Garenne, M., and E. Van de Walle. 1989. Polygyny and fertility among the Sereer of Senegal. *Population Studies: A Journal of Demography* 43:267–283.

Garg, A., and J. Morduch. 1998. Sibling rivalry and the gender gap: Evidence from child health outcomes in Ghana. *Journal of Population Economics* 11:471–493.

Geddes, R., and D. Lueck. 2002. The gains from self-ownership and the advancement of women's rights. *American Economic Review* 92:1079–1092.

Geddes, R., and P. J. Zak. 2000. *The rule of one-third.* Working paper, Fordham University.

Ghatak, M., and T. W. Guinnane. 1999. The economics of lending with joint liability: Theory and practice. *Journal of Development Economics* 60:195–228.

Gibson, M., and R. Mace. 2003. Strong mothers bear more sons in rural Ethiopia. *Proceedings of the Royal Society* 270:108–109.

Giddens, A. 1984. *The constitution of society: Outline of the theory of structuration.* Cambridge: Polity.

Gladwell, M. 2000. *The tipping point: How little things can make a big difference.* Boston: Little, Brown.

Gladwin, C. H., and D. McMillan. 1989. Is a turnaround in Africa possible without helping African women to farm? *Economic Development and Cultural Change* 37:345–369.

Glaeser, E., S. Johnson, and A. Shleifer. 2001. Coase versus the Coasians. *Quarterly Journal of Economics* 116:853–899.

Glazier, J. 1985. *Land and the uses of tradition among the Mbeere of Kenya.* Lanham, MD: University Press of America.

Gleditsch, N. P., P. Wallensteen, M. Eriksson, M. Sollenberg, and H. Strand. 2002. Armed conflict, 1946–2001: A new dataset. *Journal of Peace Research* 39:615–637.

Glewwe, P. 1999. *The economics of school quality investments in developing countries: An empirical study of Ghana.* New York: St. Martin's.

Glewwe, P., and H. Jacoby. 1995. An economic analysis of delayed primary school enrollment in a low income country: The role of early childhood nutrition. *Review of Economics and Statistics* 77:156–169.

Glick, P., and D. E. Sahn. 1997. Gender and education impacts on employment and earnings in West Africa: Evidence from Guinea. *Economic Development and Cultural Change* 45:793–823.

Gluckman, M. 1950. Kinship and marriage among the Lozi of northern Rhodesia and the Zulu of Natal. In *African systems of kinship and marriage,* edited by A. R. Radcliffe-Brown and D. Forde, 166–206. London: Oxford University Press.

Goldstein, M., A. De Janvry, and E. Sadoulet. 2002. *Is a friend in need a friend indeed? Inclusion and exclusion in mutual insurance networks in southern Ghana.* Working paper, Helsinki: World Institute for Development Economics Research, United Nations University.

Goldstein, M., and C. Udry. 2002. *Gender, land rights, and agriculture in Ghana.* Working paper, London School of Economics.

Gordon, D. 2002. *School achievement and adult death in Kwazulu Natal, South Africa.* Working paper, Berkeley: University of California at Berkeley.

Gordon, N. 1997. "Tonguing the body": Placing female circumcision within African feminist discourse. *Issue: A Journal of Opinion* 25:24–27.

Gourevitch, P. 1999. *We wish to inform you that tomorrow we will be killed with our families: Stories from Rwanda.* New York: Picador.

Gray, L., and M. Kevane. 1999. Diminished access, diverted exclusion: Women and land tenure in sub-Saharan Africa. *African Studies Review* 42:15–39.

———. 2001. Evolving tenure rights and agricultural intensification in southwestern Burkina Faso. *World Development* 29:573–587.

Gray, R. 1960. Sonjo bride-price and the question of African "wife purchase." *American Anthropologist* 62:34–57.

Gray, R. F., and P. H. Gulliver. 1964. *The family estate in Africa: Studies in the role of property in family structure and lineage continuity.* London: Routledge/Kegan Paul.

Greene, B. 1998. The institution of woman-marriage in Africa: A cross-cultural analysis. *Ethnology* 37:395–412.

Grier, B. 1992. Pawns, porters, and petty traders: Women in the transition to cash crop agriculture in colonial Ghana. *Signs* 17:304–328.

Griliches, Z. 1977. Estimating the returns to schooling: Some econometric problems. *Econometrica* 45:1–22.

Grossbard, A. 1976. An economic analysis of polygyny: The case of Maiduguri. *Current Anthropology* 17:701–707.

———. 1980. The economics of polygamy. In *Research in population economics,* vol. 2, edited by J. L. Simon and J. D. Vanzo, 321–350. Greenwich, CT: JAI.

Grossbard-Schechtman, S. 1995. Marriage market models. In *The new economics of human behavior,* edited by Tommasi and Lerulli, 92–112. Cambridge: Cambridge University Press.

Guyer, J. 1980. Food, cocoa, and the division of labour by sex in two West African societies. *Comparative Studies in Society and History* 22:355–373.

———. 1986. Beti widow inheritance and marriage law: A social history. In *Widows in African societies,* edited by B. Potash, 193–219. Palo Alto, CA: Stanford University Press.

Haanstad, E., and M. Borgerhoff Mulder. 1996. Brideprice. In *Encyclopedia of cultural anthropology.* New York: Henry Holt.

Haccou, P., and O. Glaizot. 2002. The ESS in an asymmetric generalized war of attrition with mistakes in role perception. *Journal of Theoretical Biology* 214: 329–349.

Haddad, L., and J. Hoddinott. 1994. Women's income and boy-girl anthropometric status in the Côte-d'Ivoire. *World Development* 22:543–553.

Haddad, L., and T. Reardon. 1993. Gender bias in the allocation of resources within households in Burkina-Faso: A disaggregated outlay equivalent analysis. *Journal of Development Studies* 29:260–276.

Hakansson, T. 1986. *Landless Gusii women: A result of customary land law and modern marriage patterns.* Working papers in African studies, African Studies Programme, Department of Cultural Anthropology, University of Uppsala.

———. 1994. Detachable women: Gender and kinship in the process of socio-economic change among the Gusii of Kenya. *American Ethnologist* 21:516–538.

Henrich, J., R. Boyd, S. Bowles, C. Camerer, E. Fehr, H. Gintis, and R. McElreath. 2001. In search of homo economicus: Behavioral experiments in 15 small-scale societies. *American Economic Review* 91:73–78.

Herbst, J. I. 2000. *States and power in Africa: Comparative lessons in authority and control.* Princeton, NJ: Princeton University Press.

Herskovits, M. 1937. A note on "woman marriage" in Dahomey. *Africa* 10:335–341.

Hertzberg, H. 2002. Them, too. *New Yorker,* June 10, 2002.

Hill, K., and D. M. Upchurch. 1995. Gender differences in child health: Evidence from the demographic and health surveys. *Population and Development Review* 21:127–151.

Hill, P. 1963. *The migrant cocoa-farmers of southern Ghana.* London: Cambridge University Press.

———. 1969. Hidden trade in Hausaland. *Man* 41:392–409.

———. 1970. *Studies in rural capitalism in West Africa.* Cambridge: Cambridge University Press.

Hirschmann, D., and M. Vaughan. 1984. *Women farmers of Malawi: Food production in Zomba district.* Berkeley: University of California Institute of International Studies.

Hochschild, A. 1998. *King Leopold's ghost: A story of greed, terror, and heroism in colonial Africa.* Boston: Houghton Mifflin.

Hoddinott, J. 1992. Rotten kids or manipulative parents—Are children old age security in western Kenya? *Economic Development and Cultural Change* 40:545–565.

Hoddinott, J., H. Alderman, and L. Haddad. 1997. Testing competing models of intrahousehold allocation. In *Intrahousehold resource allocation in developing countries: Models, methods, and policy,* edited by L. Haddad, J. Hoddinott, and H. Alderman, 129–141. Baltimore: Johns Hopkins University Press.

Hoddinott, J., and L. Haddad. 1995. Does female income share influence household expenditures? Evidence from Côte d'Ivoire. *Oxford Bulletin of Economics and Statistics* 57:77–96.

Hodgson, D. 1996. "My daughter . . . belongs to the government now": Marriage, Maasai and the Tanzanian state. *Canadian Journal of African Studies* 30:106–122.

Holy, L. 1974. *Neighbours and kinsmen: A study of the Berti people of Darfur.* London: C. Hurst.

Hopkins, J., C. Levin, and L. Haddad. 1994. Women's income and household expenditure patterns: gender or flow? Evidence from Niger. *American Journal of Agricultural Economics* 76:1219–1225.

Hufbauer, G. C., J. J. Schott, and K. A. Elliott. 1990. *Economic sanctions reconsidered.* Washington, DC: Institute for International Economics.

Hulme, D. 2000. Impact assessment methodologies for microfinance: Theory, experience and better practice. *World Development* 28:79–98.

Hunt, N. 1991. Noise over camouflaged polygamy, colonial morality taxation, and a woman-naming crisis in Belgian Africa. *Journal of African History* 32:471–494.

Hymowitz, C., and M. Weissman. 1978. *A history of women in America.* New York: Bantam.

International Labour Organization. 2002. Case law in Tanzania—high court. www. ilo.org/public/english/employment/gems/eeo/law/tanzania/cl_hc.htm, accessed July 15, 2003.

Jacoby, H. G. 1995. The economics of polygyny in sub-Saharan Africa: Female productivity and the demand for wives in Côte d'Ivoire. *Journal of Political Economy* 103:938–971.

James, W. 1970. Why the Uduk won't pay bridewealth. *Sudan Notes and Records* 51:75–84.

———. 1978. Matrifocus on African women. In *Defining females: The nature of women in society,* edited by S. Ardener, 140–163. New York: John Wiley and Sons.

Jenefsky, A. 1991. Permissibility of Egypt's reservations to the convention on the elimination of all forms of discrimination against women. *Maryland Journal of International Law and Trade* 15:199–234.

Jensen, R. 2002. *Fertility preferences and excess female mortality: Equal treatment, unequal outcomes?* Working paper, Harvard University.

Jones, C. 1986. Intra-household bargaining in response to the introduction of new crops: A case study from north Cameroon. In *Understanding Africa's rural households and farming systems,* edited by J. L. Moock, 105–123. Boulder, CO: Westview.

Jones, H., N. Diop, I. Askew, and I. Kabore. 1999. Female genital cutting practices in Burkina Faso and Mali and their negative health outcomes. *Studies in Family Planning* 30:219–230.

Kabeer, N. 1994. *Reversed realities: Gender hierarchies in development thought.* London: Verso.

Kamas, L., S. Baum, and A. Preston. 2001. *Altruism in anonymous and social settings: What's gender got to do with it?* Working paper, Santa Clara University, Department of Economics.

Karp, I. 1978. *Fields of change among the Iteso of Kenya.* London: Routledge and Kegan Paul.

Kaufmann, G., and D. Meekers. 1992. *A reappraisal of the status of women and nuptiality in sub-Saharan Africa.* Working paper, State College: Pennsylvania State University, Population Research Institute.

Kebede, B. 2000. *Intra-household distribution of expenditures in rural Ethiopia: A demand systems approach.* Working paper, Oxford: Centre for the Study of African Economies.

Keller, B., E. C. Phiri, and M. Milimo. 1990. Women and agricultural development. In *The dynamics of agricultural policy and reform in Zambia,* edited by A. E. A. Wood, 241–262. Ames: Iowa State University Press.

Kent, S. K. 1998. *Gender in African prehistory.* Walnut Creek, CA: AltaMira.

Kevane, M. 1996. *Qualitative impact study of credit with education in Burkina Faso.* Report #2, Davis, CA: Freedom from Hunger.

———. 1997. Land tenure and rental in western Sudan. *Land Use Policy* 14:295–310.

———. 2000. Extra-household norms and intra-household bargaining: Gender in Sudan and Burkina Faso. In *Women farmers and commercial ventures: Increasing food security in developing countries,* edited by A. Spring, 89–112. Boulder, CO: Lynne Rienner.

————. 2003. *Ratification of the Convention for the Elimination of Discrimination against Women.* Working paper, Santa Clara University, Department of Economics.

Kevane, M., and L. C. Gray. 1999. A woman's field is made at night: Gendered land rights and norms in Burkina Faso. *Feminist Economics* 5:1–26.

Kevane, M., and B. Wydick. 2001. Social norms and the time allocation of women's labor in Burkina Faso. *Review of Development Economics* 5:119–129.

Khandker, S. 1988. Determinants of women's time allocation in rural Bangladesh. *Economic Development and Cultural Change* 37:111–126.

Kimhi, A., and N. Sosner. 2000. *Intrahousehold allocation of food in southern Ethiopia.* Working paper, Rehovot: Hebrew University, Center for Agricultural Economic Research.

King, E. M., and M. A. Hill. 1993. *Women's education in developing countries: Barriers, benefits, and policies.* Baltimore: John Hopkins University Press, for the World Bank.

Klasen, S. 1996. Nutrition, health and mortality in sub-Saharan Africa: Is there a gender bias? *Journal of Development Studies* 32:913–32.

————. 1999. *Does gender inequality reduce growth and development? Evidence from cross-country regressions.* World Bank Policy Research Report on Gender and Development, working paper series, no. 7. Washington, DC: World Bank.

————. 2000. *Malnourished and surviving in South Asia, better nourished and dying young in Africa: What can explain this puzzle?* Working paper, University of Munich.

Knight, J. B., and R. Sabot. 1991. Labor market discrimination in a poor urban economy. In *Unfair advantage: Labor market discrimination in developing countries,* edited by Nancy Birdsall and Richard Sabot. Washington, DC: World Bank.

Knight, J. B., R. H. Sabot, and D. C. Hovey. 1992. Is the rate of return on primary schooling really 26 percent? *Journal of African Economies* 1:192–205.

Kobou, Georges. 2000. Le sexe du travail: Mythes et réalites de la discrimination sexuelle dans le marche du travail. In *La biographie sociale du sexe: Genre, société et politique au Cameroun,* edited by Luc Sindjoun, 273–306. Paris: Karthala; Dakar: Codeseria.

Kremer, M., and S. Jayachandran. 2002. Odious debt. *Finance and Development* 39:36–39.

Krueger, A. B., and M. Lindahl. 2001. Education for growth: Why and for whom? *Journal of Economic Literature* 39:1101–1136.

Kuate Defo, B. 1998. *Sexuality and reproductive health during adolescence in Africa: With special reference to Cameroon.* Ottawa: University of Ottawa Press.

Labouret, H. 1940. Situation matérielle, morale et coutumière de la femme dans l'Ouest-Africain. *Africa* 13:97–124.

Lachaud, J.-P. 1998. Gains feminins, allocation des biens et statut nutritionnel des enfants au Burkina Faso. *Revue d'Economie du Developpement* 2:3–53.

Lallemand, S. 1977. *Une Famille Mossi.* Paris: CNRS.

Larsen, U., and S. Yan. 2000. Does female circumcision affect infertility and fertility? A study of the Central African Republic, Côte d'Ivoire, and Tanzania. *Demography* 37:313–321.

Laslett, P., and R. Wall. 1972. *Household and family in past time.* Cambridge: Cambridge University Press.

Lavigne Delville, P. 2000. Harmonizing formal law and customary land rights in French-speaking West Africa. In *Evolving land rights, policy, and tenure in Africa,* edited by C. Toulmin and J. Quan, 97–122. London: IIED.

Leach, M. 1992. Women's crops in women's spaces: Gender relations in Mende rice farming. In *Bush base, forest farm: Culture, environment, and development,* edited by E. Croll and D. Parkin, 77–96. London: Routledge.

Le Coeur, S., and M. Khlat. 2000. Mortality related to sexuality in Africa. *Reproductive Health Matters* 8:142.

Lengeler, C., J. Cattani, and D. De Savigny. 1996. *Net gain: A new method for preventing malaria deaths,* Ottawa: International Development Research Centre.

Lesthaeghe, R., G. Kaufman, and D. Meekers. 1989. The nuptiality regimes in sub-Saharan Africa. In *Reproduction and social organization in sub-Saharan Africa,* edited by R. Lesthaeghe, 238–337. Berkeley: University of California Press.

Levine, D., and M. Kevane. 2003. Are investments in daughters lower when daughters move away? Evidence from Indonesia. *World Development* 31:1065–1084.

LeVine, S., and R. A. LeVine. 1966. *Nyansango: A Gusii community in Kenya.* New York: John Wiley and Sons.

Lichbach, M. I. 1989. An evaluation of "does economic inequality breed political conflict" studies. *World Politics* 41:431–470.

Lilja, N., and J. Sanders. 1998. Welfare impacts of technological change on women in southern Mali. *Agricultural Economics* 19:73–79.

Liljestrand, J. 1999. Reducing perinatal and maternal mortality in the world: The major challenges. *British Journal of Obstetrics and Gynaecology* 106:877–880.

Lott, J. R., and L. W. Kenny. 1999. Did women's suffrage change the size and scope of government? *Journal of Political Economy* 107:1163–1198.

Lovett, M. 1996. "She thinks she's like a man": Marriage and (de)constructing gender indentity in colonial Buha, western Tanzania, 1943–1960. *Canadian Journal of African Studies* 30:52–67.

Lowe, M. 1978. Sociobiology and sex differences. *Signs* 4:118–125.

Lund, C. 2001. Questioning some assumptions about land tenure. In *Politics, property and production in the West African Sahel: Understanding natural resources management,* edited by T. Benjaminsen and C. Lund, 144–162. Uppsala: Nordiska Afrikainstitutet.

Lundberg, S., and R. A. Pollak. 1994. Noncooperative bargaining models of marriage. *American Economic Review* 84:132–137.

Madise, N., Z. Matthews, and B. Margetts. 1999. Heterogeneity of child nutritional status between households: A comparison of six sub-Saharan African countries. *Population Studies* 53:331–343.

Maipose, G. S., and T. C. Matsheka. 2000. *Explaining African growth performance: The Botswana case study.* Working paper, Gaborone: University of Botswana.

Maitra, P., and A. Rammohan. 1999. *Why aren't all the children in school: Theory and evidence from South Africa.* Working paper, University of Sydney.

Mamdani, M. 1996. *Citizen and subject: Contemporary Africa and the legacy of late colonialism.* Princeton, NJ: Princeton University Press.

Manji, A. 1998. Gender and the politics of the land tenure reform process in Tanzania. *Journal of Modern African Studies* 36:645–667.

Manski, C. F. 1993. Identification of endogenous social effects—the reflection problem. *Review of Economic Studies* 60:531–542.

Marcus, R. 1993. *Gender and HIV/AIDS in sub-Saharan Africa: The cases of Uganda and Malawi.* Working paper, Brighton: University of Sussex Institute of Development Studies.

Marpsat, M. 1999. Models of 'neighborhood effects' in the United States: A review of recent surveys. *Population* 54:303–330.

Marx, K. [1852] 1948. *The eighteenth brumaire of Louis Napoleon.* Moscow: Foreign Language Publishing House.

Masquelier, A. 2001. *How is a girl to marry without a bed? Weddings, wealth, and women's value in an Islamic town of Niger.* Working paper, Department of Anthropology, Tulane University.

Matsuyama, K. 1992. The market size, entrepreneurship, and the big push. *Journal of the Japanese and International Economies* 6:347–364.

Mauro, P. 1995. Corruption and growth. *Quarterly Journal of Economics* 110: 681–712.

May, A. 2003. *Maasai migrations: Implications for HIV/AIDS and social change in Tanzania.* Working paper, University of Colorado.

Mbaruku, G., and S. Bergstrom. 1995. Reducing maternal mortality in Kigoma, Tanzania. *Health Policy and Planning* 10:71–78.

McIntosh, C. 2002. *Assessing the impact of policy reforms in Ugandan microfinance.* Working paper, Department of Agricultural and Resource Economics, Unversity of California at Berkeley.

McMahon, W. W. 1999. *Education and development: Measuring the social benefits.* New York: Oxford University Press.

McMillan, D. E. 1995. *Sahel visions: Planned settlement and river blindness control in Burkina Faso.* Tucson: University of Arizona Press.

McPeak, J., and C. Doss. 2002. *Are household production decisions cooperative? Evidence on migration and milk sales from northern Kenya.* Working paper, Syracuse, NY: Department of Public Administration, Maxwell School, Syracuse University.

Meekers, D. 1992. The process of marriage in African societies: A multiple indicator approach. *Population and Development Review* 18: 61–79.

Meekers, D., and N. Franklin. 1995. Women's perceptions of polygyny among the Kaguru of Tanzania. *Ethnology* 34:315–329.

Melvern, L. 2000. *A people betrayed: The role of the West in Rwanda's genocide.* London: Zed.

Miguel, E., and M. Kremer. 2001. *Worms: Education and health externalities in Kenya.* Cambridge, MA: National Bureau of Economic Research, working paper series, no. 8481:1–62.

Miguel, E., S. Satyanath, and E. Sergenti. 2003. *Economic shocks and civil conflict: An instrumental variables approach.* Working paper, Berkeley: University of California Department of Economics.

Mikell, G. 1984. Filiation, economic crisis, and the status of women in rural Ghana. *Canadian Journal of African Studies* 18:195–219.

———. 1989. *Cocoa and chaos in Ghana.* New York: Paragon House.

Miles, W. F. S. 1994. *Hausaland divided: Colonialism and independence in Nigeria and Niger.* Ithaca, NY: Cornell University Press.

Miller, B. D. 1997. *The endangered sex: Neglect of female children in rural north India.* Delhi: Oxford University Press.

Miller, P., C. Mulvey, and N. Martin. 1997. Family characteristics and the returns to schooling: Evidence on gender differences from a sample of Australian twins. *Economica* 64:119–136.

Mincer, J. 1974. *Schooling, experience, and earnings.* New York: Columbia University Press, for the National Bureau of Economic Research.

MkNelly, B., and M. Kevane. 2002. Improving design and performance of group lending: Suggestions from Burkina Faso. *World Development* 30:2017–2032.

Moll, P. G. 1996. The collapse of primary schooling returns in South Africa, 1960–90. *Oxford Bulletin of Economics and Statistics* 58:185–210.

Montiel, P. 1995. *Financial policies and economic growth: Theory, evidence, and country-specific experience from sub-Saharan Africa.* Working paper, Nairobi: African Economic Research Consortium.

Moore, S. F. 1986. *Social facts and fabrications: 'Customary' law on Kilimanjaro, 1880–1980.* Cambridge: Cambridge University Press.

Moore, W. H., R. Lindstrom, and V. Oregan. 1996. Land reform, political violence and the economic inequality political conflict nexus—a longitudinal analysis. *International Interactions* 21:335–363.

Morduch, J. 1999. The microfinance promise. *Journal of Economic Literature* 37:1569–1614.

Mulder, M. B. 1990. Kipsigis women's preferences for wealthy men—evidence for female choice in mammals. *Behavioral Ecology and Sociobiology* 27:255–264.

Munalula, M., and W. Mwenda. 1995. Case study: Women and inheritance law in Zambia. In *African women: South of the Sahara,* edited by M. Hay and S. Stichter, 93–100. New York: Longman Scientific and Technical.

Munshi, K., and J. Myaux. 1998. *Social effects in the demographic transition: Evidence from Matlab, Bangladesh.* Working paper, University of Pennsylvania.

Muntemba, m. S. 1982. Women and agricultural change in the railway region of Zambia: Dispossession and counterstrategies, 1930–1970. In *Women and work in Africa,* edited by E. Bay, 83–103. Boulder, CO: Westview.

Murphy, K. M., A. Shleifer, and R. W. Vishny. 1989. Industrialization and the big push. *Journal of Political Economy* 97:1003–1026.

Musisi, N. B. 1991. Women, elite polygyny, and Buganda state formation. *Signs* 16:757–786.

Mwangi, G. 1997. Masai woman resists tradition. *San Jose Mercury News,* October 31, 1997, 16A.

Nash, J. 1950. The bargaining problem. *Econometrica* 18:155–162.

———. 1951. Non-cooperative games. *Annals of Mathematics* 54:286–295.

———. 1953. Two-person cooperative games. *Econometrica* 21:128–140.

Navajas, S., M. Schreiner, R. L. Meyer, C. Gonzalez-Vega, and J. Rodriguez-Meza. 2000. Microcredit and the poorest of the poor: Theory and evidence from Bolivia. *World Development* 28:333–346.

Niblock, T. 2001. *"Pariah states" and sanctions in the Middle East: Iraq, Libya, Sudan.* The Middle East in the international system series. Boulder, CO: Lynne Rienner.

Nielsen, H. S. 2000. "Wage discrimination in Zambia: An extension of the Oaxaca-Blinder decomposition." *Applied Economics Letters* 7, no. 6:405–408.

Nielsen, H. S., and N. Westergård-Nielsen. 2001. Returns to schooling in less developed countries: New evidence from Zambia. *Economic Development and Cultural Change* 49:365–394.

Oaxaca, R. 1973. Male-female wage differentials in urban labor markets. *International Economic Review* 14:693–709.

Oboler, R. S. 1985. *Women, power, and economic change: The Nandi of Kenya.* Stanford, CA: Stanford University Press.

———. 1986. Nandi widows. In *Widows in African societies,* edited by B. Potash. Stanford, CA: Stanford University Press.

O'Connell, S. A., and B. J. Ndulu. 2000. *Africa's growth experience: A focus on sources of growth.* Working paper, Washington, DC: World Bank.

Okali, C. 1983. *Cocoa and kinship in Ghana: The matrilineal Akan of Ghana.* London: Kegan Paul, for the International African Institute.

Okeyo, A. P. 1980. Daughters of the lakes and rivers: Colonization and the land rights of Luo women. In *Women and colonization: Anthropological perspectives,* edited by M. Etienne and E. Leacock, 186–213. New York: Praeger.

Oppong, C., C. Okali, and B. Houghton. 1975. Women's power: Retrograde steps in Ghana. *African Studies Review* 18:71–84.

Osmani, S. R. 1990. Wage determination in rural labour markets: The theory of implicit co-operation. *Journal of Development Economics* 34:3–23.

Otsuka, K., and F. Place. 2001. *Land tenure and natural resource management: A comparative study of agrarian communities in Asia and Africa.* Baltimore: Johns Hopkins University Press.

Pageard, R. 1969. *Le droit privé des Mossi, Tradition et evolution.* Recherches voltaïques, no. 10–11. Paris: Laboratoire d'anthropologie sociale Collège de France.

Pal, M. 1995. *An examination of the Grameen bank model and its replication in Burkina Faso.* Working paper, Abidjan: African Development Bank.

Parkman, A. M. 1992. Unilateral divorce and the labor-force participation rate of married women, revisited. *American Economic Review* 82:671–678.

Père, M., and H. Desroche. 1973. *Animation féminine dans une société villageoise traditionelle: le Centre de Gaoua en Pays Lobi, Haute-Volta.* Paris: École Pratique des Hautes Études.

Peters, H. E. 1992. Marriage and divorce: Reply. *American Economic Review* 82: 686–693.

Pindyck, R. S., and D. L. Rubinfeld. 1998. *Econometric models and economic forecasts,* 4th ed. Boston: Irwin/McGraw-Hill.

Pitt, M. M., and S. R. Khandker. 1998. The impact of group-based credit programs on poor households in Bangladesh: Does the gender of participants matter? *Journal of Political Economy* 106:958–996.

Platteau, J. P. 1996. The evolutionary theory of land rights as applied to sub-Saharan Africa: A critical assessment. *Development and Change* 27:29–86.

Poewe, K. O. 1981. *Matrilineal ideology: Male-female dynamics in Luapula, Zambia.* New York: Academic, for the International African Institute.

Pollitt, E. 1996. Timing and vulnerability in research on malnutrition and cognition. *Nutrition Reviews* 54:49–56.

Pritchett, L. 2001. Where has all the education gone? *World Bank Economic Review* 15:367–391.

Prunier, G. 1998. *The Rwanda crisis: History of a genocide.* London: C. Hurst.

Psacharopoulos, G., and Z. Tzannatos. 1992. *Women's employment and pay in Latin America: Overview and methodology.* World Bank regional and sectoral studies. Working paper, Washington, DC: World Bank.

Quinn, N. 1977. Anthropological studies on women's status. *Annual Review of Anthropology* 6:181–225.

Quisumbing, A. R., L. Haddad, and C. Pena. 2001. Are women overrepresented among the poor? An analysis of poverty in 10 developing countries. *Journal of Development Economics* 66:225–269.

Quisumbing, A. R., and J. A. Maluccio. 2000. *Intrahousehold allocation and gender relations: New empirical evidence from four developing countries.* Working paper, Washington, DC: International Food Policy Research Institute.

Rabin, M. 1998. Psychology and economics. *Journal of Economic Literature* 36:11–46.

———. 2002. A perspective on psychology and economics. *European Economic Review* 46:657–685.

Rahman, A., and N. Toubia. 2000. *Female genital mutilation: A guide to laws and policies worldwide.* New York: Zed.

Ramamurthy, R. 1993. Patriarchy and the process of agricultural intensification in south India. In *Gender and political economy: Explorations of South Asian systems,* edited by A. Clark, 180–214. Delhi: Oxford University Press.

Rammohan, A., and P. Robertson. 2001. *Gender bias in education: The role of kinship and household norms in LDCs.* Working paper, Sydney: University of New South Wales.

Rao, V. 1993. The rising price of husbands: A hedonic analysis of dowry increases in rural India. *Journal of Political Economy* 101:666–677.

———. 2000. The marriage squeeze interpretation of dowry inflation: Response. *Journal of Political Economy* 108:1334–1335.

Ravallion, M. 1999. *The mystery of the vanishing benefits: Ms. Speedy Analyst's introduction to evaluation.* Working paper, World Bank.

Renne, E. P. 2001. Introduction to special issue: Sexuality and generational identities in sub-Saharan Africa. *Africa Today* 47: vii–xii.

Reno, W. 1998. *Warlord politics and African states.* Boulder, CO: Lynne Rienner.

Retel-Laurentin, A. 1973. Evasions féminines dans la Volta Noire. *Cahiers d' etudes Africaines* 19:253–298.

Roberts, P. 1988. Rural women's access to labor in West Africa. In *Patriarchy and class,* edited by S. Slichter and J. Parpart, 97–114. Boulder, CO: Westview.

Robson, A., and H. Kaplan. 2003. The evolution of human life expectancy and intelligence in hunter-gatherer economies. *American Economic Review* 93:150–169.

Rodney, W. 1982. *How Europe underdeveloped Africa.* Washington, DC: Howard University Press.

Rohatynskyj, M. 1988. Women's virture and the structure of the Mossi *Zaka. Canadian Journal of African Studies* 22:528–551.

Roos, D. L., and C. H. Gladwin. 2000. The differential effects of capitalism and patriarchy on women farmers' access to markets in Cameroon. In *Women farmers and commercial ventures: Increasing food security in developing countries,* edited by A. Spring, 65–88. Boulder, CO: Lynne Rienner.

Rosenzweig, M. R. 1995. Why are there returns to schooling? *American Economic Review* 85:153–158.

Ross, M. 2001a. *Timber booms and institutional breakdown in Southeast Asia.* Cambridge: Cambridge University Press.

———. 2001b. Does oil hinder democracy? *World Politics* 53:325–361.

Rothbarth, E. 1943. Note on a method of determining equivalent income for families of different composition. In *War-time patterns of saving and spending,* edited by Charles Madge, 123–130. Cambridge: Cambridge University Press.

Sachs, J., and A. M. Warner. 1995. *Economic convergence and economic policies.* NBER working paper, no. 5039. Cambridge, MA: National Bureau of Economic Research.

Safilios-Rothschild, C. 1985. The persistence of women's invisibility in agriculture: Theoretical and policy lessons from Lesotho and Sierra Leone. *Economic Development and Cultural Change* 33:299–317.

Samatar, A. I. 1999. *An African miracle: State and class leadership and colonial legacy in Botswana's development.* Portsmouth, NH: Heinemann.

Samuelson, P. 1956. Social indifference curves. *Quarterly Journal of Economics* 70:1–22.

Saul, M. 1989. "Separateness and relations: Autonomous income and negotiation among rural Bobo women," in *Household Economy: Reconsidering the domestic mode of production*, ed. Richard Wilk, 171–193. Boulder, Westview.

Savadogo, K., S. Coulibaly, and C. A. McCracken. 2002. *Analyzing growth in Burkina Faso over the last four decades.* Working paper, Washington, DC: World Bank.

Savvides, A. 1995. Economic growth in Africa. *World Development* 23:449–458.

Sawadogo, J.-P., and V. Stamm. 2000. Local perceptions of indigenous land tenure systems: Views of peasants, women and dignitaries in a rural province of Burkina Faso. *Journal of Modern African Studies* 38:279–294.

Schapera, I. 1938. *A handbook of Tswana law and custom.* London: Oxford University Press, for the International Institute of African Languages and Cultures.

Schoepf, B. G. 1985. *The "wild," the "lazy," and the "matriarchal": Nutrition and cultural survival in the Zairian copperbelt.* Working paper, Michigan State University.

Schroeder, R. A. 1996. "Gone to their second husbands": Marital metaphors and conjugal contracts in the Gambia's female garden sector. *Canadian Journal of African Studies* 30:69–87.

———. 1999. Community, forestry and conditionality in the Gambia. *Africa* 69:1–22.

Schultz, T. P. 2002. Why governments should invest more to educate girls. *World Development* 30:207–225.

Schultz, T. W. 1964. *Transforming traditional agriculture.* New Haven, CT: Yale University Press.

Seguino, S. 2000. Gender inequality and economic growth: A cross-country analysis. *World Development* 28:1211–1231.

Sen, A. 1981. *Poverty and famines: An essay on entitlement and deprivation.* Oxford: Oxford University Press.

———. 1990. More than 100-million women are missing (a study on women from the standpoint of demography). *New York Review of Books* 37:61–66.

———. 1999. *Development as freedom.* New York: Knopf.

Shadle, B. 2000. "Girl cases": Runaway wives, eloped daughters, and abducted women in Gusiiland, Kenay, c. 1900–c.1965. Ph.D. diss., Northwestern University.

Sheldon, K. E. 1988. Working women in Beira, Mozambique. Ph.D. diss., University of California, Los Angeles.

———. 1991. A report on a "delicate problem" concerning female garment workers in Beira, Mozambique. *Signs* 16:575–586.

Shipton, P. 1988. The Kenyan land tenure reform: Misunderstandings in the public creation of private property. In *Land and society in contemporary Africa,* edited by R. E. Downs and S. P. Reyna, 91–135. Hanover: University Press of New England.

Shipton, P., and M. Goheen. 1992. Understanding African land-holding: Power, wealth and meaning. *Africa* 62:307–325.

Sieff, D. 1990. Explaining biased sex ratios in human populations: A critique of recent studies. *Current Anthropology* 31:25–48.

Skinner, E. P. 1964. *The Mossi of the Upper Volta; The political development of a Sudanese people.* Stanford, CA: Stanford University Press.

Skoufias, E. 1993. Labor market opportunities and intrafamily time allocation in rural households in South Asia. *Journal of Development Economics* 40:277–310.

Smith, C. D., and L. Stevens. 1988. Farming and income-generation in the female-headed smallholder household: The case of a Haya village in Tanzania. *Canadian Journal of African Studies* 22:552–566.

Smith, L. C., and J.-P. Chavas. 1999. *Supply response of West African agricultural households: Implications of intrahousehold preference heterogeneity.* Working paper, Washington, DC: IFPRI.

Sommers, C. H. 2000. *The war against boys: How misguided feminism is harming our young men.* New York: Simon and Schuster.

Soyinka, W. 1996. *The open sore of a continent: A personal narrative of the Nigerian crisis.* New York: Oxford University Press.

Spiegel, A. D. 1991. Polygyny as myth—Towards understanding extramarital relations in Lesotho. *African Studies* 50:145–166.

Staudt, K. 1987. Uncaptured or unmotivated? Women and the food crisis in Africa. *Rural Sociology* 52:37–55.

Stigler, G. J., and G. S. Becker. 1977. De gustibus non est disputandum. *American Economic Review* 67:76–90.

Stone, M. P., and G. D. Stone. 2000. Kofyar women who get ahead: Incentives for agricultural commercialization in Nigeria. In *Women farmers and commercial ventures: Increasing food security in developing countries,* edited by A. Spring, 153–170. Boulder, CO: Lynne Rienner.

Stone, M. P., G. D. Stone, and R. M. Netting. 1995. The sexual division of labor in Kofyar agriculture. *American Ethnologist* 22:165–186.

Subbarao, K., and L. Raney. 1995. Social gains from female education—a cross-national study. *Economic Development and Cultural Change* 44:105–128.

Suggs, D. 2002. *A bagful of locusts and the baboon woman: Constructions of gender, change, and continuity in Botswana.* Fort Worth, TX: Harcourt Brace.

Svedberg, P. 1991. *Poverty and undernutrition in sub-Saharan Africa: Theory, evidence, policy.* Working paper, Institute for Economic Studies, Stockholm University.

———. 1996. Gender biases in sub-Saharan Africa: Reply and further evidence. *Journal of Development Studies* 32:933–943.

Swamy, A., S. Knack, Y. Lee, and O. Azfar. 2001. Gender and corruption. *Journal of Development Economics* 64:25–55.

Sweet, W. 2001. Jeremy Bentham (1748–1832). *Internet Encyclopedia of Philosophy.* www.utm.edu/research/iep/b/bentham.htm, accessed July 15, 2003.

Tambiah, S. J. 1989. Bridewealth and dowry revisited: The position of women in sub-Saharan Africa and north India. *Current Anthropology* 30:413–435.

Tansel, A. 1997. Schooling attainment, parental education, and gender in Côte d'Ivoire and Ghana. *Economic Development and Cultural Change* 45:825–856.

Taraoré, D. 1941. Yaro Ha ou marriages entre femmes chez les Bobo Nieniegue. *Journal de la Société des Africanistes* 11:197–200.

Tauxier, L. 1924. *Nouvelles notes sur le Mossi et le Gourounsi.* Paris: E. Larose.

Thiong'o', N. w. 1965. *The river between.* London: Heinemann.

Thomas, D., V. Lavy, and J. Strauss. 1996. Public policy and anthropometric outcomes in the Côte d'Ivoire. *Journal of Public Economics* 61:155–192.

Tiefenthaler, J. 1994. Multisector model of female labor force participation: Empirical evidence from Cebu Island, Philippines. *Economic Development and Cultural Change* 42:719–742.

Tornell, A., and P. R. Lane. 1999. The voracity effect. *American Economic Review* 89:22–46.

Toulmin, C., and J. Quan. 2000. *Evolving land rights, policy, and tenure in Africa.* London: IIED Natural Resources Institute.

Trivers, R., and D. Willard. 1973. Natural selection of parental ability to vary the sex ratio of offspring. *Science* 179:90–92.

Tuck, M. W. 1994. Sexuality and health in sub-Saharan Africa: An annotated bibliography. *International Journal of African Historical Studies* 27:194–195.

Turnbull, C. M. 1972. *The mountain people.* New York: Simon and Schuster.

Tzannatos, Z. 1998. Women's labor incomes, In *Women in the Third World: An encyclopedia of contemporary issues,* ed. Nelly Stromquist. New York: Garland.

———. 1999. Women and labor market changes in the global economy: Growth helps, inequalities hurt and public policy matters. *World Development* 27, no. 3:551–534.

U.S. Census Bureau. 2000. *IDB Summary Demographic Data for Rwanda.* Washington, DC: U.S. Department of Commerce.

Udry, C. 1996. Gender, agricultural productivity, and the theory of the household. *Journal of Political Economy* 104:1010–1046.

Udry, C., J. Hoddinott, H. Alderman, and L. Haddad. 1995. Gender differentials in farm productivity: Implications for household efficiency and agricultural policy. *Food Policy* 20:407–423.

Urassaa, M., J. T. Boermaa, J. Z. L. Ng'weshemia, R. Isingoc, D. Schapinka, and Y. Kumogolad. 1997. Orphanhood, child fostering and the AIDS epidemic in rural Tanzania. *Health Transition Review* 7, suppl. 2:141–153.

Usher, D. 1998. The Coase theorem is tautological, incoherent, or wrong. *Economics Letters* 61:3–11.

van Donge, J. K. 1993. Legal insecurity and land conflicts in Mgeta, Uluguru Mountains, Tanzania. *Africa* 63:196–218.

von Braun, J., and P. Webb. "The impact of new crop technology on the agricultural division of labor in a West African setting." *Economic Development and Cultural Change* 37:513–534.

von Bulow, D. 1992. Bigger than men? Gender relations and their changing meaning in Kipsigis society, Kenya. *Africa* 62:523–546.

Waciuma, C. 1994. Itega and Irua. In *Unwinding threads: Writing by women in Africa,* edited by C. Bruner, 80–85. London: Heinemann.

Wantchekon, L. 2002. *Clientelism and voting behavior: A field experiment in Benin.* Working paper, New York University.

Weiss, Y. 1997. The formation and dissolution of families: Why marry? Who marries whom? And what happens upon divorce? In *Handbook of population and family economics,* edited by M. R. Rosenzweig and O. Stark, 81–123. Amsterdam: Elsevier Science.

Weitzman, M. L. 1996. Hybridizing growth theory. *American Economic Review* 86:207–212.

White, D. R. 1988. Rethinking polygyny: Co-wives, codes, and cultural systems. *Current Anthropology* 29:529–572.

White, D. R., and M. L. Burton. 1988. Causes of polygyny: Ecology, economy, kinship, and warfare. *American Anthropologist* 90:871–887.

White, L. 1990. *The comforts of home: Prostitution in colonial Nairobi.* Chicago: University of Chicago Press.

Whitehead, A. 1981. "I'm hungry, Mum": The politics of domestic budgeting. In *Of marriage and the market,* edited by K. Young, C. Wolkowitz, and R. McCullagh, 88–111. London: CSE.

Whyte, M. K. 1978. *The status of women in preindustrial societies.* Princeton, NJ: Princeton University Press.

Wilk, R. R. 1996. *Economies and cultures: Foundations of economic anthropology.* Boulder, CO: Westview.

Winikoff, B., et al. (C. Carignan, E. Bernadik, and P. Semeraro) 1991. *Medical services to save mothers' lives: Feasible approaches to reducing maternal mortality.* Report, New York: Population Council, Programs Division.

Winter-Nelson, A. 1995. Natural resources, national income, and economic growth in Africa. *World Development* 23:1507–1519.

Wintrobe, R. 1998. *The political economy of dictatorship.* Cambridge: Cambridge University Press.

Wohlmuth, K. 1998. *Good governance and economic development: New foundations for growth in Africa.* Bremen: Institut für Weltwirtschaft und Internationales Management Fachbereich Wirtschaftswissenschaft, Universität Bremen.

Woolcock, M. J. V. 1999. Learning from failures in microfinance: What unsuccessful cases tell us about how group-based programs work. *American Journal of Economics and Sociology* 58:17–42.

World Bank. 2001. *Engendering development: Through gender equality in rights, resources, and voice.* Washington, DC: World Bank; New York: Oxford University Press.

———. 2002. *World development indicators.*Washington, DC: World Bank.

Index

235

About the Book

Women and Development in Africa explores gender issues in the context of Africa's generally poor economic performance.

Kevane begins with a broad discussion of the sources of underdevelopment in Africa and the the role of gender in economic transactions. He then presents solid evidence on the gendered realities of land rights, the control of labor, bargaining power within households, the marriage market (including a discussion of who "owns" women), and families. The final section of the book reviews specific development programs aimed at women and emphasizes the necessity of gender-sensitive structural changes to promote equitable and rapid development. Illustrative case studies are included throughout.

The theoretical and empirical evidence presented confirms that gender relations are fluid, political, and critically important for economic outcomes.

Michael Kevane is associate professor of economics at Santa Clara University.

Women and
Development in Africa